Herbert Spencer, William Godwin Moody

Land and Labor in the United States

Herbert Spencer, William Godwin Moody

Land and Labor in the United States

ISBN/EAN: 9783337723194

Printed in Europe, USA, Canada, Australia, Japan

Cover: Foto ©Suzi / pixelio.de

More available books at **www.hansebooks.com**

LAND AND LABOR

IN

THE UNITED STATES

BY

WM. GODWIN MOODY

AUTHOR OF "OUR LABOR DIFFICULTIES: THE CAUSE AND THE WAY OUT,"
"THE DISPLACEMENT OF LABOR BY IMPROVEMENTS
IN MACHINERY," ETC., ETC.

NEW YORK
CHARLES SCRIBNER'S SONS
1883

TO

Mrs. ELIZABETH THOMPSON,

THE CONSTANT FRIEND

OF THE LABORER AND THE DISTRESSED,

WHOSE SYMPATHY AND INVALUABLE ASSISTANCE,

FROM FIRST TO LAST,

HAVE SO GREATLY AIDED MY WORK,

THIS VOLUME

IS GRATEFULLY INSCRIBED

BY

THE AUTHOR.

PREFACE.

IN the preparation of this volume it has been my purpose to bring into the discussion those great factors that have been, heretofore, so uniformly overlooked, or designedly ignored. The condition of the great masses of the people — their idleness and their employment, with their consumption as well as production — appear to me to be matters of the utmost importance. The radical change in all our methods of production is another thing that seems to be of great interest, and vitally affecting the welfare of mankind. But I have failed to find that others have deemed them of sufficient moment to merit even the most casual inquiry.

It has long been a decided conviction in my mind that a knowledge of the *condition* of the people is of as great importance as the knowledge of their *number*, and I succeeded in having a clause added to the last census bill, providing for an enumeration to be made of the number who were found idle, also of the employed, and the amount of their employment during the previous year. But the method adopted in taking the census made it valueless. The workers themselves, who alone could have answered, were not inquired of, but all inquiries were directed to boardinghouse keepers and employers, who did not know and could not answer. Had it been the deliberate purpose of the Census Bureau to defeat the objects of the provision, a more certain means could not have been adopted. Failing to obtain this most important information through the census, I have been compelled to ascertain the idleness in the country by other methods.

Much the larger portion of the facts here used is the result of my personal observations and diligent inquiries, in which I have received the sympathy and encouragement of valued friends who saw the importance of the facts collected, and the line of the discussion, though they might not now altogether accept the conclusions reached. Among others I venture to give the names of the Rev. Dr. Edward Everett Hale and Rev. Minot J. Savage, Boston; Senator George F. Hoar, Massachusetts; Senator Henry W. Blair, New Hampshire; Rev. Edward Anderson, Toledo, Ohio; Hon. George William Curtis, Rev. Dr. R. Heber Newton, and Mrs. Elizabeth Thompson, New York City.

To the last named, in particular, am I indebted for that substantial aid so necessary, and yet so hard to find, that has enabled me to carry my work to the point where the reader takes it. If, as I hope, my efforts shall have the effect of opening a discussion, and pointing out a way by which humanity may be benefited, to that noble woman, fully as much as to myself, will the debt of gratitude be due.

W. G. M.

CONTENTS.

CHAPTER I.
MACHINERY IN AGRICULTURE, - - - - - 9

CHAPTER II.
THE BONANZA FARMS, - - - - - - - 31

CHAPTER III.
GROWTH AND DEVELOPMENT OF BONANZA AND TENANT FARMS, - - - - - - - - - 74

CHAPTER IV.
ENGLISH AND AMERICAN LAND HOLDINGS AND RAILROAD LAND GRANTS, - - - - - - - 88

CHAPTER V.
SUMMARY AND EFFECTIVE MEASURES FOR BREAKING UP GREAT LANDED ESTATES AND TENANT HOLDINGS, AND RESTORING THE PUBLIC DOMAIN TO THE PEOPLE, - 112

CHAPTER VI.
MACHINERY IN TEXTILES AND OTHER MANUFACTURES, 136

CHAPTER VII.
EFFECTS OF THE WAR OF THE REBELLION UPON THE LABOR OF THE COUNTRY, - - - - - - 149

CHAPTER VIII.
THE WAR OF THE REBELLION AND THE BUSINESS AND WEALTH OF THE COUNTRY, - - - - - 164

CHAPTER IX.
Did Railroad Building Cause our Industrial Distress, - - - - - - - - - 174

CHAPTER X.
Money and the Industrial Distress, - - - 181

CHAPTER XI.
Foreign Trade is no Remedy for our Industrial Distress, - - - - - - - - 198

CHAPTER XII.
Constant Work for All, with Liberal Wages, the Only Source of a Nation's Prosperity, - - 215

CHAPTER XIII.
The Relations of Trade to the Employments of the People, - - - - - - - - - 236

CHAPTER XIV.
Six Hour Law and Reasons for its Enactment, - 252

CHAPTER XV.
The Gospel of Relaxation, *by Herbert Spencer*, - - 276

CHAPTER XVI.
General Effects of the Mechanical Changes of the Past Fifty Years, and of Industrial Redistribution in the Future, - - - - - - 286

CHAPTER XVII.
Tenth Annual Report, Bureau of Statistics, for the State of Massachusetts, - - - - 307

CHAPTER XVIII.
What Shall We Do? - - - - - - - 330

LAND AND LABOR

IN

THE UNITED STATES

LAND AND LABOR.

CHAPTER I.

MACHINERY IN AGRICULTURE.

THE eminent French Archæologist, M. Louis Figuier, in his "L'Homme Primitif," says that in the Stone Age, before metals were known, all the efforts of man "must have tended to one sole aim — that of insuring his daily subsistence." So it is at this day for the large majority of mankind. The long ages that have followed that period, with the marvellous developments of civilization — the discovery of metals, the construction and improvement of tools and machinery of every nature that have increased more than an hundred fold man's power of producing all that enters into his daily sustenance and comfort — have not changed the fact that he still has but the "one sole aim — that of insuring his daily subsistence." The ratio of failures to achieve that object could not have been greater in the Stone Age than in the present; and never before, in any age, were practically one half of mankind forced out of all productive pursuits into idleness and destitution.

The discovery of metals, the construction and improvement of tools and machinery of every nature that have so wonderfully increased man's power of production, have revolutionized all the social and industrial relations of mankind in almost exact proportion to their development and use. Even the moral forces, also, are acted upon and stimulated for good or evil, in like degree, by these material discoveries and developments. This revolution is not confined to Christendom; it reaches out and extends into all societies and countries possessed of any degree or class of civilization.

If these premises be true, and they hardly admit of a doubt, it follows as a matter of necessity that we must examine, in some degree, into the nature and extent of these material developments if we really wish to obtain a correct understanding of the causes and tendencies of the world's present material distress and moral destitution. In opening this discussion it appears to be proper to lay down certain economic principles that have become fixed, and are, as nearly as possible, universally accepted as fundamental.

Adam Smith, in his Wealth of Nations, more than one hundred years ago, taught:—

That "the annual labor of every nation is the fund which originally supplies it with all the necessaries and conveniences of life which it annually consumes."

That "the demand for those who live by wages naturally increases with the increase of national wealth, and can not possibly increase without it."

That "it is not in the richest countries, but in the most thriving, or in those which are growing rich the fastest, that the wages of labor are highest."

That "the liberal reward of labor, therefore, as it is the necessary effect, so it is the natural symptom, of increasing national wealth. The scanty maintenance of the laboring poor, on the other hand, is the natural symptom that things are at a stand, and their starving condition that they are going fast backwards."

That "servants, laborers, and workmen of different kinds, make up far the greater part of any great political society. What improves the greater part can never be regarded as an inconveniency to the whole. No society can surely be flourishing and happy, of which the greater part of the members are poor and miserable. It is but equity, besides, that those who feed, clothe, and lodge the whole body of the people, should have such a share of the produce of their own labor as to be themselves tolerably well fed, clothed, and lodged."

That "it deserves to be observed that it is in the progressive state, while society is advancing to further acquisition, rather than when it has acquired its full complement of riches, that the condition of the laboring poor, of the great body of the people, seems to be the happiest and the most comfortable."

"When in any country a demand for those who live by wages — laborers, journeymen, servants of every kind — is continually increasing; when every year furnishes employment for a greater number than had been employed the year before, the workmen have no occasion to combine in order to raise their wages. The scarcity of hands occasions a competition among masters, who bid against one another, and thus voluntarily break through the natural combination of masters not to raise wages."

"But it would be otherwise in a country where the fund destined for the maintenance of labor was sensibly decaying. Every year the demand for servants and laborers would, in all the different classes of employment, be less than it had been the year before. Many who had been in the superior classes, not being able to find employment in their own business, would be glad to seek it in the lowest. The lowest class being not only overstocked with its own workmen, but with the overflowings of all the other classes, the competition for employment would be so great in it as to reduce the wages of labor to the most miserable and scanty subsistence of the laborers. Many would not be able to find employment even upon these hard terms, but 'would either starve, or be driven to seek a subsistence, either by begging, or by the perpetration of the greatest enormities."

That "the liberal reward of labor, as it is the effect of increasing wealth, so it is the cause of increasing population. To complain of it is to lament over the necessary causes and effects of the greatest prosperity."

These principles, as laid down by the greatest of human political economists, require no interpreter. But there is an older law in economics which, whether a formal declaration by the Almighty, or something that has grown out of the workings of an experience simply human, is generally received as of Divine origin, and accepted as the law of our existence, and that is: —

"In the sweat of thy face shalt thou eat bread, till thou return unto the ground."

In the light of these principles, as fixed by a higher than human power, and approved by human experience, that only in universal labor, liberally rewarded, is to be found life and prosperity, not only for the individual but for society, we will examine the facts of our present condition.

Starting from the time in which Adam Smith wrote we will endeavor to note a few of the changes in methods and increase in power of production that have resulted from the invention and use of machinery, as a basis upon which to estimate its effects on the demand for man's labor in the supply of his wants, and of his present employment. But first we will note that at the time of Adam Smith man's power of production had already been so greatly developed as to enable a fraction of the human family to provide for the wants of all, a large portion not being productively employed, but either absolutely idle, or engaged in the most destructive pursuits.

In discussing this matter it must be borne in mind that we, like every other people, have a certain amount of work to do — neither more nor less; and that is, to supply ourselves with the necessaries and comforts of life — to produce of all that is useful and beautiful to the extent of our ability to use and consume. We can not do less than that and prosper; neither can any other people. Nations, like individuals, can exist only by and through their own industries. Our people can not exist upon the industries of any other society, and no other people can be permitted to live upon us. Every independent nation can, must, and will, if wise, use its utmost power to protect its own people in the work of providing for their own wants. In view of these self evident principles there can be no greater folly than that of hoping to be permitted to produce and manufacture for others, except to a very limited extent and for short and most uncertain periods.

Having the necessity of providing for ourselves only, it follows that the amount of work required to be done, whether by muscular or mechanical force, must be measured by the amount that will supply the liberal use and consumption of our own society. If at any time before the present century we were able to produce sufficient to supply the three great wants of man

— that of food, clothing, and shelter — and contribute something to his love of luxury and the beautiful — and indisputably we were — then we have a measure by which we can gauge the extent of the change that has been wrought by the introduction of mechanical forces into the work of general production, and the effect which the use of machinery has upon the employment of muscular labor.

It must also be borne in mind that however great has been the development in inventions for the employment of machinery, or mechanical force, it has in every case been for the purpose of doing more effectively, more expeditiously, more extensively, that which was done before — for the purpose of more completely or easily satisfying man's existing wants. No inventor has yet succeeded in inventing or discovering a new want; he can only minister to those already existing, and all talk about creating new wants and new industries to employ the unemployed is absurd, unless we can steal the power of the Infinite.

It necessarily follows, then, that in exact proportion to the introduction of mechanical force, or machinery, in general production, is the release or displacement of muscular labor, unless there is at the same time a corresponding increase in the consumption of the product. But in those products where man's consumption is confined within narrow limits, as in his three great wants of food, clothing, and shelter, which have heretofore been in great measure well supplied, and which employs and has ever employed at least nine tenths of all the muscular and mechanical force expended in general production and distribution, it will be readily seen that though there has been a very considerable increase of consumption, it bears no proportion to the increase of production. This fact is so self evident that it is clearly stated in the Introduction to the Agricultural volume, United States Census Reports, 1860, page xi, as follows:—

"Thus every machine or tool which enables one farm hand to do the work of two, cheapens the product of his labor to every consumer, and relieves one in every two of the population from the duty of providing subsistence, enabling him to engage in other pursuits," etc.

The weak point in this statement is, that the author does not point out the "other pursuits" that are not similarly affected, in which the "relieved" man may "engage." No argument is required to show that where one man is enabled, by the use of machinery, to do the work of two, one is released or displaced, and must find other employment or remain idle, be it in farm work or any other. So, also, if one man becomes enabled to do the work of twenty, nineteen out of the twenty are displaced. The only exception is to be found in the cases where a corresponding increase takes place in the consumption of the products, if there are any such cases. Yet, notwithstanding the absolute certainty of this principle, nothing is more common than to hear it said that labor saving machinery creates work — that it gives more employment to manual labor, and throws no one into idleness. But it is rare that this fallacy can be found in print, in any publication carrying the least weight of authority. Perhaps the most notable instance in which this absurdity has been broadly stated, with an attempt at demonstration, is to be found on page clxiv, of volume 2, Agriculture, United Census Reports for 1860, as follows : —

"The first impression made on the popular mind, by any great improvement in machinery and locomotion, after the admission of their beneficial effects, is that they will, in some way or other, diminish the demand for labor or for other machinery. . . . . . It is now established as a general principle, that machines facilitating labor increase the amount of labor required. . . . . . There was an idea that the transportation of agricultural products [by railways] would result in diminishing the number of horses, wagoners, and steamboats. . . . . . The result, however, proves precisely the contrary. Horses have multiplied more rapidly since the introduction of locomotives than they did before. . . . . . Three fourths of all the miles of railroad have been made since 1850; and we see that since then the increase of horses has been the greatest. . . . . . Hence it seemed that railroads must diminish the number and importance of horses, but such was not the fact."

This evidence and argument are deemed by those who use them as proofs that will not leave a peg to hang a doubt upon, that no "great improvement in machinery or locomotion," will in any "way or other, diminish the demand for labor."

Those who use this argument have not yet discovered that the locomotive and railroad have come into competition with the horse only on the great roads and routes of travel and transportation for long distances, from which he has been undeniably driven, but leaving him in undisputed possession of a thousand and one other employments; whilst machinery has come in direct competition with manual labor in every place where force or power is used, from the manufac-

MACHINERY IN AGRICULTURE. 17

ture and adjustment of the finest watch mechanism, or dental work upon the teeth in the mouth of the patient, to the construction of the most stupendous works, and the removal of mountains; leaving to muscle no place without a swift, untiring, inexhaustive competitor, which in every case reduces the employment of manual labor to an extremely low point.

Among other reasons why "horses have multiplied more rapidly since the introduction of locomotives than they did before," is the fact that the locomotive in taking possession of the great roads and routes of travel and transportation for long distances, has greatly increased the travel and transportation on the lesser and shorter routes which it, as yet, has not been able to cover, and where the horse must still do the largely increased service; and in the great increase in the business and wealth of our cities and towns, requiring a multiplied service and street cars drawn by horses, with the development of luxury in the trading and moneyed classes that finds its expression in the use and cultivation of the horse. But when the locomotive comes into successful competition with the horse in general farm work, the road and express wagon, the street car, with the cartman, the pleasure carriage, the coach, under the saddle, on the race course — in every place where the power and force of the horse is now used, as it has been upon the great roads and routes of travel and transportation, then that animal may be cited to illustrate the effect of machinery upon the employment of muscle, and not before. So with the other illustrations used in this connection in the Census Report, and by others. A one sided, partial view of this matter, which is the too common view, will not meet the case.

Thus far I have utterly failed to discover that any attempt has ever been made to find to what extent machinery has taken the place of muscle in any production. So prevalent has been the idea, especially among the so called cultured and mercantile classes, that machinery does not affect the employment of manual labor, except, perhaps, to increase it, that they have not deemed it worthy of inquiry. Even those with the best opportunities of knowing the whole case appear to have been utterly blind or indifferent. In the two hundred and eighteen quarto pages of introductory matter, in the volume on Manufactures, United States Census Report for 1860, filled with a most interesting summary of developments in machinery and manufactures during the present century, I find but one instance wherein the slightest intimation is given of the effects of the introduction of any labor saving machine upon the manual labor employed. This may be found in the description of the manufacture of paper, on page cxxvi, as follows : —

"About the year 1825 the automaton paper machine of Foudrinier, imported from England, was introduced into the United States, at Springfield, Massachusetts, where the largest manufactory at that time in the United States, that of D. & J. Ames, employed twelve steam engines and more than one hundred females, besides the usual number of male hands, and used machinery patented by them for making continuous sheets, which enabled one man to do the work of thirty."

This simple statement gives a clear idea of the effect which one machine, in the manufacture of paper, had upon labor nearly sixty years ago : viz., that it released, or displaced, twenty-nine out of the thirty hands then and there employed, and compelled those displaced hands to find other employment or to remain idle.

With these preliminary remarks I will endeavor to find what has been the actual effect caused by the introduction and use of machinery in general production, upon the employment of manual labor in our country, during the present century. In doing this I shall confine myself to a few of the special employments that contribute directly to the supply of the three great wants of mankind — the production and distribution of the principal necessaries of life — assuming that what is there found to be true may with safety be taken as the basis for estimating its effects in all other productive industries.

As agriculture lies at the base of human providence we will begin there. Throughout Europe and America, until within a comparatively recent date, the implements of the farm remained extremely primitive and inefficient in form. It was at no remote period that the hoe, in its crudest shape, and the spade, equally clumsy, were the principal tools for tillage. Though the plow, or something used for that purpose, has been to some extent in use from time immemorial, that implement as we now know it is a new tool or machine. Originally nothing more than the branch or trunk of a tree, with its forked or curved end sharpened to scratch a furrow for the seed. Similar plows are now in common use throughout Mexico. Then a mere wedge with a short beam and straight handle, it became in time fitted with a movable share of wood, stone, copper, or iron, wrought to an attempted suitable form, as we find it in the hands of our Saxon ancestors. Afterwards the wooden mold board was added, with various improvements in shape, which continued in use until near the present time.

In England, in the middle of the last century, the plow was an exceedingly rude and cumbersome affair in comparison with those now in common use. It was no infrequent thing, in parts of the island, eighty years ago, to see from three to five horses, in light soils, and in heavy ones as many as seven, attached to a plow which turned about three fourths of an acre a day. The old Scotch plow was still worse, and no instance was known of plowing with less than four horses. The usual number was six, or four horses and two oxen; sometimes as many as ten or twelve were yoked to it, each pair requiring a driver.

In the early part of the present century our best plow, in general use, was of wood, iron shod, large, ill shaped and cumbersome, drawn by from one to six yoke of oxen, requiring one and often two men to hold it; another to ride on the beam to keep it in the ground; still another to keep it clear, and the drivers of the team — often four and sometimes six men, but never less than two, to turn one acre a day.

About 1740 James Small, of Berwickshire, Scotland, first introduced the iron mold board, still using wrought iron shares. In 1785 Robert Ransome, of Ipswich, introduced cast iron shares. The making of the first iron plow has been attributed to William Allan, a farmer of Lanarkshire, Scotland, in 1804;

but an iron plow was presented to the Society of Arts, in London, as early as 1773, by a Mr. Brand. The cast iron plow was introduced soon after.

The first patent issued in the United States after the organization of the Patent Office, was in June, 1797, to Charles Newbold, of Burlington, New Jersey, for a cast iron plow which combined the mold board, share, and land side, all in one casting. A series of improvements in the cast iron plow was commenced about 1810, by Josiah Ducher, of New York, some of which are still retained in use. In 1814 Jethro Wood, of Scipio, New York, was granted a patent for a cast iron plow having the mold board, share, and land side cast in three parts. Joel Nourse and his partners, of Worcester, Massachusetts, improved and perfected the cast iron plow, which, to his time, in 1836, was a comparatively rude implement.

Now we have plows of that lightness and easy draft that one man, with a single horse, in light soils, will turn two and one half acres in a day of ten hours, the plow requiring very little effort, even with one hand, to guide it. Some of our finest plows are made of polished steel, and work to the greatest perfection. Many in common use, known as sulkies, have the plow affixed to an axle, between a pair of wheels, with a comfortable seat above for the driver of the team. Others have no land side, but will cut and turn a furrow eighteen inches wide in the most perfect manner. In place of the straight coulter of our fathers, and still in common use, a steel disc is now applied. With two horses one man with these plows will break two and one half acres a day on the western prairies ; and by attaching two or more plows to the axle, forming what are known as gang plows, five or more acres a day are plowed by increasing the team. Or a traction engine is used, with the result of plowing an acre or more an hour.

It must be borne in mind that in speaking of the work days of our fathers, or the period included in the first quarter of this century, and for all time before, that not less than twelve, and more commonly fifteen or more hours a day were consumed in work, especially by the agriculturist, whilst ten to twelve hours are now, in most parts, the common time.

Thus it is seen that in the work of plowing one man to-day, with a gang plow that turns two furrows will plow five acres in a day, which would have required, in the days of our fathers, under the best conditions, the labor of two men for five days, and not unfrequently as many as four to six men for seven days. Being a difference of from one man now doing the work of ten, up to one taking the place of thirty. With a three gang or furrow plow, now in common use with teams, the difference would be fifty per cent. greater. With the steam plow, using gangs of five or more, the work accomplished would be still more widely marked. And more than this, the work is now done incomparably better than ever before.

After the plow there follows the harrow, the cultivator, and the roller, to thoroughly pulverize and prepare the soil to receive the seed. The harrow, though an old tool, has recently been so greatly improved as to more than double its efficiency. The cultivator is a new machine and most effective in its application.

The roller, which has been greatly improved, has more generally been brought into use for crushing and pulverizing clods and lumps, and leaving the ground smooth. Our best farmers claim that the improved tillage obtained by these implements increases the crop at least twenty-five per cent.

At the beginning of the present century, and to within a quite recent period, all the smaller grains were sown by hand. The sower would go into the field with his seed in a bag, slung from his shoulders. Then filling his hand from the bag, "with measured tread he throws the grain" before him as he crosses the field from one side to the other. But now a box or trough, eight feet or more in length, is attached to a pair of wheels. This trough being filled with grain any child that can drive a horse may take the seat on the machine, and in driving from side to side of the field either scatters the seed broad cast, or deposits it, as may be desired, at regular intervals in little drills which it makes. In this way a boy or girl will not only sow from seven to ten times more ground than can possibly be done by hand, but much better and with great economy of seed.

In planting corn our fathers, with a hoe, would go over the field, making at regular intervals little hills or drills; he being followed by some one, it might have been a boy, who would place upon each hill a few grains of corn, or into the drill a kernel at regular intervals. After the corn was thus placed in hill or drill the earth was drawn over it with the hoe. But now the corn planter is used, upon which a child may sit and, driving a single horse, will plant at least ten times as much as could one person by the old methods. Then, instead of using the hoe, as did our fathers, in working their corn, where a man found a long and hard day's work in hoeing half an acre, a man or boy will now seat himself upon a cultivator, with a pair of horses before him, and work one acre an hour; one man now doing with this implement as much as could be done by twenty with hoes.

When the wheat, or other small grain, was ripe for the harvest our fathers would go into the field with their sickles in their hands, and a long day of hard work would result in one fourth of an acre of grain cut and bound per man. This work is now done by machinery. Pliny, the elder, gives a description of a machine for harvesting grain used by the Gauls. It is supposed to have been in use for several centuries. During the last century several attempts were made to construct machines for reaping, but no one proved a success. Although in the early part of the present century cradles had been to some extent adopted in reaping, the sickle still remained the common implement used for that purpose in Europe and America.

The first American patent for cutting grain was issued in May, 1803, to Richard French and J. T. Hawkins, of New Jersey. Samuel Adams, of the same State, followed in 1805; J. Comfort, of Pennsylvania, and William P. Claiborn, of Virginia, in 1811; Peter Gaillard, of Pennsylvania, in 1812, and Peter Baker, of New York, in 1814. The next was the machine of Jeremiah Bailey, of Pennsylvania, in 1822; a rotary mowing machine, having six scythes attached to a shaft. Four other patents were registered in 1828, when Samuel Lane, of Hallowell, Maine, patented a machine for cutting, gathering, and thrashing grain at one operation. One other machine, that of William Manning, of Plainfield, New Jersey, registered in 1831, and having several points of resemblance to some now in use, was patented previous to that of Obed Hussey's, of Cincinnati, Ohio, in 1833. With the Hussey machine grain could be cut as fast as eight men could bind it. In June, 1834, Cyrus H. McCormick, of Virginia, received his first patent for cutting grain of all kinds by machinery. From that time to the present nearly every year has produced one or more modifications of harvesting machinery, among which may be mentioned that of Moore & Haskell, of Michigan, in 1836, which cuts, thrashes, and winnows the grain at one and the same time.

As early as 1860 four horse harvesting machines would cut twenty acres of grain in a day, leaving it spread upon the ground to be gathered and bound by hand. Now machines are used that will cut eighty acres in a day of ten hours, the team traveling at the rate of three miles an hour. One machine, controlled by one man, cutting as much as could be done by 320 men with sickles. The cutter of this machine is 24 feet long. But the machines in common use in some of the great grain fields of the West, having cutters from 12 to 16 feet in length, at the same rate of travel, cut 40 to 60 acres a day, one man now doing the work that required 160 to 200 about 60 years ago. These machines are known as headers, and cut the grain in such manner as to take little more than the heads, which are discharged into a large box, known as the header box, drawn by another team. The box when filled being at once taken to the rick and unloaded, whilst another takes its place. Other machines, that are drawn by two horses, known as self binders, cut the grain and bind it into sheaves, using both cord and wire for the binding, and throwing the sheaves to one side when bound, are also in common use, with cutters six and seven feet in length, which cut and bind 15 and 20 acres in a day, and do the work of 60 and 80 men with sickles.

In the days of our fathers the sheaves of grain were stored in the barns, and furnished a Winter's work for themselves, their boys, and their men servants, in thrashing it with flails. But now thrashing machines, driven by horse or steam power, thrashes, winnows, and sacks the grain as fast as 12 to 25 men can feed the machines, clear away the straw and chaff, and handle the sacks — turning out 1,000 to 1,500 bushels a day.

In California the machines above referred to that cut, thrash, and winnow the grain at one operation, are used. They also fill the sacks, which are left standing in rows where, but a few moments before, stood the golden grain untouched, inviting to its harvest. These machines require four men in working them, and with cutters 20 feet long harvest 50 acres a day. Here four men, with the machine and team, now do the work that would have required at least 300 within the memory of men now living.

Down to within the last year, when the corn was ready for harvest men were sent into the field to take the ripened ears from the standing stalk by hand;

but now a corn husker is used. A machine drawn by two horses will do the work of eight men; it will take one row at a time and husk, gather, and elevate the corn into a wagon as fast as the team will walk through the field. It will gather all the ears, whether the stalks stand up or are bent down. It leaves all the husks on the stalk, and it does not pull up, or cut up, or break down the stalks.

After the corn was harvested our fathers would turn a shovel upside down over a box, sit on it, and drawing the ears with force and vigor across its edge, would shell at most twenty bushels in a long day; but far more commonly not more than five, and hard work it was. Now two men will take the ordinary improved corn sheller and shell 24 bushels in an hour, or 240 bushels in a short day. Leaving out of the account the difference in the length of the days worked, this shows that six times as much is now done with this machine as our fathers could do by the old methods. With the three classes of horse power machines four men will shell 1,500, 2,000, and 3,000 bushels respectively per day of ten hours; one man and machine now doing the work of 75, 100, and 150 men, respectively, when without machinery.

Our fathers, when they wanted their wheat converted into flour or their corn into meal, would take it to the neighboring mill, generally having one run of stones, rarely more than two, where everything was handled and moved by muscular force, requiring from one to three men in each mill, and turning out what might amount to from ten to thirty barrels of flour a day, paying for the service rendered in a toll of about one eighth or tenth. Now the grain is sold and converted into flour in mills that will count their runs of stones or rolls by scores or hundreds, and their daily yield by thousands of barrels, but requiring no more men in the operations of flouring than did the mill of our fathers when the yield was but thirty barrels a day. Now the mills do their work without the assistance of man, except as a watcher. At night the mill may be, and usually is, locked up, dark, and lonely, except for the watchman and his lantern, but runs on and grinds out its flour by hundreds and thousands of barrels a night.

In our important hay crop the machine mower is first put in, one man with team cutting as much grass as could twelve men with scythes. Then follows the tedder with a man and horse to scatter and turn it, to facilitate its drying, doing the work of twenty men with the hand fork, and so much better as to reduce the time between the cutting and housing at least twenty-four hours. Then comes the horse rake, raking twenty acres a day, while a man with the ordinary hand rake can rake but two. Here the machine and man do the work of twelve, twenty, and ten men respectively, with the old appliances.

And machinery digs the potatoes, milks the cows, and makes the butter and the cheese. There is now nothing in food production without its labor saving process.

In all these agricultural operations there is a displacement of labor by invention of machines and their improvement of from one doing the work of seven in sowing grain, to twenty-four in plowing, and three hundred and twenty in cutting the grain at harvest, according to the kind of work done and the class of machinery used for the particular operation.

Scarcely less effective, in the aggregate, are the numerous minor inventions whereby the labor of the farm and the household have been saved. Implements of this kind make a large portion of the stock in trade of the makers and venders of agricultural wares.

Our fathers, with all their boys and men servants, had a full Winter's work in thrashing their wheat and other small grain, in shelling their corn, etc., and in getting their small products to mill or market. But now, after machinery has done its work in the field and barn the iron horse drags the product over its roads of steel, for hundreds and thousands of miles, at less cost and in less time than it took our fathers to transport the same to distances not greater than fifty miles. Upon those roads where formerly hundreds and thousands of men and teams were constantly employed in hauling products to market and goods to the country nowhere now is a man or team so employed. Men and animals are released from that labor; new forces have taken up the work, guided and controlled by comparatively few minds and hands. Even our cattle and hogs are no longer required to walk to the shambles; the iron horse takes them to the butcher; labor saving processes slaughter them, dress them, prepare their flesh for the market, for the table, and stop only at mastication, deglutition, and digestion.

To-day one man with the aid of machinery will

produce as much food as could be raised by the naked muscle and tools of a score of our fathers. There is now no known limit to the power of its production. In consumption there is no corresponding increase. Our fathers required, obtained, and used as many ounces of food per day as we do. It might have been different in kind and quality — nothing more.

Not long ago the farm found constant employment for all its sons, and also for many of the children of the city. But now it furnishes work for but a very small portion of its own children, and that for a few weeks or months at most in the year, and for the remainder of the twelve months employment must be had in the cities and towns, or not at all. Here we find the true reason for stagnation in the population of the older agricultural sections, and abnormal growth and crowding of the cities.

The use of machinery in general manufactures, and especially of textiles, has had an equally potent effect upon the daughters of the farm, in compelling them, also, to seek employment in the manufacturing towns and cities, because there was no longer work to be found under the old rooftree, as will be here shown.

The great revolution that has been effected in our industrial and social conditions, by the use of machinery and labor saving processes in general production, to the exclusion, in great part, of manual labor, may, perhaps, be best seen by the changes that have been wrought within a few years in all that relates to our farming interests. For which see next chapter, on the "Bonanza Farms."

CHAPTER II.

THE BONANZA FARMS.

[The matter which forms this chapter was written by the author of this volume for the Atlantic Monthly of January, 1880. It is here reproduced, with some additions, for the reason that it gives a clear account of the methods pursued in a system of agriculture that is monopolizing the lands, developing a system of monster estates, swallowing up the small holdings of the people, and undermining and destroying the small farm interests of the country.]

WITHIN the past year or two a new development in agriculture, in the great Northwest, has forced itself upon the public attention, that would seem destined to exercise a most potent influence on the production of all food products, and work a revolution in the great economies of the farm. But not enough is known of this new development to enable one to form any just estimate of either its force or extent. For the purpose of obtaining the data necessary to assist to a more correct understanding of the operations of what are known as the "Bonanza Farms," and their present and probable future effects, the writer went upon the ground to make them a study.

On reaching St. Paul I visited the Land Office of the St. Paul and Sioux City Railroad, to gather some facts in regard to Southern Minnesota. The Land Commissioner, James H. Drake, Esq., learning of the purpose of my tour in the Northwest, expressed a strong desire that I should go over their road, visit some of the great farms in its neighborhood, and see for myself. He spoke enthusiastically of the country, and particularly of the rare opportunities there presented for the investment of capital in agriculture as a first class financial operation; and also of the general and particular attention that great capitalists were giving to the matter, especially upon the line of that road, and mentioned a large number who had already embarked in the enterprise, and of others who had purchased lands with that object. I desired him to give me a list of some of the names mentioned, to which he at once responded with the following memorandum:—

"Thompson & Kendall farm, about 7,000 acres. The Rock County farm, near Luverne, Thompson & Warner, 50,000 acres, of which about 6,000 acres are under cultivation. President Drake, of St. Paul and Sioux City Railroad, has numerous farms, with tenants working on shares. General Bishop, manager of railroad, has 3,200 acres under cultivation. George I. Seney, President Metropolitan Bank, New York City, has 2,000 acres under cultivation, near Sheldon, Iowa. A. E. Orr, of David Dows & Co., New York, has a large farm on the line, and Goldsmidt, the great German banker, Frankfort-on-the-Main, has several large farms. President Drake's son, and Horace Thompson's son, are each managing large farms, and every director in the organization has his large farm with tenants cultivating the soil."

Commissioner Drake also placed in my hands a circular in which he endeavors to prove to the capitalist that investments made in the lands of that road, at current prices, and cultivated in wheat and other crops, will pay twenty per cent. upon the whole investment the first year, and fifty-five per cent. the second.

As that was just what I wanted to see and be convinced of, if it could be done, I gladly accepted his invitation and took a trip upon that road to the points he designated, and some others. After running about seventy-five miles, on the borders of a well wooded stream, we emerged upon an open, treeless, rolling prairie, not unlike the prairies of Kansas; thence, to Windom, seventy-two miles further, was a succession of prairie billows, with an occasional lakelet and some dozen apparently flourishing towns.

At Windom I found the proprietor of the Clark House ready to receive me and show several of the large farms and the country in his neighborhood. Mr. Clark, a native of Massachusetts, and there a resident until within a few years, himself owned several hundred acres of land, and was having it cultivated, mostly in wheat, by contract.

The next morning after my arrival we visited the farm of Richard Barden, Esq., about six miles to the eastward of Windom. Mr. Barden is a well known and prominent grain dealer, residing in St. Paul. But we had the good fortune to meet him on the place. He has 2,100 acres of land, 1,200 of which are in wheat, with a small amount in oats and corn. The work of the farm is done by monthly labor, under the direction of a superintendent. On the place is one small neat one story house, the residence of the superintendent, and two large barns and a long shed. The farm is stocked with a small herd of about twenty-five very fine short horned cows and two bulls, and a stud of about twenty highbred mares and horses. At the time of our visit an artist was engaged in sketching the stock for the purpose of publishing an illustrated catalogue. There is but a small amount of fencing on the place, the law in Minnesota, as in most of Kansas, allowing the fence question to be decided by the various districts.

About three miles to the south of Mr. Barden's place is the farm of Messrs. Thompson & Shummier, of 1,300 acres, with 300 acres in wheat. On the place is a fine two story double house, of wood, occupied by the proprietors. They are young men without families, and sons of well known capitalists in St. Paul. There is also a fine barn and other improvements projected. The place is well stocked, and has a small number of sheep. A good part of the work is done by the proprietors, assisted by other labor in the most busy seasons.

We next visited the farm of Thompson & Kendall, about eight miles west of Windom, and were received by Mr. Kendall. The farm contains 4,400 acres, of which 1,600 are in wheat, 245 in oats, 265 in barley, 235 in flax, 150 in buckwheat, 40 in turnips, and 40 in sundries :— total, 2,575 acres. On the place is a neat one story white cottage house, the residence of Mr. Kendall and family; also, a large two story wooden house for boarding the farm hands, offices, etc.; two large barns; ice house with ninety tons of ice; four tenement houses of one story, on portions of the farm that have been leased on shares, which will be discontinued so soon as the leases are out; a corn crib, twenty by one hundred feet, with piggery underneath; two vegetable houses to contain three thousand bushels, with other large barns, smaller buildings, sheds, and sheep pens in process of construction.

It is stocked with eighty-four head of cattle, a part being good short horns; sixty-two horses, mostly mares; one hundred and forty hogs, and two hundred and forty sheep, to be increased before winter to two thousand, and about one thousand fowls.

At the time of our visit, July 9th, fifteen men were employed. During harvest it was expected that the number would be increased to about eighty. The average number employed during the year is about thirty-five, at an average cost of about $17 per month, their board costing $4 50 per month.

The average yield of wheat, in good seasons, is not less than 20 bushels per acre; this year 12 bushels only are expected. Last year the No. 1 wheat was worth, on the farm, 70 cents; No. 4, 40 cents. (Last year, owing to heavy and unseasonable rains, alternating with hot days, much of the wheat was blasted in Southern Minnesota, and marked as No. 4.) Oats and barley promised well. Some of the fields of oats were estimated as high as 70 bushels, and barley 50 bushels to the acre. All but the wheat looked remarkably well. The large amount of flax here growing, as well as in other places, was solely for seed and the oil. The fiber, which appeared to be long and excellent, was put to no use.

In harvesting the grain fourteen self binders will be used, each cutting a swarth of six and one quarter feet and fifteen acres a day. Mr. Kendall gave me the following copy of a carefully made up detail statement of the cost per acre of wheat growing: —

ESTIMATE FOR RAISING WHEAT, FURNISHING EVERYTHING.

	$ cts. ms.
Plowing, 2¼ acres per day, $20 per month wages, 77c. per day, per acre,	31
Interest on team, $375; harness, $25; plow, $50; total, $450, per acre,	02 2
Wear and tear, 25 per cent on outfit,	11 2
Board, man per day, 20 cents; team 45 cents, per acre,	26
Stable men's labor and board, per acre,	20
(Stable men, wear and tear, and interest on team and harness, for one year included.)	
Sowing, 35 acres per day, wages $20 per month, 77c. per day,	02 2
Board, man, 20c.; team, 45c. per day, per acre,	01 9
Wear and tear on seeder, 25 per cent., per acre,	03 9
Interest, at 10 per cent.,	2
Harvesting (wire or cord binders), for wire or cord,	50
15 acres per day, wages $20 per month, 77c. per day, per acre,	05 1
Board of man, 25c.; team, 50c. per day, per acre,	05
Interest on reaper, $250, at 10 per cent., 150 acres per machine, per acre,	16
Wear and tear on reaper, at 25 per cent., $62 50, 150 acres per machine, per acre,	41 6
Shocking man, 77c. per day, 10 acres per day, and board at 25c., per acre,	10 2
Thrashing, 25 men at $2 per day, 40 acres, per acre,	1 25
Board, 25 men at 25c. a day, 40 acres, per acre,	15 6
Interest and wear and tear on thrasher and engine, per acre,	10
Marketing man, 77c., board 20c., board team, 45c., 40 acres per day, per acre,	32 5
Freight, 13c., at 20 bushels per acre,	2 60
Incidentals, including interest and wear and tear on permanent investment, per acre,	2 00
Total cost per acre,	$8 69 6

This estimate makes the cost of an acre of wheat, yielding 20 bushels, placed in Chicago, with an allowance of 10 per cent. interest on the whole investment for land, improvements, machinery, tools, and stock, and also of 25 per cent. for wear and tear of stock, tools, and machinery, and also of allowance for incidentals, to be $8 69 6, not including seed. Allowing $1 00 for seed will make the cost of one acre of wheat, yielding 20 bushels, laid down in Chicago, and paying an interest, or profit, of 10 per cent. on the entire investment, and 25 per cent. for wear and tear, etc., to be $9 70, or 48 cents a bushel. Wheat at 85 cents a bushel would give an additional or extraordinary profit of 37 cents a bushel, or $7 40 per acre, over and above the 10 per cent. included in the $9 70 of ordinary cost as shown in the above statement. At this rate the extraordinary profit of $7 40 per acre on the 1,600 acres of wheat on the farm, over and above the ordinary profit of 10 per cent. on the entire investment, would be $11,840.

But given the entire outfit of farm, stock, and tools, and putting the cost for wages and board for all work, except thrashing, at $20 a month, and thrashing at $2 a day, the cost of plowing, per acre was 31 cents; sowing, 3 cents; harvesting, 65 cents; and thrashing, $1 25: total, $2 24 per acre. Adding seed at $1 per acre would give the total cost of wheat growing at $3 24 per acre, or a little less than 21 cents per bushel, on 16 bushels to the acre, which is the general average for that State. Valuing the wheat at 70 cents a bushel, on the farm, would give a profit of 49 cents a bushel or $7 84 an acre, or $12,544 for the 1,600 acres of wheat. By either calculation it is seen that Commissioner Drake's estimate of 55 per cent. per annum profit is largely within the true figure, as the appreciation in the value of the land would much more than repay the expenditure for improvements on it. With 20 bushels to the acre the profit would be $17,216, and with 12 bushels to the acre, the amount expected this year, the profit would be $8,256. The total value of 1,600 acres of wheat, at 70 cents per bushel, and 16 bushels to the acre, is $17,920.

These being the results of actual operations Commissioner Drake's enthusiasm appears to be thoroughly justified.

From Windom to Sioux Falls, ninety-two miles, was through a country of remarkable beauty, with the land rolling in long and gentle billows covered with fine grasses, dotted in wide distances with the little improvements and shanties of the small farmers. Occasionally were seen the broad fields and large improvements of the great agricultural adventurers, and numbers of small towns on the line of the road. On my return I stopped at Luverne, two hundred and eleven miles from St. Paul, and made my way to the bluff to the north, which proved to be about three miles distant. From the edge of its sharp sides was presented a magnificent stretch of beautiful country which, from my point of view, appeared to be without swell or billow of any kind, except upon the eastern side of the valley, where there was a gentle rise to an apparently interminable plain. In this vast stretch the sparsity of population was very noticeable. Some five miles to the southeast were distinctly seen the farm buildings of the Rock County Farm, one of my objective points.

The next morning I drove to the farm of the Rock County Farming Company. It is incorporated and composed of Messrs. Thompson, Blakely, and Warner, well known capitalists of St. Paul. I was received by the superintendent, who drove me over the place and gave such information as was desired. The farm contains 21,000 acres, of which 4,625 are now under cultivation, with a large amount of land newly broken that will be seeded for next year's crop. Of this amount 3,251 acres are in wheat; 312 acres in flax; 550 acres in oats; 312 acres in barley; and 200 in corn. There are 96 horses and mules, 26 harvesters, 3 straw burning steam thrashers, and other farming implements to the total value of $15,000. On the place are two stations, about two miles apart, each having one house and two large barns, and other buildings for the care of tools, stock, etc. The house at Station One is of wood, two stories, double, painted white, and lathed and plastered, containing the office of the superintendent and boarding accommodation for a large number of men. At Station Two the house is smaller, of one and a half stories, painted brown, without lath or plaster, and fitted up specially as a boarding house for the farm hands. The farm is immediately on the line of the railroad and has two railroad stations.

The number of men employed is, for the month of March, 20; April and May, 56; June to July 20th, 40; July 21st to August 20th, 115; August 21st to November 15th, 70; November 16th to the end of February, 12. The average wages are $18 a month.

In going over the farm I had an excellent opportunity to observe the difference between good and bad cultivation. In some of the fields a portion of the wheat looked well, and would in all probability yield eighteen to twenty-two bushels to the acre; whilst the other portion was short, thin, choked with weeds, and would not yield more than ten bushels. One part had been well plowed, harrowed, and seeded, showing wheat without weeds, of fine growth and good stand. There can be no doubt that much of the partial as well as total failures that I observed might have been very much lessened, if not altogether averted, by better cultivation. Here, as in other places, the corn, oats, and barley gave better promise than the wheat, though some of the wheat fields had a very good appearance. In a number of places there were gangs of a dozen or more plows engaged in breaking new ground for next year's crop. Each plow was of the sulky pattern, with disc coulter, drawn by three mules or horses, the driver occupying a seat between the wheels. One of the plows was of a new pattern, being without a landside, and cutting a sixteen inch furrow four and a half inches deep, which it cut and turned more beautifully than any I had before seen.

On this farm, and at other points on this road, grasshoppers were doing some damage. Earlier in the season the superintendent had made a raid upon them, and showed me some heaps of a black mass, which he said were fifty-six bushels of that insect plague which he had caught in a tar machine, from the side of one quarter section.

Everywhere fruit growing appeared to be altogether neglected, and vegetable gardens and poultry were scarce.

I was informed that the large farmers on the road obtained special rates for their transportation, and that those rates were fifty per cent. below the rates charged to the small farmers ; and that their farming implements were obtained at thirty-three and one-third per cent. discount from published prices, which the small farmers were compelled to pay.

The buildings of some of the small farmers who have been there located for some four or five years, or more, had a quite comfortable appearance; but the new settlers were generally without a sign of comfort. So far as I could learn, in conversation with them and upon inquiry, there was the same distress that I had found in Kansas and other places. In speaking of this matter with the superintendent of the Rock County farm, he told me of an incident in his farm business that illustrated their poverty. Having occasion to find board for some of his men who were at work at a distance too far from either station to be there boarded, he made application to one of the small farmers in the neighborhood, who had a comfortable appearance, to board the men. Yes, he would be glad to do it; but before he took them he must get some wood, as he had none ; he had not more than enough flour for one day, nor had he groceries, and the storekeepers would not give him credit. The superintendent then applied to another farmer who had wood, and flour enough to last for a few days, but neither coffee, tea, sugar, lard, nor other groceries, and the traders also refused to credit him. But the superintendent supplied the farmer with what he needed and sent the men to him. In town I was informed that the small farmers were generally hopelessly in debt; and so I was told by some of the farmers.

Flour was selling in the towns at seven dollars per barrel. I did not anywhere along the road notice any flouring mills.

The valley of the Red River of the North in the northern part of Dakota and southern portion of Manitoba is about three hundred and fifty miles in length, north and south, and sixty miles wide, east and west, of unsurpassed fertility and beauty. The surface is nearly level, with hardly sufficient dip to afford to all parts a thorough drainage, on which account some portions of its area are unfit for cultivation without artificial drainage. But much the larger portion is well drained by the smaller water courses that empty into the Red River, giving large bodies of rich vegetable and alluvial loam well adapted to the growth of wheat, rye, barley, oats and the vegetables grown in the northern States. But it is too far north for corn. The wetter portions of the valley afford abundant grass, which is used for feeding and cut for hay. It is claimed that the capabilities of this valley are equal to the present wheat production of the whole United States. The Northern Pacific Railroad crosses the valley at Fargo, which lies upon the west side of the river, and about fifty miles above its southern end, and holds a land grant of forty miles on each side of its track. The St. Paul and Pacific road traverses the valley from south to north, about ten miles to the east of the river.

The failure of Jay Cooke & Co., in 1873, had the effect of throwing large bodies of the lands belonging to the Northern Pacific road into the hands of the holders of its securities; among them were the owners of some of the farms hereafter described.

Oliver Dalrymple, of St. Paul, the pioneer in the great farm development in this country in the Northwest, began his first operation seventeen years ago, in Minnesota, near St. Paul, where, for a number of years, he successfully cultivated a farm of 2,500 acres. At the time he commenced his work near St. Paul, in 1866, he paid $2 00 a bushel for his seed wheat, and sold his crop for $1 83; from his first crop paying for the whole investment and leaving a large surplus. After the Northern Pacific lands had passed into individual hands, as above referred to, Mr. Dalrymple entered into an arrangement with some of the holders, by which he was to undertake the management of their lands in the growing of wheat and other products. The proprietors of the lands to furnish land, stock, tools, and the capital required for seed, labor, and improvements, upon condition that when the products of the farms had paid all expenditures, with an agreed interest, he was to receive a clear title of one half of each farm with its stock and improvements.

In the spring of 1876 he commenced his operations near Castleton, upon what are now known as the Cass farm, of 6,355 acres; and the Cheney farm, of 5,200 acres. The following year work was begun on what is known as the Grandin farm, at Grandin, of 40,000 acres. Subsequently Mr. Dalrymple obtained, in his own right, the Alton farm, of 4,000 acres, adjoining the Cass farm.

On arriving at Fargo, July 12th, I at once attempted to find Mr. Dalrymple at his office in that town, but did not succeed, he being at Castleton. Most fortunately I encountered Mr. J. L. Grandin, who at once cordially invited me to a seat in his carriage and a visit to his farm, at Grandin, thirty-six miles to the north of Fargo. I gladly accepted the invitation, leaving that town about 4 P.M. and arriving at the farm at about 10 that night. During the continuance of daylight my attention was fully engrossed by the beauty of the valley and the large fields of wheat and oats, standing three to four feet high, with their heads level as a house floor. After the sun went down the mosquitoes had my undivided attention.

That portion of the farm known as the Grandin, in which Mr. Dalrymple has an interest and manages, lies on the west side of the Red River, about six miles to the north of Elm River, a tributary. It has a frontage on Red River of four miles, running back to the west some thirteen miles, and contains 28,000 acres. A portion, only, is in a solid body; on the western side some of the alternate sections being held by other parties. Some six miles further to the north, on Goose River, another tributary of the Red, is a body of 12,000 acres, which make up the 40,000 acres of the Grandin farm. Twenty-four miles to the west the Grandin Brothers, J. L., W. J., and E. B. Grandin, bankers, of Tidioute, Pennsylvania, have another tract of nearly 30,000 acres, known as the Mayville farm, in which Mr. Dalrymple has no interest. This last farm is designed for stock raising, being well supplied with water from the heads of the Elm and Goose rivers, and has at present 250 head of cattle, with some Durham stock, 2 bulls and 2 calves being of full blood, and 70 head of Cottswold sheep, the ram shearing 22 pounds of washed wool. About 200 acres are in oats and barley, with some wheat, and 600 to 800 tons of hay are cut.

J. L. Grandin is the principal owner of the 40,000 acre, or Grandin farm. At present there are on the place three stations, or points where are located the buildings necessary for the operations in their sections. Station One is located in the northeastern part of the farm, about 250 yards distant from the river. At this station are two dwellings, both of two stories and good size; one is painted white, being the residence of the farm superintendent and the foreman at that section; the other, painted brown, is fitted up specially as a boarding house for the hands. There are also two large barns, the general farm office, a large building for the storage and care of the tools, known as machinery hall, a steam feed mill, blacksmith shop, granary, vegetable storehouses, piggery, sheds, etc., in all thirteen good, substantial, well painted buildings, having the appearance, at a short distance, of a considerable village. At this station are two large wind mills, one near the superintendent's residence, the other on the bank of the river, about 300 yards distant, that forces water into a tank at the station. On the bank of the river is a storehouse for the shipment of grain, with two cars to run on a double wooden tramway, so arranged that the loaded car in descending to the boat will draw up the empty one.

Station Two is two and a half miles to the south of Station One, containing the dwelling of the foreman at that portion of the farm, and a boarding house, both smaller than at Station One; a machinery hall, a large barn, and a blacksmith shop, with other buildings, eight in all, substantial and well painted. At this station is a large water tank, filled by a wind mill on the bank of the river one half mile to the east. On the river bank, at that point, is another storehouse like that at Station One, and for the same purpose.

Station Three, one half mile south and one mile west of Station Two, has one dwelling of one and a half stories for the foreman there located, and cooking arrangements for the men there employed, who find sleeping room in the loft over machinery hall; beside which there is a large barn and other small buildings. At this station there was being erected a granary of the capacity of 50,000 bushels. The buildings of this station are of the same substantial character as the others upon the farm. The three stations are connected by telegraph and telephone, and with the general office at Station One.

The local management of the farm is under the care of a nephew of Mr. Dalrymple, of the same name, who is superintendent, with a foreman at each station. The foreman at Station One is a native of New Hampshire, and has his wife and three children with him, being the only woman and children on the whole place.

The numbers employed on the farm are, from April 1st to April 30th, 150 men; from May 1st to July

15th, 20 men; but if breaking new ground, 50; from July 16th to July 31st, 100 men; from August 1st to September 15th, 250 men; from September 16th to October 31st, 75 men; from November 1st to March 31st, 10 men.

The wages are, from November 1st to March 31st, $15 per month; from April 1st to April 30th, $18; from May 1st to July 31st, $16; from August 1st to August 15th, $2 per day; from August 16th to September 15th, $1 50 per day; from September 16th to October 31st, $18 per month.

The tools, machinery, and animals employed are, 67 plows, of which 11 are gangs of 2 plows each; 64 harrows; 32 seeders of 8 feet; 6 mowers; 34 self binding harvesters; 7 steam engines and thrashers adapted to burning straw for fuel; 50 wagons; and 125 head of horses and mules. For 30 days 30 teams of 2 horses are hired. There are on the place 100 hogs and pigs, and 30 head of cattle. This year there are 5,300 acres in cultivation, of which 4,855 acres are in wheat, 304 acres in oats, 127 acres in barley, and 9 acres in potatoes. About 1,000 tons of hay are cut.

There are 1,200 acres of new land now broken, to be seeded next year, in addition to the amount already under cultivation, giving 6,500 acres for the crop of 1880. It is the avowed intention to add to the amount under cultivation from year to year, and construct additional stations as required.

The men are called at four o'clock in the morning, breakfast, and get to work a little after five, and work till seven in the evening, with one hour at noon for dinner, making nearly thirteen hours of labor per day.

Going to the Grandin farm from the way of Fargo, one mile from the place, upon the left hand, a field of one mile square of wheat was seen, belonging to Dr. Garrett, of Philadelphia. Passing that field, with no visible division between, the wheat fields of the Grandin farm are reached, lying on both sides of the road for four continuous miles ; that on the left hand being two miles wide and on the right about a half mile to the river. A row of young elms has been set out on both sides of the road for the full four miles, and, also, about the yard of the superintendent's dwelling, at Station One. But not a fruit tree or bush was to be seen. Mr. Grandin informed me it was the intention to divide the whole farm into section lots of 640 acres each, opening roads on the section lines and planting elms on all the roads.

Every facility was afforded for the fullest observation, and to give me all the information desired. It would be difficult to find a finer sight than was presented by those magnificent fields of grain, standing breast high, taking on the golden yellow that precedes the harvest, their heads, as far as the eye could reach, standing as level and smooth as the top of a great table ; and when fanned by the wind moving in ripples and waves like the waters of a sea.

It was believed that the yield of wheat would be at least twenty bushels to the acre. Some portions, it was said, would give more than thirty bushels. It certainly was very fine. The grain grown upon the farm, and by others near the river, was shipped to Fargo by way of the Grandin line of steamers. The river, though narrow and tortuous, affording plenty of water for boats of light draft; the current appearing to run about two and a half or three miles an hour.

On my return to Fargo, by stage, I had for companions two gentlemen from Iowa, who had been examining the valley up to near the British line. They told me that farther to the north the wheat appeared to be even better than at Grandin or nearer Fargo.

On the way to that town my attention was particularly attracted by the many large fields of wheat and oats, some of them a mile square, all along the road, and away from it as far as could be seen from the top of the stage. Inquiries put to the driver gave me the information that much the larger portion belonged to men doing business in Fargo, or its neighborhood. It was doctor A, or lawyer B, or some merchant, or trader, or speculator who owned this or that field. There, as elsewhere, everybody had turned wheat growers or farmers of some kind.

Two miles east of Castleton, and eighteen west of Fargo, is the station of Dalrymple, and the sites of the Cass, Cheney, and Alton farms, forming one compact body of land, on the two sides of the road, six miles in length, north and south, and four miles in width, east and west; this body being one wheat field for the six miles, north and south, and three miles on the road, which cuts it in the center, except for a few small bodies of oats and barley.

The Cass farm, owned by Charles W. Cass, of New York City, has 6,355 acres, of which 4,327 acres are in wheat, and 350 acres in oats and barley. Newly broken ground for next year's seeding, 320 acres.

The Cheney farm, of 5,200 acres, owned by Benjamin P. Cheney, of Boston, Massachusetts, has 3,480 acres in wheat, and 320 acres in oats and barley. No new land broken.

The Alton farm, of 4,000 acres, the exclusive property of Mr. Dalrymple, has about 2,000 acres in grain (I have not the exact figures) and 1,200 acres of newly broken land.

The Cass and Cheney farms will employ, during harvest and thrashing, 235 men. The Alton in the the same ratio, or about 55 men. During the winter season each farm requires two or three men to take care of the stock and look after the machinery and buildings; say seven men. When no new land is broken not more than ten men are required on either farm between seed time and harvest; say, twenty-five men for the three farms. During seed time the three farms require about 125 men.

On the Cass farm there are thirteen seeders, thirty self binding harvesters, and five straw burning steam thrashers. The Cheney farm has nineteen seeders, twenty-six self binding harvesters, and four straw burning steam thrashers. The Alton farm has substantially the same ratio of implements to the number of acres under cultivation, and the three farms have nearly double the amount of other farming implements and work stock as is here reported in use on the Grandin place.

The four farms being under one general management, and conducted on the same principle, require the same number of men, animals, and tools for every hundred acres under cultivation, and are under substantially the same rate of expense; so that the report for the Grandin farm will closely indicate the working force and methods of the others. The accounts of each farm are kept altogether separate and distinct.

On the Cheney farm are three stations; number two having eight buildings, the other two a smaller number. The Cass farm, also, has three stations, one principal and two minor. The Alton farm has two stations, both being small.

Everywhere upon these three farms were observed the same evidences of good husbandry, substantial and well kept buildings and improvements, tools and stock that was seen on the Grandin farm. In none of the fields were weeds to be seen, nor tools grass grown and covered in the field edges and corners, nor doors nor gates hanging by single hinges.

Here as in parts of Kansas and Minnesota, are no field fencings. The face of the country is one broad, unbroken tract, except for an occasional station of the large farms, or small farm buildings.

Most persons in reading of fields described by hundreds and thousands of acres can form but little idea of their actual or comparative sizes. To assist to a better understanding of the sizes of these fields and farms I will state that Manhattan Island, the site of the City of New York, has an area of about twenty-two square miles, or 14,000 acres. The fields of grain of the three farms lying together contain an area of 10,477 acres, or about three fourths of the area of the City of New York. The Grandin farm of 40,000 acres has nearly space enough for three cities like

New York; and the whole farm property of the Grandins would furnish sites for five such cities. Whatever else may be said of these operations, they certainly are not wanting in grandeur.

It was claimed that the yield of wheat on these three farms would not be less than twenty-two bushels to the acre; some portions of the fields on the Alton farm were the finest I had seen.

A careful estimate of the cost of wheat growing on the four farms under Mr. Dalrymple's management would show a cost materially less than that given by Mr. Kendall, on the Thompson & Kendall farm, which was $3 24 per acre, land, stock, and tools being given. But calculated on the Thompson & Kendall basis — of $3 24 per acre of cost, with twenty bushels per acre of yield, at 70 cents per bushel, would give a cost of a little more than 16 cents a bushel, allowing 10 per cent. interest on entire investment and 25 per cent. for wear and tear of tools, and a net profit of $10 76 per acre. This would give a profit on the crop of wheat on the four farms of $157,763; or for the Grandin farm alone, $52,239. The total value of the whole amount of wheat, at 70 cents, would be $205,268; or for the Grandin farm, $67,970. But the proprietors confidently expect to realize not less than 90 cents a bushel for their wheat, on account of its superiority and the facilities they can command for transportation and storage. They, also, have "special railroad rates."

Between Fargo and Bismarck, a distance of 194 miles, are many farms of the size of thousands of acres that are already under partial cultivation, or are being prepared for immediate cultivation under similar conditions. Among those farthest west may be mentioned one at the Eighth Siding, 83 miles from Fargo, the farm of Adams & Russell, with 700 acres in grain. At the Thirteenth Siding, 143 miles west, the Troy farm, owned by Van Dusen, of Troy, New York, with 1,400 acres now broken for next year. At the Fourteenth Siding, 151 miles west, the farm owned by Steele, of Milwaukee, of 5,120 acres, with 750 acres in grain, and 1,200 acres of new land broken. At the Seventeenth Siding, 181 miles west, the Clark farm, owned by capitalists in Philadelphia, who are said to hold vast tracts, with 500 acres in grain and 1,000 acres of new land broken. These farms I saw from the cars, and inquiries informed me that for miles upon either side of the road, similar farms and work were to be seen.

The small farmers and their shanties in that region were not numerous; but so far as I could learn their condition was not relatively better nor worse than in other sections.

In Minnesota, as in Dakota and Kansas, a large portion of the residents of the towns, especially on the lines of the railroads, with the officers, conductors, engineers, and other employés of the roads, were generally adventurers in agriculture; holding and cultivating by contracts, shares, or otherwise such lands as they could obtain and work.

I found that in most places, from Brainerd, Minnesota, to Bismarck, Dakota, in all the great region where wheat is grown so abundantly and cheaply, first class flour, such as was made from the quality of grain there grown, was selling, from the local stores, at about seven dollars a barrel. With wheat at seventy cents a bushel, the highest price the small farmer could obtain, and flour at seven dollars a barrel, which he was compelled to pay for all that he consumed, it is readily seen that the wheat grower is compelled to give ten bushels of wheat for one barrel of flour, that contains only about four and one half bushels of the grain from which it is made. That the farmer now, instead of having his wheat converted into flour, as did our fathers, for a toll of one eighth or tenth, is compelled to submit to an extortion of more than one half, in face of the fact that machinery has greatly facilitated that operation. In Kansas I found that the toll extorted from the farmers by some of the local flouring mills amounted, in some cases, to more than seventy per cent. I did not observe any flouring mills upon the lines of those roads.

I particularly noticed the conspicuous absence of women and children upon the large farms. In no case was the permanent residence of a family to be found upon them, or anything that could be called a home, with a possible exception in the instance of Mr. Kendall, on the Thompson & Kendall farm. Even the Dalrymple families being but transient dwellers at the farms, their homes being in St. Paul. The idea of home does not pertain to them; they are simple business ventures, before which the home feature sinks out of sight.

Naturally this will save all expense of schools or churches in their neighborhood, and the schoolmaster and clergyman will there have a perpetual holiday.

But I was pleased to see that a Sunday service was held on the Grandin farm, conducted by the bookkeeper.

Throughout my tour it was noticed that there was a great abundance of unemployed labor. The morning I left the Grandin farm there were at one time thirteen men at the office door, soliciting work, a portion only obtaining it, the others tramping onwards in further search. On one of the farms I inquired of one man what pay he was receiving. He replied eight dollars, but was promised more during harvest. I then asked him where he expected to get employment after the harvest was over. He said he did not expect to be able to find any before the next spring's work commenced. The answers appeared so natural, and so like what all must have given, that I did not repeat them.

To well weigh the economic effects of the developments here considered, it must be remembered that they are yet in their infancy — that they are mainly the growth of the last half of the past and the present decade — and must make some effort to estimate the probable future development of the same forces and effects under the present rate of acceleration.* All parties engaged in these enterprises concurred in the statement that great numbers of capitalists who are already large holders of agricultural lands, as well as others who have not yet obtained any, are only wait-

---

* Since my examination of these operations the development and extension of bonanza farms has been marvellous. For statistics of this matter see chapter on "Growth and Development of Tenant and Bonanza Farms."

ing the results of the present harvest before they also enter into the business. The amounts of new land broken, in all directions, for future seeding, are very great.

The two great facts developed by these observations are, that those who have gone into wheat growing upon a large scale, making use of the most improved machinery and cheap labor, are making colossal fortunes at seventy cents per bushel for wheat, limited only by the number of acres cultivated and the skill with which the work is done; and that it may also be grown, at large profits, for less than twenty-five cents per bushel.

But that, on the other hand, the small farmers, depending mainly on their own labor, with limited capital and less machinery, are not making a comfortable subsistence, but are running behind hand and must go under; and that a further reduction in the market price for food products must hasten their end.

Before agricultural machinery had come into general use, and before the age of railroads, the farms of our fathers would average, in size, but little more than one hundred acres, with an amount of plowland equalling about fifty acres each. Very rarely did they exceed double that amount. On every such farm was there a family home, with all the ties, endearments, advantages, and improvements that the word "home" conveys to our minds. They furnished not alone homes, but employment, abundance, and comfort for a family of at least a dozen persons. Go through New England, New York, New Jersey, Pennsylvania, and Ohio, and see the great numbers of such places, all of them formerly family homesteads, lying within sight and hailing distance of each other. From a half dozen to an hundred may be seen from almost any elevated point.

Now mark the change that has already taken place and is fast obtaining in all our new and great agricultural regions. (Under the power of machinery and capital the farms have grown from the size of 100 acres, as formerly, to 1,000 acres, to 10,000 acres, to 100,000 acres, even to 500,000 acres, or nearly 800 square miles, and more, with not one home upon their vast areas;) with no one surrounding a family rooftree with all that made the old home a paradise. (Yet these huge tracts are being developed, cultivated, and made to yield as was no farm in the days of our fathers. Now, machinery and a few score or a few hundred hirelings and animals, to run and attend the machines, do the work under the eye of overseers. The hirelings)— the human animals —(are worked for a few weeks or a few months in the year, paid barely enough to live upon for the time being, and then are turned out) and driven from the place, to tramp or live as best they can, no matter what may be the want and misery of their lives, whilst the brute animals and machines are well housed and cared for. The owner of the farm has a property interest in the brute, but no interest whatever in the human animal other than that of getting the greatest possible amount of work for the least amount of compensation. The most valuable improvements are for the protection of the brutes and the machinery, whilst the human tillers of the soil have neither right nor interest in anything they see, or touch, or produce. In this way the finest sections of our country, in tracts running up to the size of eight hundred or more square miles — areas that would give fifty acres of plowland to more than a thousand families, and to our fathers would have furnished homes, ample employment, and comfort to more than ten thousand people — are now without even one home, and furnish but transient and uncertain employment to a few hundreds.

This state of things is made possible, and is obtaining, solely by and under the power and use of machinery; first in the hands of individual capitalists; then in the hands of companies; and, lastly, by corporations.

The owners of these large tracts have bonanzas, yielding great profits, not one dollar of which is expended in beautifying and permanently improving their vast estates, beyond that necessary for the care of the stock and tools, nor in sustaining a permanent population. Their homes, their pleasures, their family ties, are not upon their farms. Their wealth is flaunted in the gaieties and dissipations, or expended in building and developing some distant city or country. But the owner and cultivator of the small farm in its neighborhood, upon which he has planted his rooftree, and around which are gathered all his hopes and ambitions, finds it impossible to pay his taxes, clothe and educate, or find any comfort for his wife and little ones. The case of the small farmer is steadily going from bad to worse. The two can not exist together; the small farmer can not successfully compete with his gigantic neighbor under present conditions. He will inevitably be swallowed up. It is at best but a question of time.

Thus are vast areas, in the very heart of our country, barred and closed to the occupation and ownership of our people in small tracts, and the making of homes for a strong and thrifty population, but are made centers of weakness that are sure, soon or late, under present tendencies, to spread over the whole land.

On the large majority of these great holdings small portions only of their areas are found under present cultivation. During the first year one to three thousand acres are put under the plow, and each succeeding season an addition of one or more thousand acres is made to the amount that is worked. In this manner the proprietors declare it to be their intention to increase their business to the extent desired. The greatest number of acres under the plow, by one man, of which I have any knowledge, is in California, near Colusa, in the Sacramento valley, about one hundred miles above the city of Sacramento. Upon that farm fifty-seven thousand acres, or ninety square miles, are under cultivation, mostly in wheat. The labor is in large part Chinese.

The development of the large farm interest is by no means confined to Kansas, Minnesota, and Dakota. The sections covered in my late tour are but three points where these developments have been the most recent, as well as of great extent. In Kansas there has been a movement in the same direction of perhaps unparalleled magnitude.

James Macdonald, Esq., the travelling correspondent of the "Scotsman," a newspaper published in Scotland, in a recent publication, writes of numbers of gigantic cattle and grain farms that fell under his observation in 1877, in various parts of our great grain and meat producing sections. I make a few quotations from his "Food in the Far West," published by William P. Nimmo, London and Edinburgh. Of Texas he says : —

"Two of the largest cattle owners in this neighborhood are Mr. Allen and Mr. Butler, the former of whom has a fence along the line side for no less than twelve miles. . . . . . Mr. Butler's ranch is under the management of a young, practical, intelligent Scotchman, extends to over 27,000 acres, all enclosed, and is held in connection with an arable farm of over 900 acres a few miles farther west, where Indian corn and sugar are grown extensively and successfully." — Page 37.

On pages 42 and 43 he says : —

"Many of the large owners are nonresident, the number of squatters are few and growing but slowly, and hence the population of this district is limited and wide spread. There are a few 'broad acred squires' here. Captain King, Nueces County, possesses 150,000 acres fenced, and about 200,000 unfenced land, and owns between 40,000 and 50,000 cattle and 5,000 sheep. . . . . . Captain Kennedy, also of Nueces County, owns about 140,000 acres, all within fence, and about 40,000 cattle; while Messrs. Coleman, Matthias & Fulton, of Aransas, have 210,000 acres within fence, and own about 100,000 cattle. . . . . . Mrs. Rabb, Corpus Christi, has 50,000 acres enclosed, and owns 15,000 cattle. . . . . . There are many others who count their acres and cattle by thousands."

A farm of 350,000 acres would furnish area sufficient for twenty-five such cities as New York, on Manhattan Island.

Mr. Macdonald in writing of Kansas tells of Albert Crane's 10,000 acre farm, on page 81; of the 100,000 acres of Mr. George Grant, of London, England, page 82; and of the wheat farm of Mr. T. C. Henry, near Abilene, page 77. He also speaks of the "half cultivated homesteads that had been deserted," on the line of the Central Branch Union Pacific Railroad, and of some of the difficulties that the small farmers encounter which make success impossible page 74. On page 95 he writes: —

"The 'Cattle King' of Colorado is Mr. J. W. Iliff, of South Platte. He began cattle raising on a small scale in 1861, and now owns close on 35,000 cattle and nine ranches, extending to over 15,000 acres, and stretching for thirty miles along the north bank of the south fork of the river Platte."

Mr. Macdonald also tells of large farms in Illinois. One in Sangamon County, of 4,200 acres, belonging to Mr. Sculley, from Ireland, page 129; and another of 3,000 acres, near Berlin, known as the Grove Park farm, owned by the Messrs. Browns, page 140; and Mr. John B. Gillett, Elkhart, Macon County, has a farm of 12,000 acres, a considerable portion of which is devoted to Indian corn, the larger part being raised by tenants, page 144. He says that

"A considerable extent of this State is worked by tenants who pay a money rent of about three dollars per acre, or a certain proportion of the crops grown — a third, or a half, or two fifths." — Page 130.

California is noted for its farms of thousands of acres, and the great proportion of its area that is cultivated by tenantry. Throughout the whole extent of that portion of our western country that was not cursed by the existence of slavery upon its soil, there has, within the present and past decade, been an alarming increase in the number of great landholders who, with all the power of capital, machinery, and cheap labor, have entered into deadly competition with the small farmer. Before the census of 1870 had been taken the movement had begun throughout all the free States, as shown by the following table, exhibiting, first, the number of farms of 1,000 acres and over in the nonslaveholding States west of Ohio, in the years 1860 and 1870; and, secondly, the number of farms of the same character in the nonslaveholding States east of Ohio and including that State, as shown by the Census Reports of 1870.

	1860	1870		1860	1870
California,	262	713	Connecticut,	4	1
Illinois,	194	302	Maine,	2	0
Indiana,	74	76	Massachusetts,	0	3
Iowa,	10	38	New Hampshire,	4	6
Kansas,	1	13	New Jersey,	6	8
Michigan,	3	5	New York,	21	86
Minnesota,	0	2	Ohio,	112	69
Nebraska,	1	0	Pennsylvania,	15	76
Nevada,	2	3	Rhode Island,	0	2
Oregon,	47	88	Vermont,	11	15
Utah,	0	2			
Washington,	1	12	Total,	175	219
Wisconsin,	11	32			
Total,	606	1,286			

In the Northwestern States between 1860 and 1870

the number had more than doubled, and in th. N eastern section, the very oldest portion of the agri tural region of our country, the increase had een nineteen per cent. Of the movement in the past and present decade enough is shown in the following chap ter to demonstrate that within the last twenty years we have taken immense strides in placing our country in the position in which Europe is found after a thousand years of feudal robbery and tyranny of capital — with the lands concentrated in large tracts in the hands of the few, and cultivated by a people who are but mere slaves of the rich.

Before the end of the first quarter of the present century this thing was simply impossible in the Northern States, though it existed in the Southern as a natural feature of slavery. It was not till after labor saving machinery had approached its present marvellous development, and had displaced so great a per centage of the manual labor of the country as to practically turn one half of the workers out of all productive pursuits, that unemployed labor became so abundant and cheap as to be available in such operations. Under present conditions capital can at any time depend upon obtaining all the service required for any emergency, upon its own terms, and it has become possible, in the old free States, to profitably monopolize and cultivate vast tracts of land as herein related. Even so soon as the close of this second decade of the movement in the North, it is found to have obtained an acceleration equalled only by a body falling through space. The effects growing out of this state of things are of the most serious character, and will inevitably

ing upon our people the most terrible revolutionary
facts.

It has already begun and will complete the destruction of the small farm interests of our country, and
  out of existence the homes and homesteads of
the people. Because, under the operation of what
capitalistic economists declare to be a "beneficent
competition," and the present great division of labor,
the small farmer can not successfully compete with
his gigantic neighbor who commands unlimited resources of capital and cheap labor. The small farmer,
in this "beneficent competition," is in the same relative position to the great farmer as is the hand loom
weaver by the side of the great Pacific Mill, in Massachusetts, or the hand pressman in the midst of the
mighty machines of Printing House Square. No one
individual, nor aggregation of individuals can, by the
unaided use of his or their personal labor, under any
system of combination or cooperation, successfully
compete with unlimited combinations of machinery,
capital, and cheap labor in either weaving or printing;
neither can it be done in farming. In the case of
either the hand loom weaver, the hand pressman, or
the small farmer, they are alike dependent on their
own unaided exertions, with the tools and machinery
that each can successfully use; and upon their individual production alone must each and all subsist and
obtain the comforts of life, if they have any. But the
capitalist does not enter into the labors of either of
these employments, nor any other. He buys the
cheapest and most effective labor to be had in the
market, and uses it in such manner as to constantly

cheapen it in price, or lessen it in quantity, or both, until at this time it has become a well known fact that free labor is much cheaper than slave. That is, it is cheaper to buy labor in the market, and use it as wanted, than to be compelled to keep the laborer for the whole year at the lowest cost of food and clothing.

In this respect the condition of the small farmer is worse than that of either the weaver or printer, because the vital work of the farm is limited to two short seasons in the year — those of seed time and harvest — and by no possibility can it be extended beyond those seasons. Hence the amount of work that can be done in either the shortest or most laborious of those seasons, is the utmost measure of the product which must provide subsistence for the whole year for himself and his dependents.

Before the present great division of labor the farmer and his family, when not employed in planting and reaping, were engaged in spinning and weaving, and the other manufacturing operations of the farm household that provided the family, by their own domestic manufactures, with the food, clothing, and shelter necessary for a comfortable, and often luxurious, subsistence. But now, through the changes that have been wrought by machinery and new forces, all the domestic manufacturing industries have been irretrievably destroyed, or developed under other forms and conditions in the towns and cities, leaving to the farm only the work of producing the raw products of bread and meat. Even these raw products must go into the market for manufacture before the farmer can use the larger proportion of them for his own food, as must the raw products of cotton and wool before their growers can use them for clothing. But bread and meat do not form more than one fourth part of the subsistence of society, nor of any of its members — not even of the farmers. These principles were well understood and clearly stated by Adam Smith, as follows : —

> "When the division of labor has once been thoroughly introduced, the produce of a man's own labor can supply but a very small part of his occasional wants. The far greater part of them are supplied by the produce of other men's labor, which he purchases with the produce, or, what is the same thing, with the price of the produce of his own. But this can not be made till such time as the produce of his own labor has not only been completed, but sold." — *Wealth of Nations.*

Therefore the farmer must have such a market for his raw food products as will supply him with all the necessaries of life, or he will starve as surely as a manufacturer of cloth, or the maker of boots and shoes. But unlike any other producer the imperative laws of the seasons have limited the time for the effectual industry of the farm to about one fourth part of the year, during which period the small farmer must make provision for all his operative force for the full year, and from the fruit of the labor of himself and his own family solely, during seed time and harvest, must he provide for all their wants and comforts until the return of those seasons.

But with the capitalist farmer it is very different. The facts that I have gathered show that upon the Grandin farm, for example, during the four weeks of seed time, from April 1st to April 30th, there were

150 men employed; and for the six weeks of harvest, from August 1st to September 15th, there were 250 men, at wages that would barely support the workers during the time they worked; whilst, for the five months from November 1st to March 31st there would be only 10 men, as estimated for the coming winter; but in fact only 5 men were employed during that period of the past season, with neither woman nor child at any time.

Whilst the small farmer is compelled to feed, clothe, shelter, and altogether provide for the same number of persons for the whole year, the capitalist feeds, clothes, and shelters only about one tenth of the number, in proportion to the amount of work done or product produced, and that for less than one half of the year. In doing this the capitalist brings to his assistance the most improved and highly developed machinery, such as the small farmer can utilize to but a comparatively small degree, except through the means of coöperation.

Against the unlimited use of this combination of capital, machinery, and cheap labor the individual farmer, either singly or in communities, can not successfully contend and must go under. It is a combination of the most powerful social and economic forces known to man, and all efforts for successful competition must and will fail so long as the three remain united.

Cheap labor alone always has been, and still is, the curse of every country or people where it has or does still exist. This fact is too well known to require more than its statement. It is the one thing that degrades and blasts every people where it obtains, and to just the extent of its hold. To-day the most conspicuous social feature of China, of India, and of Mexico, is the cheapness of labor; and in these very countries we find the greatest poverty, misery, and degradation. In precisely the same degree does cheap labor degrade and make miserable all the nations of Europe where and to the extent it obtains. So it is in our own country. But, on the other hand, never were our people, nor any other, so prosperous, with so great and rapid development, as when its labor was dearest. Our distress and the distress of England have come upon us as the labor of both has been cheapened; and the greater the degree and more intimate the union between capital, machinery, and cheap labor the more rapid the increase of the distress. Their union sounds the knell of all those forms of industry, and the social development and material progress out of which have grown our institutions.

The successful development of the large farm interest has the direct and immediate effect not only of impoverishing the sections in which they exist, and robbing and skinning the lands without any compensating benefit, but of barring them to the settlement of a fixed and strong population that would cover the soil with homes of comfort for a great people. Not one dollar of the gross amount or net profit received from its products is returned and placed upon the land from which it is taken, beyond the construction of the fewest buildings necessary to shelter and protect the laborers in the working seasons, and the care of the work stock and tools. On the whole 5,300 cultivated acres of the Grandin farm there was not one family finding there a permanent home, where there should have been at least one to every fifty acres of land in crop, or one hundred and six families. This would give one hundred and six houses in place of the five that were there found; one hundred and six barns in place of three, with other buildings in like proportion, and a permanent population of at least five hundred where there is not now one fixed inhabitant, with all the accessories of household comfort and home improvement that do not now exist in the smallest degree. And so of the other 65,000 acres belonging to the same parties when it shall come into cultivation. A fixed population that would be continually adding to the wealth of the country and making demands for the school and the church, instead of a nonresident ownership that is heaping up colossal fortunes by skinning the land, impoverishing the people, making war upon women and children, and leaving the country without homes.

More than this: It will rob future generations of their patrimony in the soil. The fifty millions that the next half century will add to our population must find their homes in the already overcrowded towns or cities, or perchance among the occasional workers and servants upon the great farms. The small farmer and family homestead will have passed away, and our great agricultural regions will show the results of the "beneficent competition" that has destroyed them.

The effect of the operations of these adventurers and speculators in farming, under the power of capital and cheap labor, is not confined to the sections in which they have had their greatest development, but covers our whole country and is revolutionizing Europe. Throughout our land there is a marked decadence in small farming, with increase of poverty and distress among the farmers. So long as the farmer could find a ready market for his products, at good prices, that was indicated by wheat when in demand upon the farm at one dollar and a quarter to one dollar and fifty cents the bushel, he prospered. When Mr. Dalrymple was compelled to pay two dollars a bushel for his seed wheat, and sold his crop for one dollar and eighty-three cents, not only did he but all classes prospered — none more than the merchant and capitalist. But now, when wheat upon the farm will command only from fifty to seventy cents a bushel, not only are the small farmers of our country being ruined, but the farmers of England are being destroyed, and the agriculture of that country, also, is dragged to inevitable demoralization.

By the impoverishment of our farmers we are enabled to "beneficently compete" with the English farmer, and sell wheat in that country at less than one dollar a bushel, with profit to the foreign merchant and carrier, when the absolute cost to the British agriculturist to raise it is not less than one dollar and a half — our farmers raising but twenty bushels to the acre where the English farmers grow thirty. The result is, that by one and the same operation the small farm interest in the United States, and the general farming interests of Great Britain are both destroyed. Both countries are being dragged into revolution, and the only interests that derive even an apparent and temporary benefit in the midst of this general destruction are the bonanza farmers of our own country, with the foreign merchants in both, and the ocean carriers.

Whilst we are doing all these things it may be well for us to remember that we are giving to our Trans-Atlantic brethren some lessons in agriculture that it would be most strange if they did not improve upon. The adoption and use of our machines and methods in England and Ireland, in Hungary and Russia, in France, in Germany, and in India, will produce the same results in those countries as in this. Capital, machinery, and cheap labor will grow wheat at a cost of sixteen to twenty cents a bushel, for all the expenses of seed and labor in cultivating and harvesting, as well in Europe as in America. Already do those countries possess cheap labor in the greatest abundance, with capital and the lands concentrated in the hands of the few. The only other requisites wanting are the proper machinery and management. We stand ready to furnish both if they are not to be found at home.

How long will it be before those peoples will learn these things and begin to act upon the knowledge? How long before the obstructing hedges, ditches, cabins, tenant houses, and numerous subdivisions — all that prevents that enlargement of fields that will give scope for the use of the most effective machinery — will be removed, with the people who now occupy and cultivate the soil? How long before we shall see those lands planted, and sown, and harvested by the same methods as are the bonanza farms of the West, with the same want of fixed population and the same war upon women and children? Under the operations of our "beneficent competition," that we are forcing upon them, they will most certainly learn and act. Indeed, the work has already commenced.

The large development of the tenant system of farming is also an evil of the greatest magnitude, and a direct inheritance from the feudal system of Europe, utterly opposed to the whole spirit of our institutions. But with us it has obtained features worse than any now existing in Europe. The tenants in England hold leases and occupations that often and practically run for life, and have been held in families for generations, which gave encouragement for improvements. The holdings were practically homesteads. But with us the leases are uniformly for short terms, when taken; the holdings are generally from year to year, with no encouragement for improvements, and the farms are never deemed to be homes. In England the rent rarely reached and never exceeded one fourth the gross product. But in the United States it is commonly one half. Under the English tenant system the land is thoroughly cultivated and improved; with us it is simply skinned and impoverished. There is not one redeeming feature in the whole system.

It is evident from this statement of some of the effects that directly grow out of the combination of capital, machinery, and cheap labor in the cultivation of large bodies of land by individuals, companies, and corporations, that there has developed a system of agriculture that is in "irrepressible conflict" with the best interests of society, and must result in the destruction of one or the other. The duration of this conflict can be measured only by the elasticity of society, and the power of endurance and patience of the people. But in the final struggle that is sure to come there can be little doubt of the result. That the conflict may be averted by wise measures there can be no doubt. But our capitalistic leaders and shapers of legislation are as blind and as stubborn as the Bourbons of France, and it is a grave question whether the remedy that cured in some respects similar evils in that country must not also be applied in this.

CHAPTER III.

GROWTH AND DEVELOPMENT OF BONANZA AND TENANT FARMS.

SOME of the press utterings with regard to the operations of the bonanza farms, at the time I first called attention to the matter, in the pages of the Atlantic Monthly, appeared to have the design of hiding the facts, belittleing the development, and ridiculing any anxiety that might be excited. It was declared to be a movement of very limited extent, of temporary duration, that would leave no permanent effects.

An examination of the census reports for 1860, '70, and '80 will serve to show how limited is its extent, and whether it challenges attention or should be altogether ignored; or, rather, be flattered and extolled as one of the most beneficent developments of the age.

The census reports unfortunately give the data for only one part of the inquiry, that touching the increase in number. Of the size of those great food factories and monopolies, beyond the statement that they are of "1,000 acres and over," they give no information. Yet these holdings, by individuals alone, range up into hundreds of thousands, and in one instance, at least, into millions of acres; and when held by companies and corporations they do not diminish in size, as shown in the following chapter.

In 1860 the number of farms of 500 acres and less than 1,000 in the free States, was 3,472; in 1870, in the same States, the number was 6,951. In the year 1860 the number of farms of 1,000 acres and over, in the free States, was 791; in 1870, the number was 1,507. Showing that in the decade from 1860 to '70 the farms of 500 acres and less than 1,000 more than doubled, while those of 1,000 acres and over increased ninety and one half per cent. But taking the whole country for two decades we find that the ten years between 1870 and 1880 have been marked by a gigantic growth of the large farm interest.

In 1860 the whole number of farms of 500 acres and less than 1,000 in the United States, was 20,319; in 1870, the number was 15,873; in 1880, 75,972. Of the 1,000 acre farms and over, there were, in 1860, 5,364; in 1870, 3,720; and in 1880, 28,578. By this exhibit it is seen that in the decade from 1860 to 1870 there was a decrease in the number of both of these classes of farms of about one fourth. This decrease was confined to the late slave States, where many of the large plantations had been broken up and gone into the possession of the late slaves as tenants, and all the separate holdings were returned in the census of 1870 as distinct farms. But it is shown that during the last ten years the increase in the number of the smaller bonanza farms was nearly seven fold; while in the monster farms that are represented in the census reports as "of 1,000 acres and over," the increase has been nearly eight fold. They are simply huge food factories, whose productions are brought into direct competition with the small farmer, as were the cotton and woolen factories fifty years ago brought into competition with the household spinning wheels and looms of our mothers, and with the same result. The small farmer is also being crushed out. He is becoming a mere laborer to run the machines of the bonanza farms, or as a tramp to be reviled and cursed of all men.

Thus are tens of thousands of square miles of our best agricultural lands seized upon by the power of capital and monopoly, in the hands of individuals, companies, and corporations, upon which no one is permitted the right of making a home, or in any way obtaining an assured subsistence. But whilst these things are developing in one part of our country, in other sections are also square miles of territory upon each of which are crowded and packed from fifty to more than one hundred thousand souls, living in a state of wretchedness that beggars description. In New York City five contiguous square miles of territory may be found upon which are crammed not less than six hundred thousand human beings, sweltering and rotting in their misery, and sprouting the germs of anarchy and destruction. New York is by no means the only city thus afflicted; it is simply preeminent.

There are the people who should be occupying and holding those great tracts in small homesteads, building up a mighty people rich in all the comforts of life, and expending upon the soil and in the section that supports them the means which they obtain by its cultivation and development, instead of being found in our manufacturing towns and cities, swarming in poverty and wretchedness in tenement houses and hovels, and in the tramps that fill the country.

There is another stupendous evil that has grown out of the developments of the last half century. Instead of being able to boast, as could our fathers, that every man who tilled the soil was lord of the manor he occupied, owning no master, the last census report made a return of 1,024,701 tenant farms in our country in 1880. Since the taking of the census the increase can not have been less than twenty-five per cent., giving at this time not less than one and a quarter millions of tenant farms in the United States.

A comparison of this showing with the land holdings of Great Britain and Ireland will help to a better understanding of what these things import. The very latest statistics give the total number of holdings in England and Wales at 414,804; in Ireland, at 574,222; in Scotland, at 80,101: total, 1,069,127. Showing, that in the whole of Great Britain and Ireland, counting all the holdings as tenant occupations, which they are not, there are 200,000 less tenant farms than in the United States.

Among the owners of the tenant farms in our country are English, French, and German capitalists, non-residents, who have bought immense tracts of the railroad lands, and seized upon the alternate government sections lying within their railroad purchases, and on those tracts have commenced their bonanza operations, or planted their tenants on the American system. Among others mentioned in the chapter on bonanza farms, will be found the great German banker, Goldsmidt, of Frankfort on the Main. The New York Tribune, of December 15, 1882, gives a very recent case in the following brief item: —

PURCHASE OF COTTON LANDS IN ARKANSAS.

"LITTLE ROCK, Ark., Dec. 14. — A European company, headed by Benjamin Newgas, of Liverpool, has purchased 100,000 acres of cotton lands in Arkansas and Chicot Counties."

A still later mention of similar transactions is found in the following paragraph clipped from the Philadelphia Ledger, of January 26, 1883: —

"British capital is finding its way into western and northwestern agricultural and stockraising enterprises with a freedom and a magnitude that certainly imply an unbounded confidence in their future. It is not surprising, perhaps, that our Wall street men have had their attention arrested by it, and are disposed to accept it as an indication that John Bull is growing indifferent to western mining undertakings, and is now disposed to put his surplus capital into something that promises to be less elusive. That is the view they take of it at the Mining Exchange, where much importance is attached to a letter in yesterday's Chicago Tribune, from Ogden, Utah, which says: 'Great cattle corporations, like the railroad monopolies East, are busily engaged in filling up all unsettled territory, and rapidly swallowing all the smaller fish in the business.' The same letter adds: 'A. H. Swan, of Swan Bros., has just received (January 22d) a cablegram from parties in Edinburgh, Scotland, who have been negotiating the largest transaction for many years in their trade, requesting him to come immediately, with full power to close the bargain. He will sail next week.' The sale is a transfer of 67,000 head of cattle and a few hundred horses — the consideration being $2,500,000."

These items are merely indicators of what has al-

THE TENANT FARMS. 79

ready become a gigantic movement in the interest of alien capitalists.

Throughout all the older States, as in the new, the American plutocrat indulges in the peculiar luxury of the old feudal barons of Europe, in being able to count his tenants by scores and by hundreds. Among the number is the late Acting Vice President of the United States, who has his tenant farms scattered throughout the central part of the State of Illinois. As illustrative of the general prevalence of this feudal relic in our country I will here call special attention to a few only of the older States in the north and west, without reference to the Southern States, where it might be said that their presence is the natural outgrowth of the old slave system. In the State of Illinois the census of 1880 gives 80,244 tenant farms; in Ohio, 47,627; in New York, 39,872; in New Jersey, 8,438; and in California, 7,124. Every State and Territory in the Union furnishes its quota, generally numbered by thousands.

The condition of the tenant farmers in this country is also far worse than is that of the much pitied tenant farmers of Great Britain and Ireland. There the tenant farmer pays his rent with one fourth of his crop; here it takes one half (ranging from one third to two thirds). There the tenant farmer is usually a capitalist; here he is but little removed from the condition of a pauper. There the tenant farmer has a comfortable dwelling and farm buildings; here he has usually a miserable house only, or hovel, without one comfort, or, as in many instances, a hole in the ground.

Adam Smith describes, as follows, a condition of agriculture that formerly existed in Europe almost exactly like our present system of tenant farming:—

"In the ancient state of Europe the occupiers of land were all tenants at will. They were all, or almost all, slaves; but their slavery was of a milder kind than that known among the ancient Greeks and Romans, or even in our West Indian colonies. . . . . . To the slave cultivators of ancient times gradually succeeded a species of farming known at present [1770] in France by the name of Métayers. They are called in Latin Coloni Partiarii. They have been so long in disuse in England that at present I know no English name for them. The proprietors furnished them with the seed, cattle, and instruments of husbandry, the whole stock [capital], in short, necessary for cultivating the farm. The produce was divided equally between the proprietor and the farmer, after setting aside what was judged necessary for keeping up the stock, which was restored to the proprietor when the farmer either quitted or was turned out of the farm."

He further writes:—

"Land occupied by such tenants is properly cultivated at the expense of the proprietor as much as that occupied by slaves. . . . . . That tenure in villanage gradually wore out through the greater part of Europe. The time and manner, however, in which so important a revolution was brought about is one of the most obscure points in modern history. The church of Rome claims great merit in it; and it is certain that so early as the twelfth century, Alexander III published a bull for the general emancipation of slaves. . . . . . In France five parts out of six of the whole kingdom are said to be still [1770] occupied by this species of cultivators."— *Wealth of Nations.*

Here we have the most positive evidence that even in Europe, in her darkest period, our system of tenant farming was deemed to be a slavery too oppressive to be endured. But a more perfect picture of the conditions under which much the larger portion of the tenant farmers in our country hold their places could not well be drawn. The only points of difference between the tenures of the Métayers of the nineteenth century, under the government of the United States, and those under the feudal lords, are, that now, in some cases the proprietors do not furnish the entire stock, or capital; that the tenants often furnish all, or a portion, of the farm implements, or work stock, or both, and also of the seed; but still the proprietors, like their feudal brethren, assuredly claim and take one half of the product. But the share now received by the proprietors is not absolutely uniform, it ranging between one and two thirds, still averaging about one half. Yet in all the points in which the American system of villanage differs from that of the feudal ages in Europe, the present tenant slave suffers. The only advantage which the Métayer of to-day has over his brother of a thousand years ago, is not in a modification of the system, but in the fact that the tools now used are more effective, and he can produce a greater quantity to be divided, and thus obtain more subsistence for himself, though no greater share of the product. But for this only advantage the tenant is in no way indebted to the proprietor.

It is true that there have been cases where tenants, farming on shares and paying one half of their crops for rent, have been able to so improve their conditions as to become themselves proprietors. But such cases are found only under the most favorable circumstances of high prices and great demand, as during and shortly after the war of the rebellion, and have been so rare as to excite general comment; they in no sense represent usual conditions. The general facts are, that great destitution and constant want mark the lot of that class of farmers. Even the payment of tithes has ever been considered a burden too great to be borne by the agriculturist; and the one fifth to one fourth of his crop paid by the English farmer for rent is a principal cause of the agitations now threatening the existence of the English government. But however great may have been the burdens of the tithing system, or of the English tenants, those of the tenant farmers in the United States are five times greater than in the one case, and twice as great as in the other.

Still the notable fact remains, that the system of slavery against which Pope Alexander issued his bull, in the feudal age of Europe, exists in gigantic proportions on the soil of the United States. Here we nurse and protect by our laws a system of villanage too odious to be endured in most of Europe in her darkest days of barbarism, and against which the church of Rome hurled its thunders seven hundred years ago. But though the Métayer system long since went gradually out of use in most of Europe, it was continued in France till the last quarter of the past century, when it found its end in the horrors of the revolution of 1793, which it provoked, and of which the guillotin was the avenger.

The following is a tabulated statement of the number of tenant farms in each State and Territory of the

United States, as compiled from the Bulletins of the Census Bureau for 1880, and showing the number for that year.

NUMBER OF TENANT FARMS IN THE UNITED STATES.

	Money Rent.	Share Rent.		Money Rent.	Share Rent.
Alabama,	22,888	40,761	Missouri,	19,843	39,029
Arkansas,	9,916	19,272	Montana,	17	63
Arizona,	42	59	Nebraska,	1,943	9,476
California,	3,209	3,915	Nevada,	63	73
Colorado,	165	419	New Hampshire,	1,237	1,378
Connecticut,	1,920	1,206	New Jersey,	3,608	4,830
Dakota,	72	606	New Mexico,	22	386
Delaware,	511	3,197	New York,	18,124	21,748
Dist. of Columbia,	150	60	North Carolina,	8,644	44,078
Florida,	3,548	3,692	Ohio,	14,834	32,793
Georgia,	18,557	43,618	Oregon,	748	1,538
Idaho,	32	57	Pennsylvania,	17,049	28,273
Illinois,	20,620	59,624	Rhode Island,	989	247
Indiana,	8,582	37,468	South Carolina,	21,974	25,245
Iowa,	8,421	35,753	Tennessee,	19,266	37,930
Kansas,	4,438	18,213	Texas,	12,089	53,379
Kentucky,	16,824	27,203	Utah,	60	373
Louisiana,	6,669	10,337	Vermont,	2,164	2,598
Maine,	1,628	1,153	Virginia,	13,392	21,594
Maryland,	3,878	8,661	Washington,	209	262
Massachusetts,	2,292	848	West Virginia,	4,292	7,709
Michigan,	5,015	10,396	Wisconsin,	3,719	8,440
Minnesota,	1,251	7,202	Wyoming,	5	8
Mississippi,	17,440	27,118			
			United States,	322,357	702,244

The evidence is indisputable that we have resurrected and are rapidly developing a slavery from out of the feudal barbarisms of Europe, and which has there long been dead. But that with us it already numbers within its bonds more souls than did that slavery which cost us four years of war and half a million lives to wipe out. Will it be necessary to repeat that operation? If it should prove to be so, upon whom will the bolts of destruction surely fall?

These tenant farms are fast developing throughout the whole extent of our country, east, west, north, and south; from the Atlantic to the Pacific, from the British possessions to the Mexican line. They, as also the great bonanza farms, are mainly the growth of the last twenty years, and are multiplying with marvellous rapidity.

The great source of accretion to the number of tenant farms, in the older States, and to a large extent in the newer, also, is found in the fact that, under present conditions of competition and low prices, the small farm can not be made to support the family in anything like comfort, and the head of the household is compelled to resort to credit to obtain the necessaries of life, waiving all the comforts. This method once adopted is the sure beginning of the end. An interest account is established; more credit is required and obtained; a mortgage is given; the interest account is increased; the burdens and struggles for existence are multiplied, whilst the difficulties growing out of competition, cheapness, and bad harvests are constantly increasing, until the time is reached when the interest can no longer be paid. Then follows foreclosure, execution, and sale. Another farm is added to the tenant roll, and another household to the list of tenant occupants, or to the armies of town or city sufferers. These operations are going on all over the country.

Could the facts be definitely ascertained I have not the least doubt that they would show that at least fifty per cent. of the small farm ownerships in the older States are merely nominal. That that number, at least, of the small farmers in those States, are so deeply in debt, so covered by mortgages, that their supreme effort is to pay the constantly accruing interest, that a roof may be kept over the heads of the family — an effort that can have but the one ending.

In the newer States are found a similar condition of things. The only difference is, that there the small farmer is usually compelled to commence with what, to him, is a mountain of debt. He must obtain his land upon deferred payments, drawing interest, and can obtain no title until those deferred payments, with the interest, are paid in full. He must also obtain his farm implements on part credit, with interest, for which he mortgages his crops. Credit must help him to his farm stock, his hovel, his seed, his food, his clothing. With this load of debt must the small farmer in the newer States commence, if he is not a capitalist, or he can not even make a beginning. With such a commencement the common ending is not long in being found.

In traveling through those sections one of the most notable things that meets the attention of the observer is the great number of publications, everywhere met with, devoted exclusively to the advertising of small farm holdings, more or less improved, that are for sale. One is almost forced to the conclusion that the entire class of small farmers are compelled, from some cause, to find the best and quickest market that can be obtained, for all that they possess. A reference to the chapter on "The Bonanza Farms" will be found instructive in this connection.

The entire agricultural regions of our country are crowded with loan agents, representing capital from all the great money centers of the world, who are making loans and taking mortgages upon the farms to an amount that, in the aggregate, appears to be almost beyond calculation. In this movement the local capitalists, lawyers, and traders, appear as active coworkers. During the past season, whilst a short time in St. Lawrence County, New York, I learned of one Hebrew trader, about forty years of age, in Ogdensburg, who, as reported, first made his appearance in that city with a pack upon his back, that had, through trade, liberal credit to the farmers, interest, mortgages, and foreclosures, become the owner of sixteen farms, occupied by that number of tenants. A lawyer was pointed out who, by similar processes, was the owner of ten farms; and others in lesser degree.

These results mark the growth of what one of our ablest men most truly terms "the towering tyranny of capital," and what another, a popular political economist, insanely calls "the beneficent action of competition." Here is exhibited a development in the monopoly of the lands of our country, and an extension of the tenant system, that dwarfs to littleness anything that the world has before witnessed. In England the proudest of her aristocrats, the mightiest of her nobility, her greatest landlords, find their limits of possession a long way within two hundred thousand acres, and there are but three who hold more than one hundred thousand acres each. But in our country the possessions of individual capitalists pass far beyond the hundreds of thousands into the millions of acres, and the corporations into the tens of millions.

The tenant system of Great Britain has been the growth of ages — of more than a thousand years — fashioned and welded by the bloody swords and lawless brutalities of generations of robber barons and rulers who governed only to plunder; whose unwritten law was, "let him get who hath the power, and let him keep who can." But with us the tenant system is the growth of only about a quarter of a century, under the operations of written law, and already it has reached a magnitude that belittles the work of the feudal barons.

Surely the little finger of our plutocracy has become thicker for evil, mightier for crushing, than was ever the loins of baronial power in the time of its greatest strength.

CHAPTER IV.

ENGLISH AND AMERICAN LAND HOLDINGS AND RAILROAD LAND GRANTS.

THE following is a list of the whole number of land owners in England and Wales who are possessed of 50,000 and more acres of land each, and the actual amount of their holdings, by which it will be seen that there are but three who own more than 100,000 acres each, and no one has an estate that reaches 200,000 acres.

SIZE OF ENGLISH LAND HOLDINGS.

Names of Owners.	Acres.	Names of Owners.	Acres.
Marquis of Ailesbury,	55,051	Lord Londesborough,	52,655
Duke of Beaufort,	51,085	Earl of Lonsdale,	67,950
" Bedford,	87,507	Duke of Northumberland,	191,480
Earl of Brownlow,	57,799		
" Carlisle,	78,540	Duke of Portland,	55,259
" Cawdor,	51,538	Earl of Powis,	64,095
Duke of Cleveland,	106,650	Duke of Rutland,	70,039
Earl of Derby,	56,598	Lady Willoughby,	59,912
Duke of Devonshire,	148,620	Sir W. W. Wynn,	91,032
Lord Leconfield,	66,101	Earl of Yarborough,	55,370

But in the United States we have a saw maker, in Philadelphia, with his four million acres; two butchers in California with their eight hundred thousand

and more acres; a cattle raiser in New Mexico with his seven hundred and fifty thousand acres; and numbers of them in Texas whose acres are counted by hundreds of thousands. In the great Northwest the land holdings for agricultural purposes — for grain, grass, and vegetables — by hundreds, range to fifty thousand acres and upwards, occupied by tenants or machinery, or by both. The whole country, from the Mississippi to the Pacific, is dotted — no, they are not dots — is patched with these huge holdings. In comparison with the monopoly of the lands here shown, that of the English landlords appears quite insignificant. And yet we are only in the third decade of our movement.

One of the great sources of supply for this monstrous monopoly is found in the railroad land grants that have been so lavishly made by the general government, in tracts of tens of millions of acres each.

But there are other sources in almost every State in the Union. New Hampshire has shown her power of development in this direction up to two hundred and fifty thousand acres in the hands of one company. Texas is lavish in the creation of single holdings, individual and coparcenary, all through the hundreds of thousands to near the millions of acres. Florida wanders wildly in the millions of acres in her grants. Virginia, Tennessee, Georgia, New York, and other States do not let slip any opportunities by which these monopolies may be created.

For every purpose for which lands can be used, whether for denudation of their timber for foreign export and home consumption, for cultivation, or for grazing — for use or waste — the spirit of monopoly has become uppermost. But the most destructive and indefensible of all steps in this direction have been taken by the general government.

More than twenty years ago Congress devised and perfected a Public Land System by which the public domain was set apart for the benefit of the people. It was a measure that guaranteed to every child of the soil a portion of the heritage of our fathers, effectually barring monopoly and excluding the nonresident alien and all who had not taken the prescribed steps to become citizens. It was a solemn compact between the government and people. By the provisions of that system the lands of the nation, as they were surveyed, became subject to preëmption and occupation under conditions which enabled any one, whether man or woman, married or single, being of age and a citizen, or intending to be such, to obtain a portion of the soil of the country. Even those who went upon the lands before they were surveyed, going into absolute occupation and making improvements, were provided for when the surveys were made, being allotted the quarter sections upon which their improvements might fall. But under no conditions could any one obtain more than a limited amount, by either preëmption, purchase or tree culture, or by all three methods combined. The limit was one half section, or three hundred and twenty acres. And in every case the conditions of occupation and improvement were absolute.

Under this system monopoly was impossible. The lands went into the hands of the people; homes and communities were being planted upon our frontiers, and the frontiers were being constantly extended and advanced. The greatest cost to the settler for his land was one dollar and a quarter per acre, and a small fee for registry and patent; the whole to be paid after a term of years, without interest. And I believe that no case is known where a *bona fide* settler was ever disturbed or distressed because of inability to make his payment for the land. The system, in its truest sense, was beneficent, and was working out the best results.

But after railroad building had become established as a business that would yield good profits, and capital was reaching out, under the stimulus of great mechanical development, for profitable investment, the doors of some of our State governments were besieged for aid in railroad building, and especially for grants of the unoccupied lands along the lines of the proposed roads. Some of these efforts meeting with success naturally attracted attention from others, both capitalists and the impecunious, who began to devise means whereby the national domain might be attacked; and the halls, anterooms, and doors of Congress, for the last twenty years, have been in a state of constant siege for land grants to aid in the building of railroads. No expedient has been left untried; no plausible nor good reason that has not been urged; no means, fair or foul, honest or corrupt, that have not been resorted to to accomplish the end desired.

The following extract from one of our great dailies describes the knavery of one of the railroad land grants, and the methods pursued to make the fraud complete. No doubt it may be taken as a fair sample of not a few other swindles equally atrocious.

A BIG FRAUD. — THE SECRET HISTORY OF THE BACKBONE LAND GRANT.

A SCHEME TO STEAL 1,500,000 ACRES OF PUBLIC LAND.

HIGHLY IMPORTANT FACTS FOR CONGRESS AND FOR PRESIDENT ARTHUR.

"One million four hundred and ninety-two thousand acres of good land, worth every cent of $3,000,000 in good money, are about to be signed away to men who have no more right to the property than has Dom Pedro II, of Alcantara, Emperor of Brazil, says a Washington special to the New York Sun. The land belongs to the public domain. It forms a territory more than twice as large as the State of Rhode Island. Matters are in train to take this territory from the people of the United States, its rightful owners, and to hand it over to a few individuals who have grown both rich and audacious by similar operations. Nothing is needed now but the signature of the Secretary of the Interior to a subordinate's report and the President's formal approval. The job has traveled in darkness to its final stage. It is high time to turn on the daylight.

"Just before the Forty-First Congress adjourned it passed the Texas Pacific bill, a huge subsidy measure which had been pushed through by one of the boldest and most unscrupulous combinations ever effected in the lobby. This Act, carrying a grant of nearly 15,000,000 acres of public lands, was approved by General Grant March 3, 1871, one day before the Forty-First Congress ceased to exist. Its twenty-second section made a grant of twenty sections of land per mile in aid of the construction of the New Orleans, Baton Rouge, and Vicksburg Railroad, on condition that the whole road should be completed within five years. This road, familiarly known as the Backbone Road, was chartered by the State of Louisiana. It was to run from New Orleans to Baton Rouge, on the east bank of the Mississippi; then across the river and by way of Alexandria to

Shreveport — 318 miles in all. It was not finished within the limit of five years set by the terms of the act. It was not even begun.

Not a spadeful of earth was ever turned, not a tie cut, nor a rail nor a spike purchased. The railroad never earned its land grant. It never had existence except on the map filed in the Interior Department at Washington. The corporation itself is a defunct concern; its charter has been declared forfeited by the Legislature of Louisiana, which created it.

Just two years ago — that is to say, in the first week of January, 1881 — there was achieved in a little office in lower Broadway, in New York City, one of the most remarkable transactions in real estate of which there is any record. The directors of this extinct company, representing a railroad which never existed, sold for one dollar a million and a half acres of government land which it never owned. The purchaser was the New Orleans Pacific Railway Company, now consolidated with the Texas & Pacific.

"To the ordinary intellect this will seem like purchasing a lost opportunity from the ghost of an imaginary person. Yet it is on the strength of that amazing transfer that $3,000,000 worth of the public domain will be signed away, perhaps next month, perhaps next week, unless Congress blocks the game.

"On January 5, 1881, the President of the Backbone Company executed the deed of transfer, and the price stipulated is one dollar. But one dollar was by no means the real consideration.

"The true basis of the sale was a secret agreement that the New Orleans Pacific should issue land grant bonds for the lands to be acquired from the government, and that of these bonds the New Orleans Pacific should retain two thirds, the other third going to the ghost of the old company. This agreement was put in the form of an obligation, signed by the President of the New Orleans Pacific, to transfer to the President of the New Orleans, Baton Rouge, and Vicksburg one third of the land grant bonds. The document is now held by a trust company in New York.

"There was still another stipulation, and a very important

one. Out of the third of the new land grant bonds assigned to the managers of the old road they were to take up all the outstanding stock and bonds of the Backbone Company. These bonds amounted at a face value to between $4,000,000 and $5,000,000. They were not intended for the market, but were freely distributed among Congressmen while the bill was in its passage, with the agreement that they should be redeemed at a certain per centage of their face value. The holders of these bonds found that their claims would not be recognized and began to protest. When the syndicate, represented by ex Congressman Sypher, came to the front with $480,000 of Backbone paper, it was found that to take up all the outstanding bonds and stock of the railroad that never existed, would require more than the Backbone's one third of the New Orleans Pacific's new land grant obligations, even though that third amounted to not less than $1,000,000 in bonds.

"This disproportion of assets to liabilities compelled the settlement of twenty cents on the dollar. Contracts were duly signed by the officers of the Backbone Company to carry out this arrangement with the hungry bondholders. The obligations now out call for the redemption of the stock and bonds of the New Orleans, Baton Rouge, and Vicksburg Railroad Company in bonds of the New Orleans Pacific Railroad Company at the rate just indicated. The agreement to this effect, signed by the President of the New Orleans, Baton Rouge, and Vicksburg, is locked up in the safe of the First National Bank of New York.

"Behind the transfer of 1,492,000 acres of the people's lands from one railroad company to another railroad company for the nominal consideration of one dollar, there are, therefore, two secret contracts, duly executed, which show the real consideration of the transfer: —

"1. The obligation signed by E. B. Wheelock, President of the New Orleans Pacific, to hand back to William H. Barnum, President of the New Orleans, Baton Rouge, and Vicksburg, one third of the proceeds of the land conveyed by the latter company to the former. The New Orleans Pacific Railway

Company has now only a nominal existence. It was consolidated in June, 1881, with the Texas Pacific, the President of which is Mr. Jay Gould.

"2. An agreement signed by the President of the New Orleans, Baton Rouge, and Vicksburg to use its third of the new land grant bonds thus acquired in taking up the outstanding stock and bonds of the defunct corporation.

"A protest against the transfer was made by several members of Congress and other holders of the old corruption bonds. Attorney General Brewster was asked to prepare an opinion.

"That the opinion exists, and is dead against the rights of the people to the ownership of the forfeited land grant, is known to several who have seen and read the paper. Yet, although it is a public document, and a document of exceeding interest, it is carefully kept from the eyes of the public. The other papers in the case are also guarded with zealous care from the public eye. Judge Payson, of Illinois, read the opinion, and immediately wrote to the Secretary of the Interior asking to be heard before action was taken. Judge Payson's protest is all that now stands in the way of the speedy consummation of the great land grabbing scheme. Secretary Teller has only to accept Commissioner Hassard's report and to forward it to President Arthur for his formal approval, and to direct the Land Commissioner to issue patents for the land. That is all that remains to be done. Then the old corruption account of 1871 is settled at the nation's expense, a clear gift of about $2,000,000 is made by the nation to certain men, and the forfeited rights of a defunct corporation to 1,492,000 acres of the public domain are floated over miles of space and years of time to another and entirely different road, built on the other side of the Mississippi river, and not finished until years after the original grant was forfeited."

These operations have undoubtedly aided in the construction of some roads valuable to the nation. But let us briefly look at the cost of these roads to the nation; we may thus discover to whom they rightfully belong. I must be very brief. A full discussion of this matter would require volumes.

Some of the most prominent objects that attract the attention of one who, with a railroad map before him, attempts to study the action of government in relation to our land system, are the immense tracts of the national domain that have gone into the hands of corporations. We see a belt, eighty miles wide, extending from near Lake Superior to the Pacific Ocean, covering some of the best agricultural, pasture, and timber lands in the country, that has been granted to the Northern Pacific Railroad Company. Then we see a belt forty miles in width, from the Missouri river to near the bay of San Francisco, held by the Union and Central Pacific Railroad Companies. Near the Pacific coast we see a belt extending longitudinally through California, owned by the Western and Southern Pacific Companies; which, as is well known, are owned and controlled by the same parties that own and control the Central Pacific. And we see a belt, forty miles wide, stretching through Kansas into Colorado and New Mexico, towards Arizona and Old Mexico, that is represented by the Atchison, Topeka, and Santa Fé Railroad Company. Then another belt eighty miles in width, extending across New Mexico and Arizona to near the Pacific, represented by the Atlantic and Pacific Company, being substantially the Atchison, Topeka, and Santa Fé Company. Wherever, in the great West, we may turn our eyes, we see similar belts that are only a little inferior to those mentioned.

A brief examination of the official data touching

these land grants will materially assist to a correct understanding of the matter. I quote from "The Public Domain," Ex. Doc. 47, Part 4, H. R. 46th Congress, 3rd Session, p. 268.

"It was estimated that if the lands embraced in limits of grants to railroads to June 30, 1880, were all available, and that the corporations, State and National, built their roads, and complied with the laws, it would require 215,000,000 of acres of the public domain to satisfy the requirements of the various laws. The estimate of the General Land Office in 1878 was that it would require 187,000,000 of acres, which in all probability will be reduced by actual selection, forfeitures, etc., to 154,000,000 of acres. The present estimate is 155,504,994.59 acres."

Whatever may be the actual amount that will be finally conveyed and confirmed to railroad corporations, under the various grants, the amount which has actually been granted by Congress appears to be about 215,000,000 acres. This does not include the railroad land grants from the State of Texas, amounting to 38,457,600 acres, as given by the Chicago Tribune, which must be taken into account to make a complete showing, making a grand aggregate, in round numbers, of 255,000,000 of acres.

The best method by which to obtain a correct idea of the magnitude of these grants is by comparison. Without such aid the ordinary mind can not grasp its vastness.

For example:— The total area of Great Britain and Ireland is 74,137,600 acres, or less than one third as great as that given to railroad corporations in the United States.

For a home comparison I find that the total area

of New Hampshire, Massachusetts, Rhode Island, Connecticut, New York, New Jersey, Pennsylvania, Delaware, Maryland, Virginia, North and South Carolina, and Georgia — the thirteen original States of our Union — is 204,001,280 acres, or about fifty million acres less than have been taken from our public domain and donated to plutocrats and plunderers.

Another home illustration is that the eight great States of Pennsylvania, Ohio, Indiana, Illinois, Michigan, Wisconsin, Iowa, and Missouri, have an area of 258,549,120 acres, or but little more than has been by law filched from the lands of the people, and granted to a small band of speculating monopolists, to be used as means of extortion and robbery. The magnitude of these grants almost staggers the understanding. There is not, among all the enlightened nations of modern Europe, one that has an area which equals that of our railroad kings.

The great empire of Austro-Hungary and the kingdom of Italy, with Switzerland and the Netherlands added, have an area of 250,012,720 acres, or nearly five million acres less than are found in the empire of our railroad despots. The empire of Germany, with the kingdoms of Italy, Greece, and Portugal, and the Swiss Republic, combined, have an area of 251,163,520 acres, or four million acres less than is the area devoted to speculation by our government. France and Sweden united have an area of 238,936,000 acres, being nearly twenty million acres less than is held by a small number of railroad magnates in the United States, by favor of Congress, without restriction or limit in their use or disposition, and which are exempted from all the burdens to which all other property is subjected.

This immense area of the public domain is what has been actually donated to corporations by our general government and the State of Texas. But within the limits covered by these railroad grants is another area of equal extent that has been reserved by government for settlement under the provisions of the homestead laws. This, also, comes under the domination of the huge estates by which they are surrounded, and are being absorbed and swallowed up in the manner herein described and by the many other methods by which small holdings disappear in the presence of the great estates. Thus we see that under the peculiar provisions of the laws making these grants, they are made to cover twice the area actually conveyed, and bring under their baleful influence at least 500,000,000 acres of the public domain, instead of the 255,000,000 described in the grants. The more closely the provisions of these grants are examined, the greater is the monstrous wrong that is shown to be covered by them.

Estimated upon the basis of dollars and cents, it is seen that our government has donated to railroad corporations lands which, at its minimum rate, it now values at $600,000,000, without limit or check of any kind being provided for their disposition. It is notorious that the corporations are selling these lands, in blocks, to other speculators, foreign and domestic, in areas amounting to tens and hundreds of thousands of acres each, and also in small lots, to aliens as well as natives, at prices varying from three to ten dollars and more per acre. Thus extorting from the people billions of dollars, and building up in our midst a plutocratic power such as the world has never before known. The whole thing stands as a colossal monument of speculative madness and governmental folly.

These grants are divided among about eighty corporations. Some of the earlier and smaller grants were limited to six sections per mile, and the sale of the lands was restricted to actual settlers of one hundred and sixty acres each, at two dollars and fifty cents per acre. The first grant was made in 1850 to the State of Illinois, for the Illinois Central Railroad, and for the next twelve years all grants were made to the States, and by the States to the corporations. July 1, 1862, Congress made its first grant of lands direct to corporations, in the cases of the Union and Central Pacific companies. The change in the methods and amounts of the grants was complete and has continued to the present time. The number of sections has grown from six to forty per mile, with no restriction or limit of any nature.

Forty-one days before the passage of the Union and Central Pacific land grant Act, on May 20, 1862, Congress, after a long and fierce contest, had passed a homestead law, limiting the sales of the lands to one hundred and sixty acres each, for "actual settlement and cultivation," at one dollar and twenty-five cents per acre, to any one of age, who "is a citizen of the United States, or who shall have filed his declaration of intention to become such, as required by the naturalization laws of the United States." But utterly regardless of the beneficent land system just adopted — in no manner recognizing its existence — Congress entered upon its career of land robbery and waste, in response to the demands of corporate speculators and gamblers, that, as John Randolph, with biting sarcasm yet bitter truth, declared, have neither souls to damn nor bodies to kick, and the nation has now commenced to reap its harvest of repentance and restitution.

Of the 255,000,000 acres that have been granted by the general government and the State of Texas, quite one half has gone into the hands of what are substantially not more than five great corporations, viz. : the Central Pacific, 15,260,000 acres ; the Union Pacific, 16,115,000 acres ; the Northern Pacific, 42,000,000 acres ; the Atchison, Topeka and Santa Fé, 25,667,200 acres ; the Texas Pacific, 13,000,000 acres. Total, 112,042,000 acres.

These five corporations are really controlled and represented by not more than twenty-five men, who, out of their great wealth, their more than princely revenues derived from these grants — the gift of the government by the plunder of the people — contribute nothing for the support of government or the general welfare. This monstrous exhibition of our governmental fatuousness, or corruption, will become the wonder of nations, and pass into history as the monster fraud of the nineteenth century.

The results of these unguarded, unprotected, but monstrous donations are fraught with the greatest present damage to the people, and ultimate peril to the nation.

The first result is the practical destruction of the

beneficent homestead system — a breach of trust, on the part of the government to the present and future generations, that is without excuse, and can not be too soon corrected. Now capitalists and corporations, whether native or foreign, may acquire of our public domain, through railroad corporations, an amount that is limited only by the desire or the ability to buy. Practically a purchase is made from the railroad company of, say, two hundred of the odd numbered sections, which are the railroad lands, or 128,000 acres. The purchaser goes into occupation of the odd sections he has bought, and takes possession of the even numbered, or government sections, that lie between. In this manner he obtains 256,000 acres of that which the people had believed to be their birthright, and in which they were limited to three hundred and twenty acres each.

One half is bought from a railroad company, and the other half is sto—— [oh, no, not stolen; such people never steal. That term can be properly applied to the wretched woman that is compelled to steal a loaf to feed her famishing babes, for which she is legally sentenced, by blind justice, to ninety days in the House of Correction, whilst the children are left to —— what? Who can tell? Would it not be well to pull the bandage from off the eyes of the blind goddess, turn on the lights, and give her at least one good view of the horrors that are wrought in her name?]. No, no, the parties who obtain the people's lands in the manner described do not steal. The lands are not stolen; they are only absorbed. That is an inoffensive term that will express the idea.

I will therefore say, one half is bought from a railroad corporation and the other half is absorbed from the lands contiguous. The purchaser runs his plow through the government, or absorbed, sections, and thus takes possession. No one can reach those sections without crossing the lands that have been bought from the railroad corporations, and thus committing trespass. The only even sections that I have seen where there was even a pretense of respect for the people's rights, have been the school sections, numbered sixteen and thirty-six, which the adjoining proprietors say they will purchase when offered, but in the mean time take possession of.

The local courts confirm the possession and punish the trespass, and thus the title is quieted. Inasmuch as these proceedings are thus legalized it can not be stealing nor robbery. But somehow the people have lost all rights and monopoly is triumphant.

When the noncapitalist, or would be small farmer, finds a government section that is not covered as above described, he can obtain only what the law allows at the cost of two dollars and fifty cents an acre, instead of one dollar and twenty-five cents, as formerly. Or if he desires some of the railroad lands he must pay whatever the cupidity or power of extortion on the part of the corporations may compel; often amounting to ten, fifteen or more dollars per acre. For as settlements and society advance, the value of the land is enhanced; and this enhanced value, created by society, is the premium which the corporations are sure to extort.

They fill the countries of Europe with their agents

and circulars, advertising their lands and giving the most glowing accounts of the prosperity of the farmers in the west, the cheapness of the lands, and the certainty of quickly accumulating fortunes, and the life of comfort that follows. Multitudes are induced to abandon their connections and homes in the old country, and seek the new; some with contracts for lands in their pockets before they start, and others with barely enough to reach our shores, at once becoming additions to our multitudes of paupers.

The following extracts from Jay Gould's testimony before the New York Senate Committee, December 14, 1882, as reported in the Tribune of the following day, will shed some light upon the manner in which the great spontaneous [?] European immigrations are engineered : —

"You stated that speculation promoted immigration. How does it do this?"

"It induces the construction of railroads into new territory, and that induces the roads to send abroad to get immigrants to settle the lands."

"To what extent have you influenced immigration?"

"That's impossible to tell. We are advertising in all the lands abroad. The immigrants come, and may go on our lands or elsewhere. When I was in Europe you couldn't go anywhere but you saw agents of American land grant companies."

"Do all the roads have these agents?"

"All the land grant roads. The Union Pacific, Central Pacific, Atchison and Topeka, Kansas Pacific, Chicago and Burlington, Missouri and Nebraska, Rock Island, Missouri, Kansas and Texas, Texas Pacific, and St. Louis and Iron Mountain."

[Mr. Gould explained at length the methods used by the companies and their agents to induce emigration from the European countries.]

RAILROAD LAND GRANTS. 105

"On an average, how many immigrants does your system bring to this country?"

"I can't tell you that. The number is very large. I have under my immediate control 10,000 miles of roads, and immigration goes along 6,000 or 7,000 of them. I was out there last year and saw that towns have sprung up all over the territory."

"How much of the land has been settled?"

"I can't tell. The government's plan was to grant the railroads alternate sections, and as they are offered cheaper they are usually occupied first. The government's price is $2 50 an acre. We sell for from $3 to $6. I have known immigrants to take the virgin soil and make enough profit on their first year's crop to pay for their farm. We have never lost any money by these sales. There have been instances when lands have been thrown back on our hands, but we have always sold them again."

"Do you know what prices the western producers receive for their wheat in the local markets?"

"It varies according to the prices at Chicago and St. Louis."

"What is the average received?"

"There is a pretty wide fluctuation. They want a dollar for their wheat and are not satisfied with less. I think they get about 70 cents now."

"Through what sections of the country do your roads run, Mr. Gould?"

"Through Indiana, Ohio, Illinois, Missouri, Iowa, Kansas, Nebraska, Arkansas, and Texas."

Here is the most conclusive evidence of the way and manner in which the general government is used by a horde of speculators to aid their speculations. Here it is shown for whose benefit the State of New York is taxed to support her Emigrant Commissioners, Castle Garden, Ward's Island, and other immigrant expenditures. So with the thousand and one impositions upon the people, throughout the country, from the same cause. This also shows how it is that our country is being filled with an alien population raked out of all the corners and hives of Europe, and sent here in swarms, to occupy our public domain, and leave to the children of the soil not an acre of the heritage bequeathed by our fathers, that we may call our own. Here we have the most conclusive evidence that the monster immigrations from Europe which we, within a few years past, have been receiving, are induced by the agents of the land grant railroads, to fill up and occupy the lands of the people. For the benefit of these railroad corporations are our General, State, and Municipal Governments taxed for the support of the paupers they send to our shores, and for Emigrant Commissioners, etc. Not only are our people thus robbed of their rights in the public domain, but are mulcted in all the costs of the care and support of the multitudes that are thus thrown upon us. But the railroad companies are sure to escape all of these costs. These European hordes are planted in colonies as tenants upon the lands of some alien Crœsus or domestic plutocrat, to extend the feudal slavery already so firmly planted. Or, if they have the means to do so, to start a small farm near some land grant railroad, to be surely swallowed up by the great estates with which they are surrounded. Whilst other hordes who are not thus planted in colonies, nor obtain farms on their own account, are turned loose upon the country without occupations, or other means of subsistence, to furnish a fund of cheap labor to be drawn upon by the bonanza farmers, or others, as required.

Here we have a condition of things for which history does not furnish parallel nor precedent. For our system of tenant farming a precedent is found; and for our large landed estates something approaching parallel conditions. But for the robbery of a people, by their own government, that aliens may have unlimited enjoyment of their heritage, for the especial benefit of domestic and alien speculators, as has been done in our case, no precedent exists.

A good illustration of the wholesale robbery of the people for the benefit of alien capitalists and speculators is found in the following item clipped from the New York Tribune of March 6, 1883.

"Rumors that the Northern Pacific Railroad Company had completed the sale of some four million acres of land to a foreign syndicate have been recently revived. At the office of the railroad company it was said yesterday that the negotiations were in the same condition that they had been for several months. The company has something over four million acres of land east of the Missouri River which it has offered for sale at about $4 an acre. The lands have not been sold, it was said, but probably the syndicate would take them as soon as it had completed its arrangements."

Our homestead laws limit the sales of the public domain to lots of one hundred and sixty acres each, but railroad plutocrats are specially privileged to sell to alien and domestic monopolists in lots of millions of acres, and absorb all that joins them.

The spectacle of a great nation, in point of population and general intelligence standing first in the great sisterhood of modern civilization, in the hands of a class of speculators who control the government, waste and squander the nation's heritage, and play with the people's dearest interests as gamblers play with dice, or boys with foot balls, is not a hopeful sign of advancement. The facts are both astounding and shameful.

It appears to be the desire of these great corporations to at once absorb the whole public domain, people it with the paupers of Europe on the one side, and those of Asia on the other, and between these two millstones to grind the children of the soil into the most abject slavery. Certainly, another twenty years' development like those just passed, will leave nothing to the country worth saving, and sink our people so deep in the mire of plutocratic despotism and social degradation as to make a revolution, in our country, like the French of the last century, the greatest boon that the Almighty can bless us with.

Mr. Gould, in his testimony, says, "We have never lost any money by these sales. There have been instances when lands have been thrown back on our hands, but we have always sold them again." It was hardly necessary for Mr. Gould to have made that statement. Most certainly they sell them again, a dozen times over if they can get the chance to do so; but never refund a dime of principal or interest that have been paid, nor for improvements that have been made. It is certain that they do not lose money by those sales; nor do vendors of sewing machines, instalment furniture, and other articles under similar conditions. Such transactions are in perfect harmony with their practice in the whole matter.

Special rates, in this connection, is another weight that the people must bear. When the capitalist makes his purchase, he is able to command rates that the small purchaser would be laughed at if asked for by him. He must pay the uttermost demand and expect no favors.

Another special, and it should be an intolerable, abuse attends these gigantic land grants; and that is, that upon these great landholdings the grantees pay no taxes. Though they become the *de facto* owners of these great properties, which, by the operations of society, are constantly increasing in value, doubling and quadrupling within a few years, and from which are derived almost fabulous revenues, in the extortions which they thus force from the people, they pay not one cent for the support of government, or the welfare of society. All these burdens are thrown upon the people; they bear none of them.

Out of these great monopolies have grown many more giant evils than are here pointed out. I have by no means exhausted the catalogue. They hold the highways of the nation as well as rob the people of their patrimony; they control many of the great sources of industry and avenues of trade; and they appear to hold the government by the throat. Every interest in the country appears to be compelled to contribute to the aggrandizement of these great monopolies, that have grown out of the mistaken liberality of the people and government; and every interest in the country correspondingly suffers.

But they are standing upon a power that is at present ignorant of its real strength, and knows not yet how to use it, though the iron heels of these plutocratic monopolies are pressing deeper and deeper into the writhing flesh. It can not, will not always continue.

Fifteen years ago, in the New York constitutional convention, George William Curtis, in discussing the matter of the consolidation of railroad interest, said:—

"I presume no student of history; I presume no scholar in political science, will deny that what the great baronial power was in mediæval civilization, and what the great slaveholding oligarchy has been in our politics, the vast consolidation of capital will be in the future of this country, if the people do not interpose. Gentlemen who speak so lightly of monopolies should understand that the danger of our civilization is the towering tyranny of capital."

The developments of the last fifteen years, in the direction to which Mr. Curtis so forcibly calls attention as shown above, has given a force to his language that at this time makes it most notably significant.

The last edition of the Encyclopedia Britannica, in the article on LAND, makes some wholesome reflections on this matter very pertinent to our present condition. It shows the growth of landownership in Rome; the creation of tenants and tenantcy at will, under the name of *precarium*, and large estates capable of subdivision, which resulted in

"the long struggle of which the successive Agrarian Laws were the landmark and remedies. . . . . . A century later the Gracchi again endeavored to restore health to the body politic by a distribution of the state lands among the proletariat. The attempt was stifled in blood, but the necessity of the measure was proved by the fact that a full generation later Caius Julius Cæsar carried out the same reform.

"But the time for remedy, however, was past. The great estates (*latifundia*) had already been created; they were respected by the reformers, alike popular and imperial; and their inevitable growth inevitably swallowed up the small farms of new creation, and ultimately destroyed Rome. For its manhood was gone; the wealth of millionaires could not purchase back honesty or courage; and the defence of mercenaries failed to form a barrier against the wars of hardy northern invaders. Pliny's words, 'latifundia perdidere Italium,' embraces the truth, yet more fully made clear in many a generation after he wrote."

Are we not repeating that bit of history?

CHAPTER V.

SUMMARY AND EFFECTIVE MEASURES FOR BREAKING UP GREAT LANDED ESTATES AND TENANT HOLDINGS, AND RESTORING THE PUBLIC DOMAIN TO THE PEOPLE.

IN discussing these matters I can not see any good reason why they should take on a personal form. They are not questions of individual action, but of systems, of governmental policy. Though individuals appear as prominent exponents, or factors, in the development of these systems, it is not because of any predetermined action on their part, but because, in the general movement of society in accordance with present tendencies, these persons happen to be found floating in the eddies that are constantly catching and gathering the wealth borne by the great stream that rushes onwards. If it were not these individuals it would be others. These systems can not exist without producing the exact types and effects that now so prominently illustrate their workings. Therefore it should be plain to every one that whatever war is undertaken, because of the evils under which we suffer, it is not to be waged against persons, except so far as they attempt to defend the systems, but against the systems themselves. Remedies are not to be found or achieved by railing at or abusing plutocratic representatives, but by carefully examining the causes which have produced them, and devising other systems and regulations in society — in obtaining and enforcing laws, by the concurrent action of the people, under which present conditions can not exist; then plutocratic monopoly and power will cease to be the controlling factors.

Of late there has been a great development in the discussion of matters relating to the tenures of land, their derivations and growth, and the manner and method of their regulation. How these tenures have grown, and the brutalities and monstrous oppressions that have attended the numberless changes, acquisitions, and losses in the possession of the lands have been too often told, and are too well known, to require repetition in these pages. One point, at least, there is and can be no doubt about: — that the earth, the land, was given to man to subdue and cultivate, and from it to derive his subsistence.

The land being man's birthright, he becomes the sole arbiter and ruler of it, to use and dispose of in the manner that will best promote the purpose for which it was given. The right and duty thus created man can not divest himself of, nor in any manner limit or restrict the succeeding generations in the exercise of that continuous right and duty. Hence society, which is the concrete man, ever finds it necessary to change and modify the conditions of the occupation of lands, as the conditions and developments in its body require. Thus, when in the state of the nomadic and pastoral life, separate and distinct allotments, having the element of permanency, were undesirable, the lands became tribal property, for common use.

But when in the more advanced stages of society the wandering nomadic life has been departed from, and mankind have gathered into groups and communities, with fixed habits and greatly diversified industries and interests, as at present; when it is found that a large portion of society, from the very nature of its conditions, can not immediately occupy and make use of any part of the land, whilst other members of the body politic are altogether dependent upon fixed and permanent allotments, with every degree of necessity existing between the two extremes, it still is the right and duty of society to fix the limitations and determine the tenures by which all these variously required holdings may be obtained and retained.

Humanly speaking, existing society is the source of title, and the sole authority in all matters of change and adaptation; and so it must ever continue to be. In all civilized communities the voice and will of society finds its expression in what is called law; which, with us, is the direct creation of the people, under prescribed forms and regulations, also made by the people. Therefore, it is not of the smallest consequence what may have been the derivations through which the present tenures may have reached us; the rights of society in the matter remain the same. What might have been deemed vested rights at one time, and under the conditions then existing, may be found vested wrongs at this time and with us, and should be abolished. Our English ancestors, when framing the laws for our government, largely drew from the English code, and made it the common law. But the laws of entail and primogeniture were barred as unsuitable to our conditions. Twenty-five years ago it was deemed that the old laws which made slaves of a portion of mankind had become wrongs that should be abolished, and society washed them out in oceans of blood.

Hence, it can hardly be denied that it still remains as much the prerogative and duty of society to abolish vested wrongs as it is to protect vested rights, and that the right to do so extends to the use of whatever means may be necessary to accomplish the end desired. The question of means, also, lies within the judgment of society and the necessities of the case, as well as the determination of what are rights and what are wrongs.

Having, as I believe, thus clearly and correctly defined the true relations of man to the soil, I proceed to the discussion of the matters which form the heading to this chapter. That these questions are surrounded with difficulties must be admitted; and that diverse opinions may be honestly entertained can not be questioned. But keeping in view the principles above laid down, and man's inalienable rights, one need not go far wrong.

It has been shown that, within the last twenty-five years, there has been, in these United States, an astounding development of the old feudal system of tenant farming. That we already have in our country at least a million and a quarter of tenant farm holdings; a number far greater than is found in Great Britain and Ireland combined. It has also been shown that the systems of tenant farming of great estates, and tenantcy at will, which so largely obtain with us, was the cause of the destruction of Rome. It is hardly necessary to more than allude to the fact that the French revolution of the past century found its source in similar conditions, or that the most powerful nations and governments in Europe are being shaken to their foundations by like causes.

The spectacle now exhibited by Mr. Gladstone, at the head of the great liberal party and government of England, in his effort to clutch the throat of a kindred monster in that country, is most suggestive, and should be a timely warning.

The facts, the tendencies, and the inevitable results of our system of tenant farming, if a remedy is not found, there is not the least hope of successfully denying. Therefore the only question to be asked and answered is, What can be done about it? The answer is, end it; end it at once, before it attains greater strength and wider scope; wipe it out, even though it can only be done in blood; for if that monster lives and continues to grow the nation must die. But, fortunately, blood is not required, nor violence of any kind, nor distress to either party, landlord or tenant.

But there is another matter that must first be considered in this connection; and that is, the danger that the bonanza farms, which would become unmanageable under the operation of measures hereafter to be proposed, would be cut up into tenant farms, and thus add to the great evil of tenant farming, if provisions were not made to prevent that action.

The fact has been pointed out that the lands of the great railroad grants escape taxation, and so do the bonanza farms that have grown out of and upon the railroad lands. The railroad companies delay for years the taking of patents for the lands confirmed to them, for the special purpose of avoiding taxation. Did the railroad companies, in obtaining these grants, take the place of the government and become its agent in the disposition of the lands, upon the same terms as the government under the homestead laws, the case would be different. On these terms, at the price government has fixed for its reserved sections within the railroad grants, two and one half dollars per acre, the Northern Pacific Railroad Company, and also the Atlantic and Pacific Company, would be limited to $64,000 per mile from the sale of their lands. Inasmuch as their roads cost not more than $25,000 per mile, one who had not been educated in the ways of such grants would naturally suppose such a donation from the government all that could be desired. The other railroad grants being only forty miles wide, the receipts from the land sales would be limited to $32,000 per mile; but still an amount greater than the cost of their roads, and some have received government loans in addition.

It would have been far better for the people, and for the government, that the whole body of the lands within the railroad grants, had been donated on the homestead conditions. At the first suggestion such a proposition might be deemed extravagant. But a little reflection will quickly show that it is by no means as objectionable as the grants that have been made.

In the first place, under the homestead provisions, the railroad companies could not have created and fostered vast monopolies of the lands, nor have peopled the public domain with aliens; neither could they have wholesaled the people's heritage to alien capitalists, for speculation and colonization. The lands would still have been held for homes for our own people and the naturalized citizen. The system of tenant farming, now so prevalent, would not have received the unnatural development that has marked its growth in the last twenty years, and the railroad companies would not have raked Europe for aliens to occupy the people's lands. But the railroad companies, under the grants as they now stand, do all these things that are not possible under the homestead provisions, and extort from the people a far greater amount, in their speculative operations, than they would receive from the whole body of the lands when disposed of under the homestead provisions. The government does not need the revenues derived from the sale of the lands; from other sources there are abundant receipts to meet all expenditures. But good roads, by which every square mile of our territory may be easily reached, are of the first importance.

To no better use could the revenues derived from the sale of the public lands be put, than to the building of a system of railroads that would best promote that object, and for educational purposes. And the true interests of the railroads would be best served in having the lands along their lines occupied in small tracts by a people who owned the soil they cultivated. Under such a system monopolies of the lands would be effectually provided against, and the people would still receive all the benefits to be derived from the homestead laws, at the additional cost of one dollar and twenty-five cents per acre, paid for the advantage of possessing accessible railroad communication.

But we have not to deal with what might have been, but with what is; and our real business is to find a remedy for the evils brought upon us by the past unwise legislation. Under present conditions a general law making provision for the relinquishment, by the railroad companies to the United States, of all the lands within their grants upon the outer half thereof, on both sides of their roads, so as to reduce their grants to one half their present widths, and to receive from the government, in return for the same, other grants for the even, or present government sections, that would lie within the reduced breadth of their tracts, and bring all the railroad lands within the provisions of the homestead laws, excepting only the price, which might be fixed at two and one half dollars per acre, as at present on the government sections, would be a most expedient and just measure to both the people and the railroad companies. A measure of this kind would go very far towards correcting some of the most unjust legislation of the past twenty years, and again place the lands within reach of the people, and preserve to them, for a time, at least, what may yet remain.

And, also, in addition to the above, to make provision for a system of railroads that shall open up all the lands of the country, to be built as they may be required by corporations or individuals, devoting the lands, so far as may be necessary, to that purpose and the cause of education, under the general provisions of the homestead laws; declaring all the roads in the country that carry passengers and transport freight, to be highways, under the protection and control of the government; and providing for a board of commissioners to have general charge of the same, to regulate the charges for freight and passenger transportation, to establish regulations under which private parties and transporters of freight may attach their own cars to regular freight trains, to prevent discriminations and arbitrary management, and obtain the best possible service in our domestic intercourse and transportation, would be of inestimable benefit. Such a measure is practicable, and would afford an effective solution of the great railroad problem that is becoming so portentous, and give to the people and business of the country the protection that is required.

A measure of this character, proposed by the government, with the alternative of taxation as hereinafter provided, would soon end the land difficulties in that quarter. But, as it is now, the railroad companies obtain from the government an absolute grant of their lands as simple speculators and gamblers, to be disposed of to such parties, in such quantities, on such terms, conditions, and at such times as they see fit; giving to their purchasers bonds for deeds at such times as it may suit their pleasure to receive their patents; the taking of the patents being delayed for years and may be indefinitely.

Thus the lands of the railroad companies and their grantees, escaping all taxation, bearing none of the burdens of society, their holders stand in the position of the very worst class of speculators, who contribute nothing to the welfare of the community, but are continually absorbing its vitality. As society advances and increases, adding to and increasing the value of the lands around them, they sit still and increase correspondingly the demands they make for the use or possession of the lands which they control. They obtain grants and sell their lands to aliens and monopolizers for still further speculation; they hold them, unoccupied and unimproved, for a rise, and will allow of no improvement or occupation until they obtain their price, throwing all the taxation, all the burdens of government, upon the lands and improvements of the small farmer; upon his stock, his tools, and his crops. Also upon the little properties in the neighboring towns; the buildings and stocks of the traders; the dwellings and tools of the mechanics, etc. Upon everything visible fall the imposts of the tax gatherer, excepting only the lands of the railroad kings and the landed estates of the bonanza farmers. The weak are made to suffer whilst the strong altogether escape. It is a warfare upon society and the law protects them in it.

A similar state of things obtains throughout the country, on all vacant and unimproved lands, with this difference; that in all other parts where unimproved lands are held, whether in town, city, or country, there is an assessment for taxation, though made but nominal, for the special reason that it is unimproved. But the adjoining lands, that are improved, and the unimproved land, the moment it goes into use, must pay double, triple, and quadruple the amount of taxes that were imposed before the improving of the same. This custom tends directly to the encouragement of the speculator, and serves equally to discourage occupation and improvement. Illustrations of this matter exist everywhere.

A remarkable case in point may be found in New York City, where the ancestor of a well known family, when the city did not extend above Canal Street, buried some money in the lands miles away, in the interior of the island. As time passed population advanced northwards until it began to gather around those lands. Neither the original purchaser nor his heirs would sell any portion of the property, nor improve it. They were waiting for a still greater increase in value, paying nominal taxes upon unimproved property, and in no way contributing to the general welfare, till society had completely surrounded the land, advanced far beyond it, and given it fabulous values. Then it was improved, the rents now derived from it being princely. By that operation — a speculation in direct opposition to the welfare of the community and which society pays for — that family is possessed of the power of plutocrats, and an income of millions.

This system of taxation is not equitable. It is against public policy, and is a direct attack upon the best interests of the community. It exempts the speculator from the burdens of state, and throws them all on that portion of society that does the most to contribute to the general welfare. It legalizes and protects the dog in the manger principle in the most important relations of social economy. It exempts those who hold the lands but will not improve them, and thereby taxes the more heavily those who make the greatest improvements. It pays a premium upon gambling, and helps the gambler to capital to pursue his calling, but oppresses the energetic business man with double burdens. To effectually remedy the evils attending tenant and bonanza farming this indefensible system of taxation must be reversed. It is a system that found its origin in the dark ages of Europe when the landholders, at once lords of the soil and rulers of the realm, threw all the burdens of government upon the landless, the people of the towns and cities, who were unable to defend themselves. Those old customs have come down to us but little changed, and from mere force of habit our people have acquiesced in their use. But they possess not one element of justice; they are a tax upon the many for the benefit of the few, and that few are the vampires of society.

All unimproved lands, whether in city or country, which should be held for more than one year without being actually occupied and substantially improved, or in actual process of improvement, in a manner to correspond with the property by which it is surrounded, and to serve the purposes for which it is adapted, should be deemed speculative property, and be assessed at its true market value, and pay at least double the highest rate of taxation assessed upon the nearest improved property of like character. This increased taxation should be laid as the penalty to be paid for holding land of any description, unimproved in conformity with the conditions by which it is surrounded. The objects desired being to compel those who obtain lands for speculative purposes to pay for the privilege, and to offer a premium for the *bona fide* improvement of the lands, wherever they may be held. For the reason that the man who goes into actual occupation, and makes valuable improvements upon the land, is a public benefactor; whilst he who holds land without occupation and improvement, not only prevents others from adding to the wealth of society by making improvements thereon, but does so with the intent of extortion through the necessities of society, for which he should make some compensation, even though it be inadequate. And there is still another very important reason why unimproved lands should be thus taxed. Under the present system of taxation the legal owners of the lands compel the tenants and occupants to pay the taxes. It is a well recognized fact that under present conditions all taxes are really paid by the noncapitalists. But under the proposed system the owners of the unoccupied and unimproved lands would be compelled to pay their own taxes; there would be no tenants upon whom to throw it, and for once the speculative capitalist would be compelled to bear his own burden, and make substantial contributions to the support of government and protection of society.

The railroad companies holding the large land grants should come under the same rule. They should have the lands called for in their grants set apart and assessed to them as their roads are completed and put in running order. In case they or any of them should refuse or neglect to pay their taxes in pursuance of the provisions of the law, the land commissioner, upon being officially notified by the tax collector of such neglect or refusal, should, without delay, restore such lands to the operations of the homestead law, and make public proclamation of the same. The railroad companies that might feel aggrieved by such action to have their remedy by proceedings against the Land Office, but no action of any nature to lie against any settler who should be found in possession of any of the lands that lie within the limits of the grants so forfeited and restored to homestead occupation.

The lands of the bonanza farms should also be brought under the same provisions and penalties, with a special provision limiting the amount of land that might be deemed subject to taxation as improved land, because of *bona fide* occupation and improvement thereon, to one quarter section, or one hundred and sixty acres.

Under the provisions of a law of this nature, in connection with an effective redistribution of labor, the lands of the nation would again, and that quickly, go into the hands of the people. The railroad companies would sell their lands to the actual settler and small farmer on terms having the color of equity, and would not seek to hold them indefinitely in order to extort higher rates. Or, if they did so, they would be compelled to pay for the privilege.

The bonanza farmer would hasten to cut up and put his lands into the market for actual occupation, especially as the provisions of the law for the relief of tenant farmers would preclude all hope of further speculation in that direction.

The provisions of the law here proposed are in every sense strictly equitable, in no sense restricting the just rights and privileges of any person or class, nor depriving any of property without valuable consideration and just compensation, nor rights nor privileges that could in any manner add to the general welfare. No doubt such a law would operate to disappoint the expectations of many. But such expectations are sure to be based on the preparation and hope for further raids upon the well being of society, and they should be disappointed and defeated.

For the relief of tenant farmers a law is required that will provide for the assessment of all such property at its true market value, with provisions enabling any occupant of a tenant farm to purchase the whole or a portion of such farm upon the following terms :— In case a tenant wished to purchase the farm he occupied, or a part thereof, he should, in writing, notify the proprietor of the desire to so purchase the same, taking the property at the assessed value for purposes of taxation. By this provision the common practice of undervaluing lands to escape taxation would be broken up, and that great source of fraud would find an end. The tenant so purchasing to either pay in cash, or turn over to the proprietor his share of the crops taken from the soil, in payment therefor, at the market rates of the same at the point of delivery, and at the time of the payment or tender. In case full payment for the property should not at once be made or tendered, then and in that case the purchaser should pay to the proprietor interest upon all deferred payments at the lowest rate paid on the bonds of the general government, at the time of the passage and approval of the law under which the proceedings are taken. A tender of the payments therein provided for, if refused, should be deemed full satisfaction to the amount of the tender. Whenever a tenant should show to the satisfaction of any court of record, that the provisions of the act had been complied with, and the payments for the farm, or a portion thereof, had been fully made as provided therein, such court should issue an order to the proprietor of the said farm, to make a conveyance of the same to the said tenant; and from the time of the issuance of said order the said farm should be deemed in law the property of the tenant so purchasing.

Provision should also be made, that on and after the first day of January, 1890, all payments, without interest, for rents of tenant farms, should be deemed in law payments made for the purchase of the farm occupied by the tenant so paying or tendering; and that when an amount had been so paid, equaling the assessed value of the said farm for purposes of taxation, or for a portion thereof, the whole farm, or such part as may be fully paid for, to be selected by the tenant from the outer boundaries thereof, should be made over to the tenant under the conditions above stated.

The provisions of this proposed law are designed to suggest a system of summary actions, by which the tenant farmers may become proprietors of the lands they occupy at a fair valuation, and upon such terms as would come within their ability to meet. The whole proceedings taken to be such as would avoid the accumulations of cost, and the vexatious delays that inevitably tend to defeat all substantial relief.

The three measures here suggested, if adopted, viz.: a law restoring the public domain to the action of the homestead provisions, another regulating taxation, a law for the cure of the evil of tenant farming, and effective measures for the redistribution of labor, would certainly have the effect of calling all into active employment and removing enforced idleness and poverty from the land; of breaking up the large landed estates, and restoring the land to the people, for independent and prosperous homes; and would put an end to tenant farming.

Only one other measure is required to effectually break the back of plutocratic monopoly; and that is, a law to compel the equal division of estates among the natural heirs. Laws that permit a parent to rob any portion of his children for the benefit of others, whether in or out of the family, are just as much against public policy as to permit the betrayal of any other trust with which one may be clothed, by either human or Divine law. The parent, in this respect, stands in the relation of a trustee of interests which, under the highest obligations that unite families and bind man to man, all the children have a natural and equal right in and to, and one that a parent should not be permitted to ignore or violate. A parent should possess testamentary power for adjusting and equalizing between his heirs the benefits that may have been received and are to come; and to make provision for the care of the persons and portions of those who, for any cause, are incapable of, or unfit to care for themselves; but not for the purpose of robbing some and enriching others.

Our fathers, in the adoption of the English code, rejected the laws of primogeniture and entail. But in framing testamentary provisions in the form in which they now exist, the evils of primogeniture and entail are still practically reached. The building up and transmission of great estates, unbroken, from one generation to another, at the cost and sacrifice of natural rights in the family, and of damage to society, are as possible under our testamentary laws as under the old English system. The difference between the two is, that under the English system an entail once created may continue indefinitely, through many generations, and of which every one has full knowledge as to its nature and scope. But under our testamentary laws a new will is required for every generation, which has the dubious advantage, if desired, of preventing all knowledge of its bequests until after the death of the testator, and permits the consummation of many a device of deviltry without possibility of detection until too late for remedy. Where estates are settled under the provisions of our laws, without the intervention of wills, substantial justice is obtained; but the unlimited power that is permitted for the unrestricted and arbitrary disposition of properties by means of wills, is a constant invitation to such action as will defeat the only equitable provisions in our testamentary system, and the perpetration of the greatest wrongs. But the reason in this connection, which stands preëminently above all others, why estates should be equally divided among the natural heirs, is, to prevent the accumulation and transmission of great properties, unbroken, from one generation to another.

The measures here proposed are truly national; they all pertain to the "general welfare of the United States," and can not be left to the diverse and non-action of the several States. Absolute uniformity is required in these matters, that we may be truly a homogeneous people — a nation. Indeed, the measure which is most important of all, if it be possible to separate them and say which is most important, can not, by any possibility, be made operative in any one State without the cooperation of all. They are all national in their scope, and must be made national in action.

It will be said that these proposed measures would be unwarranted innovations; that the laws and customs which it is proposed to change are of time honored precedents; that they have existed in their present written and unwritten forms for generations; that they are hoary with age.

That is the very point — they *are* hoary with age; their roots are found firmly embedded in the despotisms and brutalities of the dark ages; they are the outgrowths of barbarism that have been perpetuated in tyranny. It is because they are so hoary with age that they are tainted with oppression and smell so strongly of blood. It is time that they were buried, and that something more merciful, more just, more equal, should take their places.

Adam Smith, in relation to some of these matters,

in the following quotations gives a very clear insight into their origin : —

"When the German and Scythian nations overran the western part of the Roman empire, the confusion which followed so great a revolution lasted for several centuries. The rapine and violence which the barbarians exercised against the ancient inhabitants, interrupted the commerce between the towns and the country. The towns were deserted, and the country was left uncultivated, and the western provinces of Europe, which had enjoyed a considerable degree of opulence under the Roman empire, sunk into the lowest state of poverty and barbarism. During the continuance of those confusions, the chiefs and principal leaders of those nations acquired or usurped to themselves the greater part of the lands of those countries. A great part of them was uncultivated; but no part of them, whether cultivated or uncultivated, was left without a proprietor. All of them were engrossed, and the greater part by a few great proprietors.

"This original engrossing of uncultivated lands, though a great, might have been but a transient evil. They might have soon been divided again, and broke into small parcels either by succession or by alienation. The law of primogeniture hindered them from being divided by succession; the introduction of entails prevented their being broke into small parcels by alienation.

"When land, like movables, is considered as the means only of subsistence and enjoyment, the natural law of succession divides it, like them, among all the children of the family; of all whom the subsistence and enjoyment may be supposed equally dear to the father. This natural law of succession accordingly took place among the Romans, who made no more distinction between elder and younger, between male and female, in the inheritance of lands than we do in the distribution of movables. But when land was considered as the means, not of subsistence merely, but of power and protection, it was thought better that it should descend undivided to one. In those disorderly times every great landlord was a sort of petty prince. His tenants were his subjects. He was their judge, and in some respects their legislator in peace, and their leader in war. He made war at his own discretion, frequently against his neighbor, and sometimes against his sovereign. The security of a landed estate, therefore, the protection which its owner could afford to those who dwelt on it, depended upon its greatness. To divide it was to ruin it, and to expose every part of it to be oppressed and swallowed up by the incursions of its neighbors. The law of primogeniture, therefore, came to take place, not immediately, indeed, but in process of time, in the succession of landed estates, for the same reasons that it has generally taken place in that of monarchies, though not always at their first institution. . . . . . Hence the origin of the right of primogeniture, and of what is called lineal succession.

"Laws frequently continue in force long after the circumstances which first gave occasion to them, and which could alone render them reasonable, are no more. In the present state of Europe the proprietor of a single acre of land is as perfectly secure of his possession as the proprietor of a hundred thousand. The right of primogeniture, however, still continues, and as of all institutions it is the fittest to support the pride of family distinctions, it is likely to endure for many centuries. In every other respect nothing can be more contrary to the real interest of a numerous family than a right which, in order to enrich one, beggars all the rest of the children.

"Entails are the natural consequence of the law of primogeniture. . . . . . They are formed upon the most absurd of all suppositions, the supposition that every successive generation of men have not an equal right to the earth, and to all that it possesses; but that the present generation should be restrained and regulated according to the fancy of those who died perhaps five hundred years ago." — *Wealth of Nations.*

This is the soil out of which have grown, and these are the nurserymen who have cultivated and matured the laws and customs under which we are developing. There have been some changes in the instruments used and methods of procedure, but the results are practically the same. The hands of the great proprietors are no longer shielded with gauntlets of iron, but are covered with softest kid, tipped with finest furs. But the kid and furs beautifully disguise a vast increase of active crushing power. They no longer seize the sword as the weapon of oppression, but wield the pen, which is mightier, and are supported by an army of economic teachers who have studied only in the schools of feudalism. These teachers have not yet learned anything of the great developments of the present century, nor of their causes or effects, but like the barbarians they represent, would force the people to believe "that the more the rich may gain in wealth the more the poor may gain in comfort."

Having transplanted from the old feudal nurseries their laws, and made them our own, it follows, as a matter of necessity, that we must reach the same results, and we find them in our tenant farms, our great land holdings, our monopolies, the wealth and power of the few, and the miseries of the many. Our laws and teachers having prepared the way and laid the foundation for these great social evils, they have come upon us with the inexorable certainty of fate. Do the conditions under which we live require the longer continuance of a system founded under the circumstances described, and with such results? There can be but one answer.

It must be apparent to every thoughtful person that a system of land and labor laws that found its origin in the barbarisms and confusions of the middle ages, out of which have grown all the evils described, is not a good foundation for the development and growth of Republican Institutions, nor the elevation and improvement of the masses. Feudal Laws and Republican Institutions, with us, are irreconcilable; one or the other must and will be changed. The present tendencies are all in the direction of the concentration of all the elements of wealth and power in the hands of the few, and degradation of the masses. These were the peculiar features of feudalism, and have ever marked the periods of greatest distress and decadence with every people. Can we hope to escape the necessary consequence of our own barbarous and unjust system if we persist in retaining it?

In the remedial measures here proposed there is no taint of socialism; in it I fail to find any hope of improved conditions. Nor is there the least color of communism; that, to me, is far less hopeful than socialism. Neither can any action of agrarian laws place our people in the position which would achieve the best results for humanity.

What we require is the freest and fullest exercise of independent family and individual relations, in all business, educational, and social affairs, within a range and under such limitations as will best protect the weak from the natural encroachments of the strong, and enable all to share in the blessings of well regulated society. Unquestionably, it is in this manner that the "general welfare of the United States" can be best promoted.

In seeking remedies for the cure of the evils herein

described, the fact must be fully recognized that however great these evils may be, they are the direct result of the action or nonaction of society, for which it is alone responsible; and that if, in applying its remedies, actual and undeserved damage should be inflicted, provision for indemnification should be made. But in no case can society become responsible for the failure of any speculation or attack upon the true interests of mankind. That whilst confiscations are uncalled for and unjustifiable, the further sacrifice of the interests of society for the benefit of the few can not and will not be endured.

CHAPTER VI.

MACHINERY IN TEXTILE AND OTHER MANUFACTURES.

PREVIOUS to the last quarter of the past century the work of carding of wool and cotton, of spinning of yarn, and weaving of all textiles, were the operations of purely hand labor. In England, in 1763, High invented the spinning jenny. Crompton, in 1775, introduced the mule spinner, and in 1790 Arkwright introduced the power loom. These inventions, with the introduction of Watt's engine, in 1783, in steam carding and spinning, and Bell's cylinder printing, in 1775, mark the commencement of the world's use of machinery in textile manufactures.

From the very earliest period in the history of the American Colonies, not only was domestic or household manufactures almost universal, but companies were engaged in the spinning of flax, wool, and cotton. In 1638 a company of Yorkshiremen settled in Rowley, Massachusetts, and engaged in the business; and in 1640 the General Court of that Colony encouraged that industry by bounties, followed almost immediately by the Assembly of Connecticut.

As early as 1775 a spinning jenny was put in operation in Philadelphia, followed by beginnings to manufacture by machinery in 1780, in Worcester, Massachusetts; in East Bridgewater, in 1786; in Beverly, in 1787; in Providence, Rhode Island, in the same year, and in Baltimore in 1789. From that time until 1813, though there was great development and progress made in carding and spinning by machinery, the weaving had been altogether confined to hand looms, and much the larger part of the carding and spinning done in our country was upon the hand card and spinning wheel.

At the beginning of the present century substantially all our textiles were made by hand labor, and in the main continued to be so made during the next twenty-five years. Throughout our country every farm house possessed its loom and spinning wheels. From the sheep reared upon the farm was the wool taken and carded by our mothers, ready for spinning. The flax grown upon the place was by our fathers broken and hatcheled by hand, and made ready for the women folk, who, day after day, week after week, month in and month out, for fully or more than one half of the year, were all constantly employed in carding, in spinning, and in weaving the woolen and linen cloths that clothed the family, or were traded at the store for tea, and coffee, and sugar, or other necessaries or luxuries of life. The household music of that time was the hum of the large spinning wheel, that rose and fell as the spinner receded or advanced, in concert with the more steady flow of the tones of the flax wheel, as with foot on treadle other members of the family, or women servants, spun the flax which was changed to linen yarn or thread. At the same time the constantly repeated rattle of the shuttle could be heard as the dexterous hand sent it flying through the warp, to add another thread to the web, followed by the stroke of the swinging beam. In most of our towns and cities hand carding, spinning, and weaving were established trades, giving employment to large numbers of men, women, and children.

In 1813 Francis C. Lowell and Paul Moody made the first successful introduction of the power loom in a factory which they built in Waltham, Massachusetts, containing 1,700 spindles. During the same year the Scotch loom and engine and dressing machine were introduced in Providence, Rhode Island, by William Gilmour, from Glasgow. The next operation was by P. T. Jackson, Nathan Appleton, Kirk Boott, and others, in 1822, in East Chelmsford, now Lowell, Massachusetts. From that time to this there has been a constant and rapid development in the invention, improvement, and application of machinery in every description of textile manufactures. We will examine some of the leading facts upon this point.

The Frankford yarn mill, in Philadelphia, during the month of July, 1877, in all its operations, from the receipt of the raw material to the delivery of the finished product, employed 151 persons of both sexes and all ages. In the twenty-three and a half days in which the mill run during that month there was produced 1,723,433 skeins of yarn, containing 840 yards each, which gave for the month a fraction over 822,547 miles in length of yarn, or 35,002 miles a day. It would require 61,603 women, with the old hand cards and spinning wheels, to produce the same amount in the same length of time, 1,000 yards of yarn, carded and spun, having been a day's task for a day of ten hours, with those old machines. In my essay upon "Our Labor Difficulties" it is estimated that it would require 100,000 women, with the old hand cards and spinning wheels, to have produced the amount of yarn here reported.

At the time of publishing that essay I had been unable to find any person who had been accustomed to the use of the old machines and tools, and who knew what a day's work by our mothers amounted to, or any authority upon that point. But in March, 1878, Aunt Tabitha, the spinner at the Spinning Bees of the Old South Exhibition, in Boston, gave me the desired information, and I am glad to be able to place the amount on record. Her formula for stating the day's work for carders and spinners when she was a girl was, that 40 threads, 2 yards long, made a knot, 7 knots made a skein, and 5 skeins of warp, or 6 skeins of filling, were a day's work for a spinner; and that it took as long to card the cotton or wool as to spin it. A day's work in those times was 15 to 16 hours. This statement gives for an average day's work by our mothers about 3,080 yards for two persons, one carding and the other spinning, in 15 hours; or, say, 1,000 yards in 10 hours for one person performing both operations. Upon this basis I make my estimate. I was also informed by Mr. Richard Garced, the proprietor of the mill, that he was then employing only one half the number of hands that were employed in 1872, though turning out fully as much work, having since that time refurnished the mill with new machinery.

This statement shows a displacement of 50 per cent. of the former employés in that mill by improvements in its machinery in the five years between 1872 and 1877; and that one person, with improved machinery, now fills the place and does the work that required 408 carders and spinners with the tools and machinery in common use at the close of the first quarter of the present century.

At a meeting of the New England Cotton Manufacturers Association, held in Boston, October 5, 1876, Mr. Wm. A. Burke, Treasurer of the Lowell Machine Shop Company, read a paper upon the "Cost of Manufacturing Drillings and Standard Sheetings in 1838 and 1876." In this paper Mr. Burke took the Boott Mill No. 1, in Lowell, as a type for his illustration. In this mill, in 1838, there were 232 operatives employed $12\frac{3}{4}$ hours a day for 24 days in May, who produced 208,606 yards of cloth. But in 1876, 90 operatives, the number then employed, working 10 hours a day, produced 204,863 yards. Reducing the $12\frac{3}{4}$ hours of 1838 to 10 hours a day, the working time of 1876, shows that it would have required 295 operatives in 1838, working 10 hours a day, to produce but a small fraction more than 90 operatives produced in the same number of days, in the same mill, in 1876. Here is shown a displacement, by improvements in the machinery of one mill, within the last 40 years, of 70 per cent. of the manual labor in the production of cotton fabrics. Mr. Burke stated that "this improvement," i. e., the displacement of muscle, "had been obtained by larger mills, improvements in the construction and workmanship of machinery, and many important inventions and attachments to save labor and perfect work; the number of looms a weaver is now able to tend having more than doubled. In 1838 two looms to a weaver was the rule, though there were cases of three or more being tended by one person. Now, the practice is for four to six, and even eight looms to be run by one weaver," etc. He further stated that, "Since 1861 all the mills owned by the Boott Cotton Mills have been renovated and enlarged, supplied with additional motive power, new shafting, and an entirely new suit of machinery, of the latest construction, arranged for the greatest economy in operating;" which means for the least possible employment of manual labor.

Mr. Edward Atkinson, of Boston, during the discussion at that meeting, said, "A man who owned a mill of the style of 1838 to-day would be a bankrupt. He could not run it. The whole success depends on the constant adoption of new and improved machinery. The machines have become more distinctly self operative, requiring only to be kept in order, and kept up by oversight, rather than by the actual work of those who tend them."

In Fall River the rule is eight looms to the weaver, run at a speed that gives 44 cuts of 45 yards each per week, making 1,980 yards per week for each weaver, or 330 yards a day. Our mothers could weave upon their looms about 3 yards in 10 hours of work. So that in weaving there has been not only a displacement of 75 per cent. of muscle in our mills in the last 40 years, mostly within the last 15, but to-day one girl weaver with her improved machine looms stands in the place that would have required 100 women in our mothers' time to fill.

The development in the production of cotton goods, by improvements in machinery, with the displacement of muscular labor, is exhibited by the Massachusetts reports of 1875, which show that the average time worked by factory operatives was then very nearly 9 months in the year, and for 10 hours a day. In the year ending with May, 1865, work was constant, for 12 or more hours daily. Making the adjustment here required, both for lost time and shorter hours, in order that a true comparative exhibit may be obtained, will show that while it required the labor of 24,151 operatives, in 1865, to produce 175,875,934 yards of cloth, in 1875, 31,707 operatives, working the same number of hours daily as were worked in 1865, would produce 874,780,874 yards. That while the product has increased 397 per cent., the increase in manual labor had been only 31 per cent.; that is to say, that the increase in product had been more than twelve times greater than the increased employment of labor, in the preceding ten years.

In woolen goods, the Reports of the Massachusetts Bureau of Statistics of Labor, for 1875, states that, in 1865, 18,753 operatives produced 46,008,141 yards; but that in 1875, 90,208,280 yards were produced by 19,076 operatives. This shows an apparent increase in muscular employment of 283 operatives. But to make a true comparative showing by this statement a most important adjustment is necessary. In 1865 the working time was not less than 12 hours a day; but in 1875 it was by statute limited to 10. But making the same adjustment in woolens as has been made in cottons, and for the same reasons, will show that while it required 18,753 operatives in 1865 to produce 46,008,141 yards of cloth, in 1875, 11,550 operatives would have produced 90,208,280 yards in the same time. Showing at once, not only an absolute reduction of 38 per cent. in the muscular labor employed, but an increase of 98 per cent. in the product. These great developments in cotton and woolen textiles were for the ten years from 1865 to 1875. For the eight years since 1875 the increase in production from the continued improvements in machinery has continued, but probably not in so marked a degree. The statistics upon this point by the Census of 1880 I have not yet been able to reach.

In these two great productions of cotton and woolen cloths, though there had been an increased average product of nearly 450 per cent. in one decade, there was, in the same period, an absolute decrease in muscular employment equal to the labor of 353 operatives.

Full 40 years ago machine cards, spinners, and looms had utterly destroyed all our domestic or household manufactures, and compelled those who were engaged in them, the sons and daughters of our farms and rural districts, to find employment in the mills of our manufacturing towns and cities, or to live in idleness and consequent misery. Since that time 70 per cent. of the hand labor then required in the mills in the production of textile fabrics has been displaced by improvements in their machinery, whilst, at the same time, production has been greatly increased. What has been done in the Philadelphia yarn mill, and in the Boott mills, in Lowell, has been done and is still doing in every mill in our country.

In every business or industry requiring force there is found a substitution of mechanical in place of muscular power similar to that which has been shown to have taken place in agriculture and in the production of textile fabrics. It will be sufficient for the present purpose to briefly refer to the general results attained in a few of the myriad industries in which machinery is now the great producing agent.

There is no direction in which mechanical force has wrought a greater revolution than in that of the production and manufacture of iron and steel, and the adaptation of those two metals to all the varied uses of mankind. So great and multifarious have been the advances in their use, in every direction — in the construction of naval and merchant shipping; in colossal artillery and in all the enginery of war; in bridges, railways, locomotives, steam engines, farming implements, and tools of every description, down to what is by no means the least ingenious, wonderful, or useful — the production of the stamped pots, pans, plates, basins, cups, and the thousand and one other uses to which iron and steel are applied, under the power of mechanical force, that they defy description or examination. The stride of the present century, from the primitive blast furnace and blacksmith's forge and anvil, with the crude and inefficient hand bellows, to the gigantic rolling mills, machine shops, and pot and pan factories of to-day are marvels of the age, and make it quite impossible to form a just idea of how great has been the advance in this class of mechanical power over that of the muscular force of the past century.

In boot and shoe making one man, with the tools and machinery now in use in that industry, turns out three thousand pairs of boots and shoes in a year, where fifty years ago he could produce not more than two hundred pairs.

In building and carpentry the planing machine will do the work of at least fifteen to twenty men with hand planes; the circular saw more than fills the place of a dozen men with hand saws; the molding machine will cut more moldings than can ten men with the old tools. So with the jig saw, the band saw, the mortising machine, and the many other machines in use in wood work.

The sewing machine has taken the place of the hand needle, one woman now doing the work that but a short time ago would require at least a dozen.

Machinery, in some half dozen establishments in our country, now makes the watches for the world, having quite demoralized that great industry in Switzerland, France, and England.

In printing, at the beginning of the century, all the books, papers, and other work, were done upon the hand press, directly from the type. The limit of production, from one press, worked by two men, was two hundred and fifty impressions an hour, of two pages not larger than one side of the New York Sun; thus limiting the possible issue of any daily paper to about two thousand copies. The presses now in common use in our large newspaper establishments will give thirty thousand impressions, or fifteen thousand perfected papers in an hour, all nicely folded, with no limit as to size. To-day, by the improvement in the presses, and the invention and use of the processes of stereotyping, with no change in type setting, in the great newspaper establishments, seventy-five men are actually doing the work that would have required the labor of at least ten thousand to accomplish at the beginning of the present century, and which may be extended to double and quadruple the present amount by the labor of half a dozen additional men.

So in every direction has machinery supplanted the use of muscle in the work of production and distribution, and wherever else force is used, solely for the purpose of man's consumption. Even in the horse car stables in Philadelphia, machinery has been brought into use to run the brushes in cleansing the horses, with a large saving of manual labor.

These illustrations should sufficiently indicate the revolution that has been wrought in the production of everything that enters into man's consumption — the displacement of muscle by the use of machinery — and the imperative necessity that has arisen to devise some means by which consumption shall be correspondingly developed, if possible, and that man be protected from the evils of idleness.

Before 1860, more than twenty years ago, the inventions and improvements in machinery had created armies of idlers and beggars who filled the country with their cries for work. But the operations of the war of the rebellion suddenly called all the idlers into active employment, and for four years there was work for all. But during and since the war the power of machinery has been much more than doubled; the number of idlers has been increased in like proportion, and again the cry for work comes up from millions of our people and fills the whole land. Under present tendencies the idleness must increase and the cry swell in volume and force, for at no previous time has the continued displacement of muscle by machinery been so rapid as at the present. The whole movement, from the beginning, has been marked by a constant acceleration, and at no time more distinctly than within the last twenty years.

To-day there is heard the wailing of great multitudes for work — for work that they may live. It comes from the strong and from the weak; from the skilled and from the unskilled; from the old and the young; from the cultured and from the uncultured; from mothers and from daughters; from fathers and from sons; even from babes and infants of six and eight years. The wail is everywhere — on our streets, at our doors, in our halls and houses; in our churches, and offices, and factories, and shops, and stores — for "work, work or we die." For want of it our people are dying daily; some by the slow process of starvation, others by their own hands. The same want fills our streets with prostitution and crime; our insane asylums to overflowing, and our reformatories and penal institutions beyond their capacity. It is the direct cause of the increase of all the evils of intemperance, and the great barrier to every reform. It is heard in every country, but in none so loudly as in our own.

Manifestly the great increase in man's productive

power, and ability to provide for and "insure his daily subsistence," has not been attended by a correspondingly improved condition of the great masses of the people, and an advance in the general tone of society; but, on the contrary, it has served to suddenly place enormous wealth in the hands of the few, and to bring corresponding destitution and distress on the many.

CHAPTER VII.

EFFECTS OF THE WAR OF THE REBELLION UPON THE LABOR OF THE COUNTRY.

THE war of the rebellion marks a period of very important changes in our industrial and social conditions, coming upon us, as it did, after forty years of mechanical development in the direction and with the effects herein partially described. The beginning of the year 1861 found the people of our country in the greatest distress, which had been for years increasing and intensifying. Thousands of operatives were out of employment and destitute, begging, clamoring for bread, and perishing with cold and hunger; whilst those who were fully or partially employed were in receipt of wages that would hardly supply the barest necessaries of life. Trade and business of every nature suffered in common with the industries of the country, and distress and demoralization everywhere prevailed. Whilst the country was in this condition hostilities commenced, and a call was made for 75,000 men in the North; shortly afterwards 300,000 more were enlisted; then more, and more, until all the late idle and partially employed men and women in the country had been gathered into the army, or some industry, and were paid an amount that enabled all to live more liberally, more comfortably than ever before. Not for full forty years had our people in the North been so generally employed, nor so abundantly supplied with all the necessaries and conveniences of life as during the last three years of the war of the rebellion, and for a short period after its close. Only one thing marred the general happiness — the sickness, wounds, and deaths that war carries to so many households.

The first half of the year 1865 found all the men and women in our country in active and remunerative employment — none were idle. The four years of universal employment in the northern States enabled all to pay the indebtednesses and square the accounts of the period before the war, and enter the second half of 1865 with no private debts, but largely increased powers of production and distribution.

One would think that, with this statement of facts, the future of our people must have been all that could be desired. But with the close of the war there came a change of the greatest importance. During the first months of the year 1865 all were employed and receiving compensations that gave to all a generous support; but at the close of the year millions had been thrown out of employment into idleness, and left without any industrial means of subsistence.

I have made an effort to see how great was the number who so quickly passed from well compensated employments into absolute idleness — from plenty to penury.

Whilst in Washington, during the winter of 1878 and '79, I obtained from the Secretaries of War and the Navy, from the Quartermaster General and heads of other bureaux, the best estimates obtainable within a limited time of the forces employed by government in the war of the rebellion, and the reduction which has since been made. I can not do better than to quote in full the statement of Quartermaster General Meigs: —

WAR DEPARTMENT — QUARTERMASTER GENERAL'S OFFICE.

Washington, D. C., January 13, 1879.

It is estimated that at the close of the rebellion there were in the armies of the United States not less than 1,300,000 enlisted men, 487,000 horses, 305,000 mules, and 130,000 civilians, hired as teamsters, laborers, and servants to officers, etc., to do the civil work of the army in the Quartermaster's Department.

This is exclusive of all those citizens who were employed upon railroads not under military management, in mills and factories, and workshops, building wagons and cars, and making cloth and clothing, or gathering crops of grain, hay, and other agricultural products to be consumed by the army.

Nor does it include the persons employed by the Engineer Department, the Ordnance Department, or the Commissary Department. It includes only the enlisted men and officers, their servants, and the civilians hired and paid by the Quartermaster's Department.

M. C. MEIGS,
Quartermaster General,
Br'v't Major General, U. S. A.

MR. W. GODWIN MOODY,
Boston, Mass.

At the time of receiving the above statement General Meigs said to me that his observation and experience during the war convinced him that at least one fifth of the able bodied men of the North were enlisted or employed in the immediate service of the army, and that another fifth were employed in furnishing them with material and subsistence.

To the above figures, as received from the Quartermaster General, I add 9,834 employed in the Ordnance bureau of the War Department, 11,025 in the bureau of Engineers, and 82,270 employed in the Navy Department; making a total of 1,533,129 men employed by government in those departments at or near the close of the war. The number employed in the bureau of the Commissary of Subsistence, and of the Pay Office, which I did not obtain, would no doubt increase the total number to fully 1,550,000 men, at that time in those services, as against 25,000 men now in the army, and about 7,000 in the navy. Neither was I able to obtain any statement as to the number employed in the construction of heavy ordnance for the army or navy, nor for vessels of war, where furnished by private individuals or companies.

These statements and estimates show that in the North alone at least one million five hundred thousand soldiers, and civilians with the armies who had been employed in the service of the government, by the close of the war of the rebellion found their occupations gone and themselves in idleness.

An equal number of persons, as estimated by Quartermaster General Meigs, and as generally estimated in the European armies, were employed in the supply of war material and subsistence; or, as stated by a late Secretary of the Interior, in September, 1878, in his Cincinnati speech, in the "large industries ministering to the work of destruction." To this host must be added the great numbers employed in the Sanitary and Christian Commissions, and other voluntary organizations, receiving their employment and subsistence through the operations of the war; traders and camp followers, and armies of fugitives and refugees, estimated by hundreds of thousands; in all swelling the grand total of those dependent on the war for employment and subsistence to fully three and one half millions of persons in the North, or quite one half of its whole industrial population, who, in 1865, by the ending of the war were deprived of their employments and means of subsistence, and thrown into idleness.

By adding to this amount the number who were similarly affected in the South, we find that we have had in our country more than four millions who found their occupations gone by the close of the war, and who were compelled to find new employments or remain idle.

These enormous bodies of men, animals, and the machinery that were used in the destructive employments of the war, were the tremendous forces that, to find employment and subsistence, were at once hurled back upon the peaceful industries of the country, that had already been developed far beyond the normal requirements of the people by the abnormal demands of the preceding four years.

It must be noted that at the time when one half of the producing force of the North had been taken from the normal industries of peace, and were employed in the occupations of war, with its enormous consumption and destruction, the other half, who still remained in the peaceful industries, not only fully supplied all the demands of society and more than made good all the waste and destruction of the war, but they also enabled the whole people to live in greater abundance and comfort than ever before. One half of our people furnished abundant subsistence and comfort for the whole at the very time when the normal and abnormal demands for consumption were the greatest; and, consequently, at the close of the war there was no demand for the services of those who had been engaged in it either as enlisted men or otherwise, to help in the work of providing for the sustenance and comfort of society.

An incident marking the great development and power of our normal industries during the war, and the abundance and wealth of our products, was, that in the midst of the most tremendous throes of that great struggle, when it was learned that the work people of Lancashire were hungry and in great distress for want of cotton to work upon, our southern ports being blockaded and little cotton exported, we loaded three ships with cargoes of food from our wealth of abundance, and sent the means of life and comfort to a suffering and distant people. Still more recently the people of Lancashire and all England have again been hungry and distressed, with plenty of cotton and other material to work upon; but our people, though in a state of profound peace and burdened with the greatest abundance of everything necessary for the life and comfort of all, were still too poor to feed our own hungry or help their distress. Our people are also idle and poorly paid.

The great industrial change that reduced four millions of persons from abundant employment to idleness was mainly accomplished within one hundred and twenty days after the signing of the capitulation at Appomatox Court House. A change greater, more rapidly made, and of more momentous consequences than the world ever before witnessed; an event that demoralized our whole industrial and trade interests.

The idleness that was developed by this great and sudden change came upon us in the very hight of our greatest prosperity; it was like a flood, with its waters spread over the face of the whole country, which are still rising and washing and wearing away the foundations of all prosperity and filling the nation with ruined fortunes and dead and blasted hopes.

It is not possible for the condition of things here noted to occur under the European systems. The great armies of those nations are never disbanded en masse, and turned in upon the nation to find employment or be idle, as best they may. There, in peace as in war, the great body of men who are not required in productive pursuits find occupation and sustenance under their military systems, and thus are those nations, in very large measure, preserved from those perils by which we are surrounded. If, at the close of the late Franco-German war the great armies of those nations had been at once, and permanently disbanded, the industrial distress which now exists in each would have so multiplied as inevitably to have destroyed both. These economic facts and principles are well understood and acted upon by the governing powers in Europe; but our ward politicians and feudal economists have yet to obtain their first idea of these self evident principles.

Of the great number thus enforced to idleness, from the armies and abnormal industries of the North alone, at least two and one half millions were men immediately dependent upon their employments for subsistence for themselves and their families, or others relying on them for support. Out of this two and one half millions of unemployed men not more than five hundred thousand ever found employment in new or more largely developed industries — in railroad building and municipal work (see Edward Atkinson's Industrial Redistribution in the International Review), and that for a very short period, which ended in 1873, leaving entirely unaccounted for at least two million persons.

The returned soldiers were of the most able men in our country, developed and disciplined by military service, who could not and would not remain idle if work could be found or made. The workmen thrown out of the abnormal industries were the equals of those still engaged in the normal employments, and they, also, could exist only by work. The absolute necessities of all compelled the effort to find employment somewhere, in something, that they and those dependent on them might live.

So far as possible the machinery and muscle that had been "ministering to the work of destruction" were turned to the work of ministering to the normal wants and comforts of society. Many went to the western lands and became farmers; hundreds of thousands sought trade and brokerage as middlemen, as will be seen in the enormous increase of traders shown in the chapter on money; still others dipped into any and every speculation that could be devised. Yet many failed in finding or devising any employment, and remained idle, whilst with all there has been the utmost uncertainty in all their employments.

Although at the close of the war almost every person had some small means at command, it could not long continue as their only support, and at best was altogether insufficient to establish new businesses, when the opportunities were found to do so. Therefore all such enterprises were almost wholly dependent upon credit for their start and development, and all came in direct competition with like industries and employments that were already, and had long been, abundantly supplying the people's normal demands, and had the immediate effect of lessening the employment of many, by dividing between two or more the work or business previously done by one, and wholly displacing others. The result was an era of the wildest speculation and credit, with the inflation of many a bubble, based on the prosperity and gains of the past four years.

The producers and manufacturers of the products which enter into the normal consumption of the people continually multiplied their products by improvements in their machinery, which has been more than doubled in its productive capacity within the last eighteen years, and now requires less than one half the amount of manual labor that was required in 1865 to produce an equal amount of subsistence; in this way reducing by at least one half the amount of muscular employment at that time required. This great development in mechanical power is briefly shown in the chapters on Machinery in Agriculture and Machinery in Textiles and other Manufactures.

It was after the close of the war that the struggle for work again commenced between the idle and the employed. To obtain employment the idle would work for less than current rates; then would follow strikes with their losses and failures. Then, again, those but recently thrown out of employment in their turn were compelled to get it again by still another cutting under. At that time, also, commenced the organization of the great army of tramps. A grinding, cutting competition was developed which had the direct effect of both lowering wages and lessening employment. Debts were increased; consumption was lessened; production was largely developed; the grinding competition grew heavier; idleness increased; strikes were more frequent; tramps were constantly enlisted. All these operations were being accelerated until 1873, when a great panic was created by the paralysis of that year. Railroad building suddenly contracted to small proportions, and municipal work stopped in great part, both adding largely to the numbers then unemployed. Speculation and credit received a severe check; employment more rapidly diminished; furnaces, mills, shops, and all the hives of industry either closed or reduced the number of their operatives, and cut down their wages — using less of muscular force and more of mechanical — but still crowding the markets with vast stocks of every conceivable product, for which there was little or no sale.

Still wages and incomes are being reduced; still our people are growing poorer and poorer; still failures and disasters are multiplying; still strikes are more frequent and destructive; still the army of tramps is increasing, and the people are growing more and more desperate. And it must be so, for the forces and influences which made this condition possible are as active as ever. At this time the amount of idle or unemployed manual labor can not be safely estimated at less than double what it was immediately after the close of the war, with wages at about one third, when employment is obtained.

Everywhere the evidences are increasing that our people have reached the point where, in the language of Adam Smith:—

"Many are not able to find employment even upon these hard terms, but must either starve, or be driven to seek a subsistence by begging, or by the perpetration of the greatest enormities." — *Wealth of Nations.*

And he emphatically declares that:—

"The scanty maintenance of the laboring poor is the natural symptom that things are at a stand, and their starving condition that they [things in general] are going fast backwards."— *Ibid.*

These great military and industrial operations were events that did not transpire in a corner, neither did the succeeding incidents. They were of too great magnitude to be hidden; but were of the most public character and known by all men. Examine the facts and judge of them by the light of the principles above laid down, and see where our folly and madness are dragging us.

In August, 1878, I filed with the Hewitt Labor Committee a statement of the unemployed in Massachusetts, as carefully made up from the reports of the Labor Bureau of that State, from 1865 to 1875, which showed that, in 1875, there were 92,042 persons, belonging to the industrial classes in that State, unaccounted for and without employment. This statement did not include any portion of the 62,294 enrolled men returned to the State from the army in the latter half of 1865 and in 1866, and who do not appear in the industrial reports. A continuation of the examination from 1875 to 1878, on the same basis and authority, shows the nonemployment at that time of 130,713 persons. By bringing into the account the "large numbers or recruits to the ranks of labor," from the 56,117 dependents, "living at home," "a class not furnishing competitors four years ago," but who are now forced into those ranks (see statement of Col. Carroll D. Wright, Chief of Bureau of Statistics of Labor, of August, 1878), with the abnormal increase of those ranks from the 62,294 soldiers heretofore referred to, will swell the amount to more than 200,000 persons at that time unemployed in the old Commonwealth of Massachusetts.

An idleness of 200,000 in Massachusetts indicates an amount equal to that of 5,500,000 persons in the United States. Do not misunderstand this statement. It is not that this great host get no employment whatever; but that the amount of time lost by those who are only partially employed, added to those who really get no employment, equals the time for labor of more than 5,500,000 people.

By making an adjustment of the difference in working time for the two periods of 1865 and 1875, being

12 hours a day for the first period and 10 hours for the last; and also making the required allowance for the average time lost, from partial employment, by work people in all industries, amounting to fully one fourth, as shown by the Massachusetts statistical reports, we find that though the population in the ten years following 1865, increased to the amount of 384,881 persons, the amount of employed muscular force fell off to the extent of 77,000. That whilst the increase in the production of cotton fabrics was from 175,875,934 yards in 1865 to 874,780,874 yards in 1875, or nearly five fold, the actual increase (not the reported) in the muscular force employed was from 24,151 persons to 31,707, or about one fourth; in woolen goods there was an increase from 46,008,141 yards in 1865 to 90,208,280 yards in 1875, and an absolute decrease of more than one third of the manual labor employed — from 18,753 persons to 11,550. Of boots and shoes there were made in 1865, 31,870,581 pairs against 59,762,866 pairs in 1875, with an absolute decrease in the muscular force employed of nearly one half, being from 52,821 persons in 1865 to 28,854 in 1875. That is, the number of persons set down as representing the muscular force employed in 1875, if working now twelve hours per day, as was the usual time in 1865, in the above three industries, with constant employment, would produce the enormously increased products of 1875. Since 1875 the development in increase of production and decrease in muscular employment has in no respect lessened. The industries here considered are the leading industries in Massachusetts, and no doubt may be accepted as a

basis for estimating all. It will be observed that whilst in these three industries there is shown an enormous increase in production, there is an absolute decrease in manual employment equal to that of 25,000 persons. A most startling fact, affording abundant food for thought.

Not being yet able to obtain the corresponding statistics for 1880, I am compelled to rely upon those for 1875. They sufficiently mark the tendencies, which have in no respect diminished since that time; but, on the contrary, have notably increased in many directions. The Massachusetts returns are here used for the reason that they are more complete and more perfectly show the advances that are made in mechanical production, than do those from any other quarter.

In all their essential features these two exhibits, that from the military operations and that from the Massachusetts Labor Bureau, sustain each other, the army estimate indicating six millions, and the Massachusetts estimate indicating five and one half million persons as representing the idleness in our country; and they are confirmed by the incidents that have marked the progress of our distress; by the constant increase in idleness of our people; by the reduction in wages; by the vast unsaleable stocks of products of every nature; by the multitudes of manufacturing, commercial, and financial failures; by the idle and half occupied mills, factories, and workshops of every kind; by the unoccupied stores and dwellings that line our streets; by the contraction in incomes; by the shrinkage in values of every nature; by the idleness of large capitals; by the reduction in interest, by and through all of which we have sunk to a point where values and business are twenty per cent. below that of 1860, the period of the greatest depression and distress before the war. And still our course downward does not pause nor diminish; still the waters of our deluge of idleness are rising higher and higher.

The concrete wisdom and experience of all ages have crystallized into the proverb, that "idleness is the root of all evil." Certain it is, that the starting point of our present distress was the enforced idleness that followed the close of the war; the end — when and where shall we reach it?

The facts here presented have been obtainable by any who desired them, and require no high coloring to fully exhibit their hideous features. Yet these great factors are studiously hidden, ignored, misrepresented, and falsified. Our national, state, and municipal politicians, hounded on by the class of political economists who control a large portion of the press, are in full cry for a greater reduction in salaries and wages, greater reduction in working force, especially of those who now obtain the least compensation, in all departments of government employ, and among the clerks, the workmen, the teachers in our schools, our laborers — in every place where another worker can be forced into idleness, or another dollar can be taken from his scanty income. In every possible way driving our people into deeper depths of idleness and poverty, and our country more rapidly to perdition — all upon the plea of retrenchment and economy.

CHAPTER VIII.

THE WAR OF THE REBELLION AND THE BUSINESS AND WEALTH OF THE COUNTRY.

FROM time to time, within the past few years, when some of our prominent politicians have thought it necessary to offer some explanation of the causes that have operated to produce the evil times that have come upon us, society has been invited to accept some most remarkable conclusions. So misleading have been these conclusions, so wanting in every basis of fact and the simplest principles of logic, and so often are they repeated, that it seems very proper that some of them should be examined.

A late Secretary of the Interior, in a speech at Cincinnati, in September, 1878, said that "the real cause of our distress . . . . . were great wars, resulting in an immense destruction and waste of wealth; large industries ministering to the work of destruction instead of producing additional wealth," etc.

An able writer says of the war that "it destroyed millions of property, actually wiped out of existence this vast amount of wealth which it had taken years to produce. It obliged us to run in debt."

When so eminent and so able a man as Carl Schurz

can give currency to such fallacies we need not be surprised that so many others should be equally deluded. It is true that our war of the rebellion was a great event and greatly affected our industries. It is also true that our industrial distress is a great disaster, and that it comes after the war has closed. But it is not true that the distress is in consequence of the war. It may as well be said that the sun is the cause of darkness. On the contrary, and the truth is, that the only period of great industrial prosperity — the only period when our people have all been actively employed and in receipt of compensations that permitted of anything like comfort for all — that they have known for full fifty years, was during and the direct result of the war, and that the distress came upon us because the industrial conditions of the war were not continued, nor other provision made for the employment of those who were engaged in it. It must be borne in mind that the conditions of prosperity that came upon us during the war were purely industrial and trade; and that the conditions of distress that followed and have so constantly increased to the present time, are also trade and industrial, having no relation whatever to the carnage and destruction of war, except so far as they made additional demands upon the productive industries.

Adam Smith says: —

"Manufactures during the war will have a double demand upon them. . . . . . In the midst of the most destructive foreign war the greater part of manufactures may flourish greatly; and, on the contrary, they may decline on the return of peace. The different state of many different branches of the British manufactures during the late war, and for some time after the peace, may serve as an illustration of what has just been said." *Wealth of Nations.*

Never were the manufacturers and working classes of England more prosperous than during the Napoleonic wars, except for the period in 1810–11, when British commerce was shut out from the continent, and also when excluded from the United States. But the close of the war, in 1815, was followed by a long period of the greatest industrial and trade distress. In our own country, previous to 1837, there had for years been developing a rapid change in all our methods of production, with growth in idleness and increase of speculation, credit, and business failures, which culminated in the great panic of that year and a general suspension of specie payments. After that panic, notwithstanding the many financial devices and political schemes, the idleness and distress increased until the commencement of the Mexican war, when the roar of the first gun fired at Palo Alto awoke our people to activity and industry. The idlers, in tens of thousands, were enrolled in the armies and sent to the front, and other tens of thousands found employment in supplying and sustaining the forces at home and abroad. The wheels of industry were set in motion throughout the country; our people generally found employment, and general prosperity attended every business. But when that war closed the men employed in the armies, and the persons who had been engaged in supplying war material and sustenance, found their occupations gone, and they were again, as before the war, compelled to depend upon the normal industries for employment and subsistence. Then again commenced the struggle for work, with increasing distress and another panic in 1857.

During the industrial transitions here referred to our monetary system had undergone no change. Our medium of exchange was gold and silver, with State bank issues redeemable in United States coin.

Let us briefly review some of the most prominent industrial facts of the late war of the rebellion, commencing with the panic of 1857, which was similar to that of 1873, only less in degree, but from similar causes. For years our producing capacity had been marvellously increasing; our productions had vastly multiplied, and at the same time we were importing, in great variety and enormous quantities, of nearly everything that entered into our consumption. In these two ways we were accumulating and piling up immense stocks of products for which a market could not be found. Already great numbers had been thrown out of employment. Our markets had been forced; prices fell; our credit had been strained to the utmost; goods could not be sold; debts could not be paid, and the crash of 1857 was the result, as the crash of 1873 was the result of like conditions.

1860 found us suffering a great industrial and commercial distress; large numbers of our people were idle in our towns and cities, begging from door to door, vainly seeking employment, whilst our stores and warehouses were gorged with products, offered at unprecedentedly low prices, with little or no sale. The people were almost hopelessly in debt, and the government nearly bankrupt. In this condition the opening of the war, in 1861, found us — with vast stocks of products, foreign and domestic, crushing the life out of us because they were not sold and consumed ; thus preventing the employment of the people in reproduction, and compelling them to idleness.

Now what was then our greatest economic need ? Why, the consumption of these goods, that there might be a demand for additional production, that the people might be employed, and thus be enabled to enter the market as purchasers and consumers.

This is exactly what the war did. All the idle men in our country were quickly brought into government service, together with large numbers who could be well spared from the peaceful pursuits. This gave our whole people active employment, with means to become active consumers. The result was that the large stocks on hand quickly disappeared before the consumption of our masses ; a great demand was created for additional production, and new demands for large supplies of war material. The success and welfare of our industries depended upon the quick consumption or destruction (in this connection the words are synonymous) of all those products, and they were all consumed in the manner indicated.

This general and active consumption created an immense trade and traffic of every nature, giving activity and prosperity to every interest. Instead of causing a "waste and destruction of wealth" the war showered wealth on all by consuming and destroying all those products which must be consumed in order to obtain pay for their production. So long as they were unconsumed they were a crushing weight ; their consumption gave life and activity to every industry in the work of reproduction. Upon this point Adam Smith is very clear. He says : —

"Consumption is the sole end and purpose of all production; and the interest of the producer ought to be attended to only so far as it may be necessary for promoting that of the consumer. The maxim is so perfectly self evident that it would be absurd to attempt to prove it. But the mercantile system . . . . . seems to consider production and not consumption, as the ultimate end and object of all industry and commerce." — *Wealth of Nations.*

He further says : —

"The goods of the merchant yield him no revenue or profit till he sells them for money, and the money yields him as little till it is again exchanged for goods. His capital continually going from him in one shape, and returning to him in another; and it is only by means of such circulation, or successive changes, that it can yield him any profit." — *Ibid.*

There can be no misunderstanding Adam Smith on the point of the relations of production and consumption. The "large industries that ministered to the work of destruction" called into activity the dormant energies of our people, and through their employment increased the volume of business and trade to a degree that enabled all, during the short period of that war, to live well and comfortably, to erect monuments of prosperity that will last for ages, and come out of the contest, in 1865, as Secretary McCulloch truly said, almost wholly out of debt. Had these large industries produced only that "additional wealth" which should remain unconsumed, they would simply have added to the great burden of unmarketed, unconsumed products that had so long been crushing the life out of every industry, and would inevitably have intensified the business distress that existed before the war. But the quick consumption, or destruction, of their products gave life and activity to every interest, and filled the land with comfort and wealth.

The war destroyed not one dollar of property that did not absolutely depend upon its destruction to pay for its production. If it took years to produce that which was destroyed, it only shows how long the payment for its production had been deferred. Nothing was wiped out. There was simply a conversion from the useless to the useful.

The only possible reason that can exist for the production of a single bale of cotton cloth, or one bushel of wheat, or one pair of shoes, is the life and comfort which are obtained by and through their use and consumption. Unused, unconsumed, they fail to repay the labor and cost of production, or in any manner to contribute to the sustenance of life, the comfort of mankind, or the wealth of society. But it is in their use, their consumption, that all the required conditions are found. And, manifestly, the quicker they are brought into use and consumption, the sooner will the producer and trader reap their reward and profit. It is consumption that makes the demand for reproduction, that fixes the value of products, creates the volume of trade, and pays both producer and trader. Production and consumption, growth and destruction, are the law of progress and development; and this talk of wiping wealth out of existence, except by and through idleness, by stagnation, by the loss of that consumption which requires constant reproduction, is the sheerest nonsense. Production and cumulation create stagnation and death, whilst production and consumption give life and development.

The war gave to the people four years of full employment, the only time they have been fully employed during the last fifty years, thus enabling them to pay their debts, and conferring prosperity on all.

There is an unerring instinct in the minds of the people that if we could only have another great war, we should be again prosperous. The *why* and the *how* they do not consider. It is only the *result* that they feel. Neither do they see that the same result may be obtained without war, and be made permanent. It was not the killing of our fellow men that gave or added to our prosperity.

When the war closed three and one half millions of men and women in the North alone, who had been employed in the armies, and in their support, were thrown out of employment and into idleness. It was at this point, when this great deluge of idleness came upon us, that our difficulties began. During the continuance of the war no one in the North wanted food, or clothing, or shelter, because he could not get work, or because his wages would not pay for an abundance of either. But when it closed at least three millions of working people and their dependents were at once deprived of the means of buying in the markets for consumption, except upon credit, or by competing in and compelling a division of employment in all our normal industries. That is, stated more simply, these three millions of men and women, except a small portion, and that for a very limited time, have found but partial employment, and that only by the displacement of others.

In no sense was the war the cause of our present industrial distress, as I have clearly shown by the facts and operations presented. On the contrary, it broke the tendency to idleness and distress which began with us more than fifty years ago. It gave employment to the idle, food to the hungry, clothing to the naked, shelter to the roofless, and prosperity to all. When the war closed we simply went back again to the idleness and distress of four and five years before — we began again where we left off at its commencement — and are surely reaping the legitimate results of our wilful refusal to profit by the industrial lessons of the war, which are so little understood and so constantly perverted by our modern economists.

By the barbarism of war we are clearly taught the lesson that whenever the masses are brought into active employment — whenever they are placed in the condition that will enable them to make their consumption the greatest — that that condition is immediately followed by the greatest prosperity of all classes and individuals, and especially is it the harvest season of the capitalist and the manufacturer. But that, on the other hand, whenever the masses are least employed, whenever their ability to obtain for consumption is reduced to the lowest point, there closely follows the greatest distress in society, from which the capitalists and manufacturers are by no means exempted. The destruction of human life is in no way involved in the industrial problem; that is the barbaric feature that may well be eliminated; it is not necessarily connected with the case. The whole matter rests upon the two points of the actual and constant employment of the masses and their compensation. The time of their daily employment is not a factor in the case, except so far as it shall determine whether sufficient is or is not produced to meet the consumption of society when in its most prosperous condition. With these simple factors, it does not seem difficult to discover a way out of our distress, and an economic law that may be as well understood, and as easily applied, as the law that governs in any other matter.

If the operations of the war of the rebellion shall have the effect of discovering to us the way out of our present distress, and an economic law that shall lift society out of its ruts of slavery to fallacies and false economies, to renewed and permanent prosperity and development, it will have conferred upon the world a much greater blessing than can be found in lifting the negro alone out of bondage, and make one almost tempted to apologize for the barbarism of that war.

CHAPTER IX.

DID RAILROAD BUILDING CAUSE OUR INDUSTRIAL DISTRESS?

OUR late Secretary of the Interior, in his Cincinnati speech, hereinbefore referred to, charged the cause of our industrial distress not only to "great wars resulting in immense destruction of wealth," but, in addition, to "excessive enterprise, such as the building of railroads where they were not needed—running from point nowhere to point nowhere."

The editor of one of the great journals published in Chicago, Horace White, Esq., in testifying before the Hewitt Labor Committee, in August, 1878, also charged our distress to excessive railroad building. When such men lead in fallacies a multitude is sure to follow. Let us also examine this charge and see what there is in it.

In what way did the employment of a large number of men, after the close of the war, in building railroads, cause our industrial distress?

Edward Atkinson, of Boston, says that 250,000 men (see Industrial Redistribution, in International Review), being only one twelfth of those discharged from the armies of the North alone, and the industries which sustained them, were so employed. Did the keeping of that number of men out of idleness, giving them employment, and consequently the means of buying food and clothing, and other necessaries and comforts of life, bring misery upon our whole country, or assist in doing it? Did the employment of one twelfth of those discharged from the armies, and their attendant industries, bring poverty and distress, not only upon the other eleven twelfths, but upon our whole people?

The idea is a fit companion for that which charges the cause of our distress upon the war. It has not one fact, or grain of common sense, to sustain it. It is a gross perversion of the results of labor, of industry, of enterprise.

The truth is, the industry that was developed in railroad construction delayed to just that extent the general distress that is now upon us. The capital that was thus used set into activity the wheels of industry in many avocations, and acted beneficially on all. The great trouble was, that railroad building was almost our only industrial development, and the other eleven twelfths who had been in government employ were compelled to divide the work with those already employed, or remain idle. In railroad building there was no "destruction of wealth," no "large industries ministering to the work of destruction," but large industries creating that which ministered to the wants of man; the making of something useful where nothing before existed.

Not a dollar of capital that was thus expended was lost, or wiped out of existence. It went to draw out of the earth the coal and the ore that was wrought into iron. It built furnaces, mills, shops, and dwellings; it wrought in wood and metal; it cultivated the soil; it furnished food and clothing, pleasure and instruction; it built highways, opened up vast extents of country to settlement and development, and in every way ministered to the wants of man, and then returned, every dollar of it, not one cent lost, again to the capitalist. It might not have been to the same individual; at most it had but changed hands; but none of it remained in the pockets of the working people; it all returned to the capitalist.

A portion, only, of the interest which it has paid are the additional roads that have been built, the furnaces, mills, dwellings, stores, and everything which remain unconsumed. The capital that was used in the building of these roads is still in the hands of the capitalist, and in addition all these evidences of increased material wealth.

Capital in activity assisted in doing this; capital brought into activity labor, and, being divided and distributed, moved and excited the industries of the people, and gave to the masses the means to enter into the market and make use and consume of all of the products of industry. In this way capital was an agent by which all this was accomplished. Nothing was destroyed, nothing lost, nothing wiped out of existence, as is charged on the war, but very much was added to the means which should contribute to man's welfare, and solely by the application of man's industry.

That which entered into and was consumed in the

creation of these railroads, and all that grew out of their construction, was the labor of man — and so it is in all that man produces and consumes; it is labor only that enters into the construction, crystallizes, and there remains, an addition to material wealth, whilst the capital always returns to the capitalist — and the true reason why our great industrial distress came upon us is found in the fact that only one twelfth of the late army employés found uncompetitive employment, while the other eleven twelfths remained in idleness, or by constant competition with those already employed forced a continual reduction in wages, uncertainty in and partial employment, a reduction in the means of living, a lessening of consumption, with continual decrease in the demand for manual labor in production. It is this great weight of idleness that is crushing the life out of us.

The allegation that excessive railroad building was a cause of our general distress, is not true. It was that enterprise that delayed and made more gradual its approach. The charge that we built "railroads running from point nowhere to point nowhere," as well as the whole allegation against railroads, had its origin in the Northern Pacific, where the great financial panic of 1873 first developed; a road which had then only 585 miles completed, with starting points of no mean importance, and running through and opening up, so far as completed, as good a region of country as can be found in the valley of the Mississippi. If that road did not then pay dividends, it was simply in the same condition as some of the oldest and best roads in our country.

During the four years of the war, from 1862 to 1865, inclusive, there were built 3,799 miles of road; during the next four years, 11,759 miles; and in the next four years, ending with 1873, 23,467 miles. Of this 35,226 miles of railroad built during the eight years which followed the war, 1,480 miles were in the Eastern States, being an increase of nearly 40 per cent. in that section; in the Middle States, 5,104 miles, and nearly 60 per cent. increase; in the Southern States, 3,877 miles, and 42½ per cent. increase; in the Western States, 22,833 miles, an increase of 171 per cent.; and in the Pacific States, 1,932 miles, being an increase of nearly ten fold. Which and how many of these roads were not needed? It must be easy to point them out, and it would make a most interesting and instructive exhibit.

The industry that built this vast extent of railroad (that would reach one and one half times around the world), and incidentally the great number of furnaces, forges, mills, machinery, and structures of many kinds, and that created the great demands for food, clothing, shelter, and other necessaries that were used and consumed in the sustenance of the operatives, were not the cause of our great industrial distress, because they have all been created without the consumption or destruction of any portion of the material wealth or capital that before existed, and are just so much added to the means for providing for man's necessities and comforts.

The following extract from an editorial in the Chicago Times, of October, 1882, is in the same line of fallacious statement as that of the late Secretary of the Interior. In commenting upon the railroad construction for the year, the writer says : —

"At the same rate of construction for the current quarter the total trackage laid for the year would be about 10,700 miles. This construction, assuming the actual cost to be $25,000 per mile, on the average — and it is probably not far from that — will involve the conversion of $270,000,000 of circulating capital into fixed capital."

What does this writer mean ? "Circulating capital" is generally understood to be money. Does he intend to be understood as saying that $270,000,000, in money, have changed their nature and been "converted" into iron, and wood, and roadbeds ; and consequently, that there is just so much "circulating capital" lost to the world ? Oh, no, he does not intend to say that. But that is the meaning of the language used, or it has no meaning. It is that kind of "conversion" that would make it "fixed," i. e., immovable.

The statement is a pure fallacy, without a grain of sense to sustain it. The truth is, that not one dollar of capital, of any nature, has been converted into railroads. All such capital has simply been temporarily used in the construction of the roads, as were the wheelbarrows of the laborers, and still remain as "circulating capital" for further, or other uses, as do also the old wheelbarrows, if not worn out ; a liability to which "circulating capital" is not incident.

Labor is the only "capital" that has undergone a "conversion," and become "fixed" in the railroads that have been built. In that "conversion" the labor that built those roads has gone into the hands of the capitalist as "fixed capital," upon which to obtain additional amounts of "circulating capital" by the methods too well known to require explanation here.

The two statements here commented upon may be accepted as fair samples of the fallacies that are being continually given to the public as facts, by the popular economists of the present period.

CHAPTER X.

MONEY AND THE INDUSTRIAL DISTRESS.

WHAT is money and what are its uses? Adam Smith says:—

"Money is neither a material to work upon, nor a tool to work with; and though the wages of the workman are commonly paid to him in money, his real revenue, like that of all other men, consists, not in the money, but in the money's worth; not in the metal pieces, but in what can be got for them."

"Money, by means of which the whole revenue of society is regularly distributed among all its different members, makes itself no part of that revenue. The great wheel of circulation is altogether different from the goods which are circulated by means of it. The revenue of society consists altogether in those goods, and not in the wheel which circulates them."— *Wealth of Nations.*

In the United States there are great numbers who charge all our industrial difficulties upon a contraction of the currency, a lessening of the volume of money; and other great numbers who have insisted that all that was needed to restore prosperity to all interests was the resumption of specie payments, the making of our money to harmonize with that of all other commercial nations. Some insisting that the greater the volume of money, hard or soft, the greater the prosperity. Others have been equally positive that gold, only, must be the standard of values, and with that all our industrial distress would disappear.

If these two classes would but fairly examine the facts of our present distress, and look abroad and see that the same distress is prevailing in every civilized country of the globe, with the conditions under which it obtains, they would be compelled to admit that money has nothing to do with it, either as cause or remedy.

I fully recognize the use and value of money as a medium of exchange, a representative of values — nothing more. I also appreciate the necessity of having our medium of exchange, our money, of equal value and character with that of other commercial nations, so long as we remain a member of that family; and, also, the great value of an unfluctuating, uniform currency at home. In trade, in commerce, in all financial transactions, these things appear to me indispensable for security and success. But these are matters of trade, of commerce, and finance — of the great wheel of circulation, and not of the goods which are circulated — matters which I do not here propose to discuss. Our industrial production and consumption, and the trade that grows out of these two things, are very different matters. These last things have to do with labor, work, employment — the production and use of that which is needful and useful to man for his existence, comfort, and development, among which is "money" itself, *and which is the only fiction.*

Heretofore all our discussions have been about "money, money," and "trade, trade," never once recognizing the fact that all trade is absolutely dependent upon the use and consumption of the products of industry, and that the millions are the real consumers; that their consumption is the source and measure of all trade. Neither do they appear to appreciate the industrial revolution that has changed the whole social and political condition of all Christendom, nor the relations of trade to the conditions of the whole people. About one hundred years ago all trade was substantially confined to, and dependent upon not more than a tenth part of the people. Adam Smith then said foreign trade was "to supply, at as easy a rate as possible, the great men with the conveniences and luxuries which they wanted." But now it takes in the whole of the masses of civilization, and all trade is dependent upon their condition. Our political economists have dealt solely with a matter which lies upon the surface of political and social organization — with money — that which is merely the conventional representative of real values — the medium of exchange in place of barter. They have not yet seen, and will not understand, that the real values — the fruits of the industries of mankind, their production and consumption — are what demand the most careful examination and thorough understanding.

We have evidence that money is not the cause of our present distress in the fact that Canada, divided from us by an imaginary line, is suffering the same distress, with no fluctuations in her currency. In England there is the greatest distress, but there has been no change in her financial policy for more than fifty years; but her industrial methods have been completely revolutionized. Germany has recently greatly strengthened her finances, but her industries are paralyzed. France suffers in her manufactures, and her workmen are enduring the greatest destitution, but there have been no great financial changes. Every nation and people on earth that have civilized industries and commerce have been more or less affected by the world's industrial revolution; and to the exact extent to which each country has been affected by this revolution, is the amount of distress in that country. Ours is the only nation where there have been changes in the money system, and financial follies; but in our industries we suffer in common with the whole world, whether our money is hard or soft, gold or greenbacks.

The great industrial revolution is in the use of machinery — mechanical forces in place of muscular — in general production. Money will not and can not change the relations of machinery to muscle. The increase of the volume of our money will not change the ratio of the employment of these two forces; neither would the reduction of our money to one tenth the present volume. Every one, whether possessed of much or little, will make use of that force which is most effective and of least cost. And so it should be.

At the close of the war, in 1865, as is alleged by the advocates of an increased volume of currency, there was in circulation nearly $1,800,000,000 of circulating medium. During the previous four years all the people in our country had been actively employed; the consumption of products had been enormous; the demand for reproduction had been in proportion, and duly met. The volume of trade had been so great as to compel the utmost activity. All prospered; capitalists, agriculturists, manufacturers, merchants, traders, carriers, workingmen, and laborers, all had been fully employed; all consumed liberally, paid promptly, and were contented. Money would then readily command an interest as high as eight, ten, and twelve per cent. But the close of the war quickly changed the course of all these operations. From the armies, North and South, together with "the industries that ministered to the work of destruction," there were thrown out of employment at least four millions of persons, in very large part men, with two or more dependents, whose means of subsistence were thus at once terminated.

Then followed the demoralization in all our industries, with the era of speculation and credit already described. Soon the market of consumption by our industrial classes was utterly lost and destroyed, except as it was sustained from the diminished and diminishing resources of those who still obtained employment, and by running in debt. Production did not diminish, but rather increased, and solely for speculation, creating a burden that soon became insupportable — building a monstrous pyramid, standing on its apex, of idleness, unsaleable products, and debts that could not be paid, until, in 1873, it became too ponderous to be longer held up by money, credit, or other means, when it fell, crushing the railroad and municipal work in the common ruin. Ever since that time there has been a wail, "This is the result of contraction, the work of Hugh McCulloch and John

Sherman. If we only could have had more money our pyramid would not have fallen."

A friend and correspondent in Philadelphia, one of the best and most widely known of its industrial statisticians and scientists, and, withal, one who can only see in the contraction of the currency a sufficient cause for our distress, writes to me, saying: — "I confess this calamity coming in time of peace, upon a condition of unequaled prosperity, is a mystery to me."

This class of mourners have not yet learned that first fundamental principle in political economy so clearly laid down by Adam Smith, that "the annual labor of every nation is the fund which originally supplies it with all the necessaries and conveniences of life which it annually consumes." If this be true then necessarily the trade and wealth of a people increases or diminishes as that fund of labor is employed or remains idle, and in proportion to the wages or interest which it draws or receives in its use. Neither have they yet been able to discover that it was at the very hight of our greatest prosperity, when, as they allege, we had a volume of currency amounting to nearly two billions of dollars, that substantially one half of our great fund of labor — that for a number of years had been so fully employed, drawing good interest — was at once thrown out of use, receiving no interest, whilst the half that continued employed was largely reduced in value, and received a greatly diminished interest in lower wages.

It was solely to pay the interest on this great labor fund when so generally employed, twenty years ago, that the demand for a greatly increased volume of currency was created. It was the interest that was paid upon the labor fund that went at once into circulation and created the great body of trade of that period. When a large part of this labor fund went out of use there was a sudden stoppage of interest on that portion, with an equal lessening in the amount of trade, and reduction in the amount of consumption and demand for reproduction. These great industrial events, the most notable ever witnessed by any country, in any age, our present political economists have not been able to see nor to understand. What caused the great demand for reproduction at that period; how the great consumption was sustained, and from whence came the support of the enormous domestic trade, were matters by them unknown or unconsidered; and when calamity came they were equally ignorant of the cause. They have yet to learn the great economic fact that it is the labor fund that feeds and sustains all other funds; that without that fund there can be no other. That every consumer is an economic mint that converts the products of labor into the gold that enriches society, and the amount of such conversion, or coinage, is in exact ratio with the number and capacity of the mints at work. The large and active employment of the labor fund of the nation at that time gave us our great trade and industrial prosperity. It was that that made labor valuable and caused it to command good interest, as does the active demand and use of the money fund give it value and increase the rate of its interest.

Neither do our wise economists see that immediately after the close of the war we were suddenly overwhelmed with a deluge of idleness which has been constantly increasing in volume; and that since the bursting of that deluge the contraction of the currency has not at any time equalled the falling off in the home trade and consumption, until now, with, as is claimed, a largely reduced volume of money, millions of it are vainly seeking investment in business enterprises at less than one half the interest it commanded eighteen and twenty years ago, and have been invested in United States three per cent. bonds to the amount of hundreds of millions of dollars. It was more than twelve years after the close of the war that specie payments were resumed, and for the last four years gold and paper money have stood at par. But during all this time business and values have surely declined, until now we are far below any period within the last twenty-five years; and still the tendency is downward.

At the close of the Mexican war, when our whole circulating medium was redeemable in coin, the general condition of the country was prosperous, the people being mostly employed. But when the armies that had been engaged in that war, and the industries that sustained them, had been thrown back upon the normal employments of the country, there was a growth of idleness and business distress, like that since the war of the rebellion, but which was greatly mitigated by the large emigration to the gold fields of California, in 1849, and the following years, and by the yield from the mines. Yet, notwithstanding the relief that was there found, the industrial distress that followed the close of the Mexican war resulted in the panic of

1857, in which year there were 4,932 failures, followed by a general suspension of specie payments. Still the idleness and distress increased, and business failures continued. During the last year of that period of great idleness, 1861, there were 6,993 failures; but the next year, 1862, when the people became generally employed, the number of failures fell to 1,652. As the employment of the masses increased prosperity developed; in 1863, the failures were 495; in 1864, 520; and in 1865, the number was 530. In this last year the millions who had been employed in the occupations of the war were thrown back upon the normal industries for employment, with the resulting idleness and business distress shown in the following table of failures, being for twenty-six years, from 1857 to 1882, carefully made up from the reports of the Commercial Agency of Messrs. R. G. Dun & Co. of New York. These statistics are collected from the large corps of branch agencies connected with that house, and are designed and believed to include approximately the whole number of business concerns in the United States, engaged in trade or commerce, excepting a considerable portion of the strictly petty traders. Banks, bankers, stock operators, insurance, real estate, the professions, as the medical and legal, manufacturers, builders, contractors, etc., are not included.

It will be noticed that since 1865 the increase in the number of yearly failures was nearly constant to 1878, like the increase in idleness, whatever may have been the condition of the currency, whether hard or soft, plenty or scarce; but since that year there have been greater fluctuations, though at very high figures.

LAND AND LABOR.

TABLE OF MERCANTILE FAILURES FOR TWENTY-SIX YEARS.

Year.	Number in Business.	Number of Failures.	Amount of Liabilities.	Percentage of Failures.
1857		4,932	$291,750,000	
1858		4,225	95,749,000	
1859		3,913	64,394,000	
1860		3,676	79,807,000	
1861		6,993	207,210,000	
1862		1,652	23,049,000	
1863		495	7,899,000	
1864		520	8,579,000	
1865		530	17,625,000	
1866	160,303	1,505	53,783,000	1 in every 106
1867	205,000	2,780	96,666,000	1 in every 74
1868	276,000	2,608	63,694,000	1 in every 105
1869	355,000	2,799	75,054,000	1 in every 126
1870	427,292	3,546	88,242,000	1 in every 120
1871	476,018	2,915	85,252,000	1 in every 163
1872	532,236	4,069	121,056,000	1 in every 130
1873	562,054	5,183	228,499,000	1 in every 108
1874	608,904	5,830	155,239,000	1 in every 103
1875	644,389	7,740	201,000,000	1 in every 83
1876	680,072	9,092	191,117,000	1 in every 75
1877	652,006	8,872	190,669,936	1 in every 73
1878	674,741	10,478	234,383,132	1 in every 64
1879		6,658	98,149,053	
1880		4,735	65,752,000	
1861		5,582	81,155,932	
1882	822,256	6,738	101,547,564	

Messrs. R. G. Dun & Co., in their circular for 1882, make the following comments: —

"The marked increase in the number of failures in the last two years can have only one interpretation, viz.: — that the risks of business, and the losses by bad debts, are increasing in greater proportion than the growth in the volume of trade, or the possibilities of profit."

Here we see that notwithstanding the constant efforts that are being made to guard against mercantile failures, by the restriction and limitation of credits, and by the establishment of a vast and perfected system of espionage, through numerous mercantile agencies, that enables the patrons of those great establishments to learn the business standing of every considerable trader in the country, that the number of failures reported each year unmistakably proves that a chronic state of commercial demoralization exists that is most disheartening. No better evidence is needed to conclusively show the rottenness of the industrial system upon which all our trade is standing. And the foregoing table, in the clearest and most forcible manner, also tells the story of the cause and cure of the world's industrial distress.

Commencing with 1857, a period of great industrial idleness, we find broad columns of failures and liabilities, which hold and increase until the people are brought into general employment, when they suddenly contract to less than one tenth of their former volume. This remarkable shrinkage in failures continues until the people are once more thrown into idleness, when these columns again, and almost at once, began to assume their former huge proportions. For thirteen years they almost constantly grew broader and heavier, as the idleness and destitution increased, till they reached 10,478 failures, and liabilities to the amount of $234,383,132; since which time the number of failures have fluctuated between five and ten thousand per annum.

Making due allowance for the difficulty of obtaining complete financial returns from the States in rebellion, this table presents a graphic diagram — a perfect picture — of the effect upon general business caused by the employment or nonemployment of the masses. So would a similar table of the period between 1837 and 1857, with the Mexican war in the middle, if it could be obtained, though less grand in its proportions. And so will any period of general employment of the masses, from whatever cause, or in whatever country, sandwiched between two periods of great idleness. There is an economic law governing these matters as inflexible as the law that governs the siderial system.

This table also shows the extraordinary increase of traders — middlemen, between the producers and consumers — immediately after the close of the war, and which has continued to the present time, caused by large numbers being forced out of the abnormal industries of the war into idleness, and the necessity of finding something to do, as stated in the chapter on "The Economic Effects of the War of the Rebellion." In 1866 the number of traders is shown to be 160,303, being 1 to every 222 inhabitants, or every 37 of our voting population. In 1867 the number had risen to 205,000, being 1 to every 177 inhabitants, or every 29 voters. In 1870 it was 427,292, being 1 trader to every 89 inhabitants, or every 15 voters; in 1878 they had increased to 674,741, being 1 to every 72 inhabitants, or every 12 voters; and in 1882 the number of traders, reckoning each trading company or house as one trader, had reached to 852,256, being 1 to every 61 inhabitants, or 1 to every 10 voters.

It must be noted that in this statement is given only the number of business houses that have sufficient business importance to appear on the books of Messrs. R. G. Dun & Co., and that, on an average, each business concern has at least two members, some having half a dozen or more. But we will say two, which give 1,704,512 persons, or one in every six of our voting population engaged in notable trade, leaving out of the account the hosts of petty traders, brokers, bankers, stock jobbers or gamblers, speculators, those in real estate and insurance, as well as accountants, clerks, salesmen, etc., here unconsidered, that must amount to nearly or quite an equal number, making fully one fourth of our people engaged in pursuits that are in no sense productive. The sarcasm of Napoleon that England was but a "nation of shop keepers" it appears may be far better applied to us, with the addition of "and gamblers." But when the people are driven out of the productive employments they must seek other business, and what else is to be found? This exhibit clearly shows that the influences which caused the abnormal increase of traders in the first five years following the war, are still active.

Thus it is seen that while the inhabitants have increased not more than 35 per cent., the proportion of traders to population has increased about 370 per cent., or more than ten times faster than the increase of population, as appears by the foregoing table of failures. But the increase in the other nonproductive pursuits is beyond the power of calculation. This may possibly explain why it is that at this time the producer gets so little for his products, whilst the consumer must give so much. Between the producers and consumers stand these great armies of nonproducers, who appear to be remarkably well fed, clothed, and housed, notwithstanding their numerous failures.

With the close of the harvest of 1879 a speculative movement in breadstuffs and provisions was inaugurated, induced, as generally believed, by the foreign demand, which, however, for wheat, was not greater than that of 1878, whilst the production was largely in excess of that year. This speculation advanced the trade price of some of those staples to the home consumers from thirty to one hundred per cent. The advance, though well understood to be purely speculative, reacted upon other articles of general consumption, also causing a rise in their cost to society.

In 1881 there was a large advance in all food products, with crops very considerably short of those of the previous year, and an increase of failures to 5,582; 1882 brought abundant crops, lower prices to the producer, but largely increased cost to the consumer, and 6,738 failures. And now, as I write, February, 1883, the great increase of failures since the beginning of the year, with the stagnation of general trade, the rapid increase of idleness from the shutting down of many large industrial operations, and the rapid decline in wages, seem to indicate that this year will be marked for its exceptional general distress.

It is certain that to just the extent of the increased cost of the articles of general consumption to the masses is the advance an additional deprivation to the productive classes, because there is no improvement in their general condition that could induce a larger consumption even under the late lower costs, and must reduce it under the present higher prices. There is neither a general increase in the number of those finding employment nor in the wages received. But the contrary is the fact. Therefore the increased cost of the staples of subsistence becomes a serious additional burden upon the mass of our people. The small farmer and workingman, whose labor went into their production, derive no benefit from the increase in the trade price. Whatever benefits have resulted have remained almost solely with the foreign trader and speculator. Yet even as I write the press, from one end of the country to the other, call the present condition a return of business prosperity.

Concurrent with the commencement of the fever of speculation, in 1879, there was developed an unparalleled movement in railroad building, mainly in the great West, and covering quite the entire portion of the national domain that remains open to either agricultural or mining use. Indeed, there can be no doubt that the movement largely finds its support in the rivalry between great capitalists to at once gain possession of all the lands that remain under government title.

To a thoughtful observer it must be apparent that these speculative movements, as well as all others of a similar character, were created and sustained purely in the interest of classes that are opposed to the general welfare of the country — that live upon the miseries of society and fatten upon its distresses. How unsafe are the teachings of those classes, and how their interests conflict with the interests of society,

Adam Smith did not fail to point out with the greatest clearness.

In the very nature of things the speculation in and exportation of food products can not always continue. The English and European seasons will not always remain bad; neither can England nor any other country long exist and depend upon foreign importations for any considerable portion of the food that feeds her people. She must raise her own bread and meat. The very first return of good seasons and harvests with that people who now receive so largely from us, will throw back upon ourselves the enormous amounts that we now export, and cause such a demoralization in our trade and industries as will shake us as we have not yet been shaken. Even if this does not happen during the coming year it must come soon. But whether it comes soon or late the present fever of speculation can not long continue, and is sure to be succeeded by inevitable prostration, as did the speculative mania that followed the close of the war of the rebellion.

When prosperity returns it will come upon us as before: by springing from the root, not from the top — the growth will be upwards, not downwards. As in the years that followed 1861, it will have its foundation in the improved condition of the masses, not in food speculations and stock gambling. The tens of millions of gold that have been received from England, and grasped and hoarded by our great capitalists, will go no farther in relieving the distress of the industrial classes than the hundreds of millions that have already been invested in United States bonds.

It is certain that money, whether hard or soft, much

or little, did not create and will not relieve our distress. There is a power greater, mightier than it, that has wrought these great changes. No amount of fallacy or sophistry, of dodging or ignoring, of arrogance or stupidity, of falsehood or calumny, can hide the fact that all our distress is chargeable to the crime which, by any means, deprives man of the opportunity to "eat bread in the sweat of his face," and forces him into idleness. This is the one great factor, either always kept out of view, or belittled, or belied, but which certainly underlies the whole matter. If idleness be the root of all evil, then must employment be the parent of all good.

CHAPTER XI.

FOREIGN TRADE IS NO REMEDY FOR OUR INDUSTRIAL DISTRESS.

[A portion of the matter forming this chapter I prepared for the Atlantic Monthly of August, 1879, where it may be found under the title of "Foreign Trade no Cure for Hard Times."]

A VERY large number of well meaning people believe that the only remedy for our industrial distress is to be found in foreign trade — by selling our manufactures and products of every nature in foreign markets — by manufacturing and producing for all the world — by making our country the workshop of the world, and our people the world's providers.

Suppose it were to our interest, and the interest of the world, that it should be so, how can it be done? The answer quickly comes, By manufacturing and producing cheaper and better than any other people — or, to sell a better article, at a less price, than any competitor. By the power of cheapness to drive all other producers and manufacturers out of the market — to undersell all others.

Let us see what this means, and what we have to compete with, for it is by competition only that foreign markets can be obtained. I take up the "Statesman," of India, to learn the working time in their cotton mills. From that paper I quote:—

"The Bengal cotton mills work fourteen hours per day, and the Bowriah cotton mills twenty hours per day, as well as Sundays; and some of the Calcutta mills are lit up with gas and work day and night, as well as Sundays. Undoubtedly the machinery, working day and night, can not but last for a very few years; consequently the poor shareholders will have soon to renew the machinery."

The amount of wages paid is not stated; but it is well known that wages in India, like wages in China, are very low — in the neighborhood of ten cents a day.

To obtain a foreign market, in textiles, we must, therefore, compete with fourteen, twenty, and twenty-four hours a day of work, for seven days in the week, with wages at ten cents a day, or sixty or seventy cents a week. There is a lamentation in this extract over the wear and tear of machinery and "the poor shareholders." But the wear and tear of poor workers do not enter into the account. Laborers are of no more value or cost to the manufacturer in India than in the United States. It costs no more to replenish humanity there than here. When one working man or woman is worn out and disappears, no doubt a dozen or more are found competing for the vacant place, in India, as in the United States and all the countries of Europe.

This picture of manufactures in India will answer for China, for South America, Central America, and Mexico. They are all struggling for the same position, and they all have England, Germany, France, and the United States to help them onward, by supplying them with the required machinery, and experts to teach its use. A Hindoo boy or girl can run a machine as well as the Anglo Saxon; and so, also, can a native of China and of South America.

England, until recently, controlled the market of India — that is, did its manufacturing, etc. It is trying to do the same thing for the other countries named, and no doubt is meeting with equal success. But India has recently learned something. By the use of machinery she now produces and manufactures for herself. She has driven and is driving British manufactures out of her markets, and is already seeking a foreign market for her own machine products. So it is with us, who, but a generation ago, were England's greatest and best customer. So it will be with every other country. It is true that England has still a large foreign market, which we are trying to get by underselling her. England, to keep the market she has, is compelled to get her work done so cheap that her people are starving. We are doing the same thing. The reports we daily receive of the distress in that country are simply terrible. With us it is but little better. Great efforts are made by our political economists, among them a late Secretary of State, to show that our work people are living in abundance and comfort. In evidence of this claim our foreign consuls and agents, with others, find that whilst the European laborer is starving, in England, for example, on from three to eight shillings a day, the American workingman will get from sixpence to two shillings more per diem, and has every reason to be contented with his greatly superior condition. That the wages received by the American workingman, when at work, will not provide the necessaries of life, is a matter of no consequence; and the great amount of idleness to which he is subject, when no wages are received, are of still less importance. He must be contented with the asserted fact that his wages are greater than is paid for the same work in Europe. The American workingman, in his misery, must find all the comforts he requires in the fact that other workmen are in still worse condition. This is the full extent to which the remedies of our statesmen and political economists have yet reached. But we are doing all we can to make our people still poorer, to work for still lower wages, that we may undersell, not only England, but India; for to succeed we must undersell the cheapest.

No matter what it costs us, that is the price, and the only price, at which we can obtain foreign markets for our manufactures and products, and we must pay it. On these conditions, and no other, we have been able to increase our domestic exports for foreign consumption from $136,940,248, for the year ending June 30, 1865, to $680,709,258, for the year ending June 30, 1878, and to $749,911,309 for the year ending December 30, 1882, of which less than one hundred millions were of our manufactures for either year; being an increase, in seventeen years, of $612,971,061; but we will call it, in round numbers, six hundred millions of dollars, of both raw and manufactured products, or one hundred millions of dollars of manufactured products alone. The value of the exports of manufactures of cotton is given as $11,438,660 for 1878, and $13,180,044, for 1882; of wool and its manufactures, $542,342 for 1878, and $391,674 for 1882;

iron and steel and their manufactures, $13,968,275 for 1878, and $19,029,759 for 1882 ; and boots and shoes, $468,436 for 1878, and $527,914 for 1882 ; total, $26,417,713 for 1878, and $33,129,391 for 1882. It is in these four products that the great effort has been made to force the cost of production to the lowest possible point, by paying the smallest wages, that we may successfully compete in foreign markets. Most certainly the increase in the four years from 1878 to 1882 is not very encouraging.

Thus, after seventeen years of national effort — of legislation, of subsidizing, of treaties and conventions of every nature, and superhuman efforts at cheap production, by the reduction of wages and salaries, the substitution of machinery for muscle, and the throwing of millions into idleness — we have got so far below the cost of manufacturing and producing in India, in Brazil, in England, or any other country, as to increase or make a foreign market for our manufactures to the amount of, say, one hundred million dollars, and of our general products of, say six hundred millions of dollars per annum.

Has it paid ? Does it now pay ?

Let us see the cost. We have all the factors necessary for thorough examination and illustration. We have at this time, in our whole country, at least fourteen millions belonging to the great industrial class — that is, to those dependent on their salaries or wages for subsistence. Of this class only will we speak, excluding those persons who, as officials in civil or governmental employ, or as superintendents or foremen, or those in professional or clerical positions, who hold exceptional employments and receive exceptional salaries.

Seventeen years ago, at the time of the close of the war of the rebellion, there were of this class, in the North alone, about seven millions, in large part males.

The wages paid to the industrial classes are very nearly the exact measure of the amount contributed by those classes to the trade of society. Almost certainly is that the case where the amount of wages falls within one thousand dollars a year. Even where small savings are made, and stored in savings institutions, it is soon withdrawn and goes into the volume of trade in some shape.

Upon the basis here laid down we will see how our foreign trade pays as compared with our home traffic.

Before the close of the war, and for sometime afterwards, all who found employment received as compensation, upon an average, at least two and one half dollars, gold value, a day, or seven hundred and fifty dollars for a year of three hundred days. At this rate the seven millions belonging to the great industrial class, in the North, contributed, in the first half of 1865, at the rate of five and one quarter billions of dollars per annum to the home trade of consumption.

At the same rate, with our present fourteen millions in our whole country belonging to the great industrial class and who should be in active employment, our home traffic would swell to the enormous amount of ten and one half billions of dollars per annum. But it is only about one quarter that amount.

Among these fourteen millions there is an amount of idleness that equals the full time of six million persons, leaving full employment for but about eight millions. At this time the average wages paid to workers, when employed, is less than one dollar a day; but we will estimate at one dollar, or three hundred dollars a year, which, for eight million persons, give a trade of two billions four hundred million dollars per annum.

This must be the measure of that part of our home traffic now derived from the industrial classes, because it is not possible that they should contribute anything more than the wages they receive.

Here is shown an annual loss to the trade of home consumption, by the industrial classes, caused by their increasing idleness and constant reduction in wages, within the last seventeen years, that amounts to the enormous sum of over eight billions of dollars per annum, and an absolute decrease of two billions eight hundred and fifty millions of dollars per annum during the same period, though the number of consumers during that time, and in those classes have fully doubled. That is, that the seven millions of fully employed, well paid persons, seventeen years ago, created more than double the amount of business that is now created by fourteen millions of persons of the same character and capacity, when only partially employed and but poorly paid.

But if it be insisted that the whole of the great industrial class must enter into the computation, and be considered as contributing something to trade, as nearly all do some work at some time, and consume something, then sixty cents a day is the utmost that can be allowed for the average earnings of all, which results in substantially the same showing.

The amount of present wages is based on the Massachusetts Labor reports.

This great contrast between two billions four hundred millions, and ten billions five hundred millions, is just the difference, in dollars, between the home consumption of fourteen millions of partially employed, poorly paid persons, and their dependents, and that of the same persons when all are employed and well paid, leaving altogether out of the account the amount of destitution and misery in the one case, and the comfort, happiness, and improvement in the other. It is the home trade contrast shown by more than fifty millions of the most generally educated and advanced people on earth, when the industrial classes are all employed, at good wages, and the time when nearly half are practically idle, and those who do work are ground to the lowest cent.

The contrast in the quantity of products consumed at home by each individual now and sixteen and eighteen years ago, may be determined by learning the number of furnaces, forges, factories, mills, and workshops of every nature now standing idle, or but partially employed; the reduction of the number of employés in all establishments as compared with the production; the immense stocks of products now on hand for which there is little or no demand; the large exportation of home products, and the difference in the number of consumers in the two periods. The factors that enter into this contrast are too many and too complicated to be satisfactorily considered in a limited space; I therefore simply call attention to the point.

A home trade of consumption, by the industrial masses of our people, amounting to ten and one half billions of dollars, appears to be an object worth striving for, and cultivating, and sustaining by all the power of our government and people. Not so, think and teach many of our would be statesmen and political economists.

At this time the idleness in our country causes a loss in the home trade of consumption of over eight billions of dollars per annum. "But what of that," reply our modern statesmen and foreign traders; "have we not gained in our foreign export trade to the amount of six hundred millions of dollars? Have we not the foreign trade balance in our favor? What do eight billions lost to home traffic, and the comfort and wealth of the people signify, when we can get an increase in our foreign trade of six hundred millions of dollars in seventeen years, with a favorable foreign trade balance?" The foreign trade balance was in our favor in 1878, but in 1882 it was against us. It is subject to constant fluctuations; but in neither case does it lessen the national evils nor increase the benefits of foreign trade.

But if we add this six hundred millions of foreign trade we have gained, to the two and one half billions we have saved, we shall find that it gives a total trade at the present time, home and foreign, of three billions of dollars, against five and a quarter billions in 1865, and ten and one half billions we should now have, if all our people were employed.

Does it pay?

Every dollar of foreign trade that we have gained, if

because of the cheapness of the manufactures exported, has been at the cost of at least eighty dollars of home traffic. Or, if because of the cheapness of the whole export, raw and manufactured, it has been at the cost of more than thirteen dollars of our home trade, with the incalculable poverty and misery brought upon our people by idleness and low wages, whilst in the pursuit of this maddest of all follies, foreign markets for the consumption of our manufactures. In this mad pursuit we have found a foreign consumption for those products which, only because of their cheapness — of the manufactures of cotton, wool and its manufactures, iron and steel and their manufactures, and boots and shoes — can be sold to the amount of $33,129,391 per annum. This is substantially our only offset for the loss, in and through cheap production, of fully $8,000,000,000 per annum of the home trade of our own people — an amount equal to nearly twice the whole cost to the nation of the war of the rebellion — for no doubt our food products and raw cotton, our petroleum, our agricultural and other machinery, with most of our smaller products, would find a foreign market even if the most liberal wages were paid in their production.

The millions of little streams that flowed from the labor and wages of the masses who were employed sixteen and eighteen years ago, created the great flood that filled the reservoir from which were drawn all the fortunes, all the wealth, all the comfort, all the material progress that so signally marked the decade of 1862 to 1872. But the sudden throwing of three millions of the great industrial class out of their abnormal employments of the war, back upon the normal industries which were already full, and where they were not wanted, started a demoralization in all our industries, and a rapid decline and shriveling of all our business interests that, though for a time hidden by the fever of credit and speculation that followed the war, have brought our industries and trade to a lower point than ever before, and still we seek lower depths.

Does foreign trade pay at the cost at which we purchase it? Are six hundred millions of foreign trade, which we have gained, worth more, in dollars and cents, than eight billions of home traffic, which we have lost? This is the question, squarely put, with the evidence on which it is based.

The truth is, there can be no greater folly perpetrated by our nation than that of seeking to employ, or in any way to benefit, our own people by producing or manufacturing for any other. The reasons why it is so are abundant and obvious. I will give a few.

1. No people without domestic industries can possibly be permanent or profitable purchasers of foreign products. It is with a nation as with individuals — by and through its industries, only, can it exist and become a purchaser in any market.

2. Every nation that sustains an industry must and will employ that industry in producing that which enters directly into the consumption of its own people. That nation which is compelled to depend on the foreigner for either food, clothing, or lodging, is wanting in some of the elements of permanent prosperity.

3. Every country advanced in its civilization must

have the elements within itself for self support; and if it be wanting in any of the mechanical appliances of the age necessary to develop its resources, those appliances will be obtained and utilized.

4. There is no large and permanent market for our manufactures with any advanced people; all such must and will manufacture for themselves, and are even now seeking foreign markets for their own products. Whenever our manufactures and products, or those of any other people, come into serious competition with their own at home, they are sure to be excluded or heavily taxed. The law of self preservation compels it.

5. Our present chief effort is to find markets with those populations that are not yet fully developed in their use of the latest mechanical methods of production. All such are either too poor or too exclusive to become profitable consumers of the products of our civilization. It is only by developing advanced industries in the midst of those peoples that their condition can be changed or improved; and that will be done to the exclusion of any considerable foreign consumption.

More than four years ago the following item appeared in the columns of the New York Tribune of February 24, 1879. Is it possible that there is any one so blind that between the lines of this item he can not read the future of trade in more things than cotton fabrics?

COTTON MILLS FOR CHINA.

LONDON, Saturday, Feb. 22, 1879.

The Post's Berlin correspondent says: "The Chinese Government have purchased machinery and engaged experienced engineers and spinners in Germany to establish cotton mills in China, so as to free that country from dependence upon English and Russian imports."

Though China is somewhat tardy in her action we may be certain that she will be thorough. Not only the English and Russians, but all others, will find that market not closed to cottons alone, but to everything that that people consume. More than this; the time is not far distant when textiles from Chinese machine looms; iron, and steel, and cutlery, from Chinese furnaces, forges, and workshops, with everything that machinery and cheap labor can produce, will crowd every market. The four hundred millions of China, with the two hundred and fifty millions of India — the crowded and pauperized populations of Asia — will offer the cup of cheap machine labor, filled to the brim, to our lips, and force us to drink it to the dregs, if we do not learn wisdom. It is in Asia, if anywhere, that the world is to find its workshop. There are the masses — all the conditions necessary to develop the power of cheapness to perfection, and those conditions will be used. For years we have been doing our utmost to teach the Chinese shoemaking, spinning and weaving, engine driving, machine building, and other arts, in California, Massachusetts, and other States, and we may be sure they will make good use of their lessons, all being under contract to be returned to China, dead or alive. There is no people on earth with more patient skill and better adapted to the use of machinery than the Chinese; and it is from that people in particular, that the industrial world must protect itself. What the Chinese government is doing for China, Dom Pedro is doing for Brazil, but it may be, in a different form. That country, like every other, in order to prosper and develop must do its own work; this fact its intelligent ruler thoroughly understands and acts upon.

We have our own work to do and no other. It is the only work we can control, and is our only dependence. Is it wise to neglect or sacrifice it for the purpose of grasping what we can not hold, even if we could once get it? We have our own market to supply, and our trade at home, and there is no other over which we can, by any possibility, have full command. This market and the consequent trade may be almost indefinitely extended. Is it wise to destroy it in pursuit of an *ignis fatuus?*

With our industries and home traffic rehabilitated there can be no doubt that our foreign trade would largely increase in some directions. But it would be of a character very unlike the present, and based on a very different foundation. It would be a trade resting on the wealth of the people, and not living on their poverty; a trade that would add to our comfort, and not increase our miseries. Our best consumers and customers are at home. It is our home market that furnishes, or that can be made to furnish, an inexhaustible source of wealth and comfort for all; whilst a general foreign market for our products can be obtained only at the cost of more than ten dollars of home trade for one of foreign, with the pauperizing of our people and the destruction of our institutions.

But all the evils of foreign trade are by no means confined to the effort for successful competition in obtaining foreign markets. The compelling of our people to compete with the cheap slave or free labor of Europe and Asia, and of the islands of the East and of the West, for the supply of whatever may enter into our own consumption, is an evil of the greatest magnitude. One fact alone in this connection, should be enough to cause us to bar our doors to all foreign products that can be produced upon our own soil.

Our imports of merchandise for the year 1882, are reported at $752,843,507. Included in this amount are the following items: —

LIST OF SPECIAL ARTICLES OF IMPORTATION, WITH THEIR INVOICE VALUES.

Breadstuffs and other farinaceous food,	$17,487,737
Manufactures of cotton,	36,093,169
Eggs,	2,645,610
Earthen, stone, and China ware,	7,507,046
Flax, and manufactures of,	19,907,928
Glass and glass ware,	7,443,211
Hides, other than furs,	27,237,065
Hemp, and manufactures of,	5,975,859
Iron and steel, and manufactures of,	49,209,964
Leather and manufactures of,	13,197,523
Potatoes,	3,827,142
Provisions,	2,395,493
Silk, manufactures of,	41,415,984
Soda, salts of,	5,400,269
Sugar and molasses,	101,806,697
Tobacco and manufactures of,	9,053,903
Watches, materials and movements,	2,793,273
Wines, spirits, cordials,	10,540,476
Wood, manufactures of,	11,019,549
Wool and manufactures of,	53,784,800
Total,	$418,739,198

The above amount is the foreign valuation fixed for exportation and to avoid duties, and must be quite or fully doubled to represent the true value in our markets; which shows an importation to the value of eight hundred millions of dollars, of products that can be as well produced in our own country as on any other portion of the globe. There are other articles not here specified, but of large importance.

Whilst we are making these vast importations, the product of the slave and pauper labor of other countries, we have millions of our own people who are suffering every distress, even to death itself, for want of the very work of which they are thus robbed. This is the whole matter in a single paragraph. Is it not clearly a case of that monstrous madness of which only an American politician and the popular political economist are capable?

Add to these facts that other which is equally potent, viz.:— That the production of these various articles at home, by our own people, and of every other that can be here produced, would increase the amount of trade incident thereto to a degree at least ten fold greater than is now derived by us from their importation, puts the folly, the criminality, of our present policy in still stronger light.

Whilst our markets are open to the products of the slaves and paupers of the world, there can be no improvement with us; we are brought into direct competition with them, and our people are forced to their level. The weight of the world's poverty is more than we can carry. Left to ourselves, giving that protection to all interests, without exception, that will guarantee to every industry the full benefit to be derived from our own developments, would at once place us upon the highway to prosperity, and shower the blessings of universal industry on all alike.

These are the invulnerable grounds that should be taken by all who have a sincere desire for the good of society in general, or of any of its members. In them there is not necessarily one particle of sentiment or philanthropy. Our distresses are not the work of sentiment, but of material conditions. So, also, the measures here suggested, may be looked upon as matters of the purest material interest, under the guidance of the simplest elements of common sense; but still they are in full harmony with every principle of humanity and social advancement.

CHAPTER XII.

CONSTANT WORK FOR ALL, WITH LIBERAL WAGES, THE ONLY SOURCE OF A NATION'S PROSPERITY.

BY constant work is not meant labor for the whole of every day, but that every day there shall be that amount of employment that will supply all the requirements of society, and furnish the laborer with liberal subsistence. Of the value of labor in the creation of wealth I quote high authority.

"It was not by gold or by silver, but by labor, that all the wealth of the world was originally purchased."

"Though the manufacturer has his wages advanced to him by his master, he, in reality, costs him no expense, the whole value of those wages being generally restored, together with a profit, in the improved value of the subject upon which his labor is bestowed. But the maintenance of a menial servant never is restored. A man grows rich by employing a multitude of manufacturers; he grows poor by maintaining a multitude of menial servants." — *Wealth of Nations.*

"Dr. Smith perceived that the universal agent in the creation of wealth is labor; which in every case produces it." — M. GARNIER, *in the Introduction to Edinburgh edition of 1817, Wealth of Nations.*

The principle here so clearly laid down, of the truth of which, in its fullest sense, there can not be a shadow of doubt by the careful student of economic laws, that it is by labor only, and not by gold or by silver, that all wealth is created, does not at this time appear to be generally recognized. On the contrary, among our most popular economists, and with the mass of manufacturers and producers, the effort appears, as by common consent, to be directed to the creation of wealth by means of mechanical tools and forces, without the use of labor — manual labor be it always understood — or by the use of the smallest possible amount, and at the least possible compensation. With what success, and with what effect upon society, the universal industrial and business distress clearly show.

The experience of the world invariably proves that whenever and wherever the people have been most generally employed, and best compensated, then and there has society been most prosperous, and increase of wealth and all moral and material development the most rapid. But that, on the other hand, whenever the people have been least employed, and the lowest wages received, then and there has society made the least progress, and endured the greatest distress. That whenever any nation or people has been suffering great distress, with stagnation and disaster in all business, the bringing of the masses into general employment, with good wages, have always had the immediate effect of restoring prosperity to every interest, and giving life and activity to every development.

In the history of our own people we have had two demonstrations of the truth of these propositions; one of them the most remarkable within the history of man. Previous to 1861 there had been gradually growing upon us a condition of great industrial and business distress, so that in 1860 there were multitudes out of employment — those having work receiving the smallest possible compensation — with great destitution in all our larger towns and cities. In 1857 there were 4,932 failures, and in 1861 the number had increased to 6,993. But in that year the large armies that were formed absorbed great numbers of the unemployed. The old industries were made active, and new industries were created, which also made additional demand for laborers, and tended directly to the increase of wages, larger consumption of the necessaries of life, activity in trade, with greatly developed production. The result of these operations was general prosperity, indicated by the reduction of the number of failures in 1862, from 6,993 of the previous year, to 1,652, being a falling off of 5,341 in one year, and of 1,157 in the next, there having been only 495 failures in 1863, and for the next two years a change from that figure of but 35.

For four years following the summer of 1861 there was an increasing demand for the employment of the people, with an increase of wages, and fully corresponding increase in the prosperity and development of society. How great was that development and prosperity the Hon. Daniel Needham, United States Bank Examiner for Massachusetts, has told in an address delivered by him before a meeting of the Woonsocket, Rhode Island, Horticultural and Industrial Association, October 3, 1877, as reported in the Massachusetts Ploughman, of October 13th, of that year. His description is so thoroughly truthful — so generally covers the ground — and his authority so unimpeachable, that its facts are commended to the careful study of all.

"There was a growth and development of business in the northern and western portions of the United States, such as no nation ever experienced before. There was building of new mills, and enlarging old ones; there was adding tens of thousands of spindles to the thousands already running; there was adding steam engines to aid water power, and the adoption of new machinery, which increased to a fabulous extent the capacity to manufacture cotton and woolen fabrics.

"There was the establishment of hundreds of banks — the building of thousands of miles of railroad — settling new countries — cutting down forests — building cities in most distant portions of the Republic — and opening communication by railroad with the Pacific Coast.

"The history of those ten years of industrial growth and prosperity would fill many volumes.

"Wages advanced as the industries increased. Workers in iron, and steel, and brass, and wood, and stone were as greatly in demand as workers in cotton and wool. The common coarse domestic cottons sold for fifty and sixty cents a yard, and woolen goods doubled, and trebled, and quadrupled in value.

"Adding, as did these exorbitant prices, to the cost of living, wages kept pace with the goods, and our wives and children dressed better than before. The cost of the absolute necessaries of life were also in keeping with woolen and cotton goods. Flour, sugar, rice, coffee, tea, rents — all kept pace in the great inflation; and families indulged not only in the necessaries, but in the luxuries, and everybody had abundance. Never before was there such apparent prosperity. There were no men wanting work who failed to find it; and the laborer, even in the most ordinary avocation of life, fixed his own price.

"Mechanics commanded from three to six dollars a day; common field laborers demanded and realized from two and one half to three dollars; professional men doubled their charges, and church committees recommended of their own accord increase of salaries to their pastors.

"What days were these for America and Americans! We may well look back upon them with wonder and astonishment! They grew upon us so rapidly that we never stopped to consider that they might not always continue. But they had their culmination. In 1873 the great storm which this unparalleled expansion had been gathering burst upon the country, and from that day to this things have been growing worse rather than better."

In this graphic narration of the great prosperity that so quickly came upon us, one other marked feature of the time might very properly have received special mention, viz.: that never before did all investments of capital in manufactures, transportation, distribution, or other legitimate enterprises, pay so great an interest; dividends upon actual earnings rarely falling below ten or fifteen, and often exceeding fifty per cent. per annum.

It will be specially noted that no attempt is made to show the cause of this marvellous "industrial growth and prosperity." It is merely said that it "grew upon us so rapidly that we never stopped to consider." And it is equally true that we have not yet stopped to consider either the cause of this sudden and sweeping "prosperity," or the nearly equal suddenness, and as wide spread following, of the adversity and distress that "from that day to this have been growing worse rather than better." No man can be so foolish, and least of all men the one who so well describes the facts of our great "industrial growth and prosperity that would fill many volumes," as for an instant to suppose, or, much more, to say, that those great events were without causes, in every way commensurate with the effects that followed. Causes as great, as wide spread, and as sweeping; which, if any one failed to see them, it could only be because of wilful blindness, or not wishing to know them.

It is there said that "never before was there such apparent prosperity." It is certain that never before did any so brief a period leave such indelible marks of the genuineness and realness of its prosperity as were left by that period; and the attempt to belittle it is but a sign of the general fatuity. It is also called a "great inflation."

Inflation, indeed! Was there ever anything more substantial, more real, than the vast developments that marked the period under discussion? Was it all accomplished by windy and gaseous distensions? Was there no better foundation for the great prosperity which "we may well look back upon with wonder and astonishment?" These occasional deprecations and belittleings are but the echoes of the common fatuousness that marks the general reference to those times.

Just previous to the commencement of that period, in 1861, our government was nearly bankrupt, being unable to obtain a loan at less than twelve per cent., and our people were ground to the earth with debt. Within four years thereafter, at the close of 1865, all the great changes and progress above noted had been fully developed, or were in process of development; our national credit was established on a firmer basis than ever before, and Secretary McCulloch officially reported that our people were substantially out of debt. Was there nothing real in all that? Was it merely inflation? "Our wives and children dressed better than before; families indulged not only in the necessaries, but in the luxuries, and everybody had abundance." And that was done without running in debt, said Secretary McCulloch. Was it merely inflation? Nothing but wind?

For some years before and down to the sudden commencement of this prosperous period there were large numbers of our people without employment, and consequently without the means of living — hungry and nearly naked — begging their food from door to door, or in other ways living upon charity. The very first incident that marked the beginning of that period of prosperity was the bringing of these idle people into employment, until "there were no men wanting work who failed to find it." This is the great initial fact that governed the whole matter, and should not for a moment be lost sight of. But our orator does not appear to see that it possesses any significance. Then followed all the succeeding incidents as follow the workings of the parts of a great machine, or the operations of a great factory after the engine is put in motion, or the motive power is applied. "Wages advanced as the industries increased. Workers in iron, and steel, and brass, and wood, and stone were as greatly in demand as workers in cotton and wool. Mechanics commanded from three to six dollars a day; common field laborers demanded and realized from two and one half to three dollars; professional men doubled their charges, and church committees recommended of their own accord increase of salaries to their pastors." Then, also, came an immediate rise in prices for all that entered into the use and consumption of man. "The common domestic cottons sold for fifty and sixty cents a yard, and woolen goods doubled, trebled, and quadrupled in value. Flour, sugar, rice, coffee, tea, rents — all kept pace in the great *advance*," and all investments of capital in industrial enterprises paid large dividends; some even as much as one hundred per cent. per annum. Well might the lecturer exclaim, "What days were these for America and Americans!" for "never before was there such *real* prosperity."

The motive power that produced these results was the labor of the masses, and the incidents of that period of prosperity followed each other in the exact order here indicated with the immutable certainty of cause and effect.

Our lecturer further said : — "In 1873 the great storm which this unparalleled expansion had been gathering burst upon the country." Here commences the great fallacies into which he, in common with most others, have fallen. The beginning of the storm was not in 1873, nor even its culmination, which is not yet reached. It was upon us in force in 1867, and constantly gained in fury till 1873. It is true that in that year the storm which had been raging for seven years brought down some of our tallest steeples; this caused the general panic. But previous to the fall of these towers thousands of other structures had been brought to the earth whose foundations were as well laid, and whose edifices were as useful to the society which surrounded them, as the tallest of the fallen spires. In 1866 the failures had nearly trebled the number in 1865; in 1867 the number was more than five times greater, being 2,780 against 530 in 1865. The percentage of failures in 1867 rose to the extraordinary rate of 1 in every 74, a rate that was not again reached until 1877. In 1872 there were 4,069 failures, and in 1873, the year of the panic, there were 5,183, being 1,810 less than in 1861, at the close of the great distress before the war, and 158 less than the falling off in the next year, 1862, after the people had been brought into general employment. In the seven years preceding 1873 there had been 20,222 failures, and from 1865 to this time there has been a nearly constant yearly augmentation.

The storm really commenced in 1865, and the very first incident which marked its beginning was the sudden throwing of three millions of persons, in the North alone, out of employment into idleness; as the first incident at the beginning of our prosperous period was the bringing into employment of the great body of the then unemployed. The throwing of these great numbers out of employment was followed by there being *many* "men wanting work who failed to find it;" by wages being reduced and demand for laborers decreased; by workers in iron, and steel, and brass, and wood, and stone being as little in demand as workers in cotton and wool. Mechanics now, when they can get work, are fortunate to obtain from one to one and a half dollars a day, in place of three to six, as in the period of our general prosperity; common field laborers are glad to get seventy-five cents and one dollar, where formerly they received two and one half to three; professional men have reduced their charges by more than one half, and church committees are compelled to reduce the salaries of their pastors. The common coarse domestic cottons that sold for fifty and sixty cents a yard when all were employed, now sell for five and six cents, and woolen goods have fallen one half and three fourths in value. But yet our wives and children can not dress as well as before; families can not indulge even in the necessaries, omitting all luxuries, and no one has abundance. Investments of capital in manufactures, transportation, distribution, and other legitimate enterprises, often prove absolute losses; many hardly pay expenses, and very few pay even five or six per cent. per annum. What a contrast! What terrible days are these for America and Americans! "We may well look upon them with wonder and astonishment!" and seriously inquire what has brought them upon us?

Most certainly the causes which lay at the foundation of our present distress are the very opposites of the causes which gave us our great prosperity. We have seen that the very first incident at the beginning of our period of prosperity was the removal of all from idleness to employment; and the very first incident at the beginning of our distress was the change of multitudes from active, well paid employment, into idleness. In each case those great changes have been followed by effects that are inseparable and in strict harmony with fundamental economic laws, well known to every true economic student, and laid down by Adam Smith in the simplest and clearest language, that "it was not by gold or by silver, but by labor, that all the wealth of the world was originally purchased;" and that "a man grows rich by employing a multitude of manufacturers."

Most certainly if it is by labor that all the wealth of the world is created, and if a man grows rich by employing a multitude of workmen, then the converse of these propositions must be true, that it is because labor is not employed, or only to a very small extent — because of the great amount of idleness — that the world is distressed and man is made poor.

It is an indisputable fact that when our industrial classes have been most generally employed, and in receipt of the most liberal compensations, that period has been marked with the most general prosperity and society has made the greatest advancement. But that, on the other hand, when the people have been least employed, and in receipt of the smallest compensations, then is the time of greatest adversity and society absolutely goes backward. That the last is our present condition is manifest to every thoughtful person. Even in the works of those who make it their business to show that we are now enjoying a period of unusual prosperity there is the clearest evidence of the great distress by which we are surrounded. In the Tenth Annual Report of the Bureau of Labor Statistics for Massachusetts is found the following testimony upon this point, from both manufacturers and workmen in that State, in answer to inquiries from the Bureau: —

"We think the question will be, Can they [the workmen] get employment at all?" — *Agricultural Implements*, (b) page 148.

"We have to rush through such styles as fashion dictates,

giving us about eight months full time and four months dull trade." — *Boots and Shoes*, (a) page 149.

"During the last five years the trouble has been in not having work enough to give reasonable employment to body and mind. The uncertainty of values, and the consequent fitfulness of trade — each man buying what he has previously sold — have deprived each employer and employé of the regularity needed to realize any profit in the business." — *Ibid*, (b) page 149.

"The difficulty of keeping our employés at work steadily any number of hours per day throughout the year is one of the greatest disadvantages under which our business labors. It is only for a short time each season that we can have the balance of work and workmen properly adjusted. The demand for goods, for a time, is greater than we can supply; while for a much larger part of the year we have more men than we need." —*Ibid.*, (d) page 149.

"Our busy or hurried season begins now early in March, and usually ends by the first or middle of July. For the past few months we have not only reduced the hours of labor, but our force, waiting for a solution of the question so important to manufacturers; viz., What can be done to assist the distribution and consumption of our manufactures at living prices?" —*Carriages*, page 150.

"Our season extends only over a small part of the year, beginning usually in February, closing in June, a very few being made in August and September. Many of our employés can not obtain other work for the balance of the year when not employed in our branch of business." — *Straw Goods*, (b) page 155.

"Since October, 1873, we, with other tack manufacturers, have averaged only two thirds time." — *Tacks*, page 155.

"In times of great business depression, such as we have been going through for the last three or four years, the working people especially are led to believe there must be something radically wrong in the management of our business industries to cause such depression. Things seem to get worse rather than better, and as yet no one seems to know the remedy." — *Textiles*, (g) page 159.

"The wages of operatives are now very low, with a strong prospect of going lower before Spring. Mills are running with a smaller number of hands than ever before." — *Ibid.*, (*h*) page 161.

"As the best prices manufacturers can afford to pay during the present depression is barely sufficient to support most of the families, any reduction in that amount will inevitably result in the misery and starvation of some of them. This mill has run every hour it was possible under the law during the last five years, only stopping for necessary repairs; and we have made no profits, only keeping our operatives alive." — *Ibid.*, (*k*) pages 161-2.

In answer to some of the inquiries addressed to workmen, the following replies were received in relation to their condition.

"9. *a. Do you live as well as you did five years ago?*

"In answer, 138 said, 'I do not;' 6 replied, 'Not half as well;' and 3, 'Not quite as well.' On the other hand, 62 said, 'Yes;' 10, 'Nearly the same;' and 4, 'Better;' 7 did not answer the inquiry.

"9. *b. If not (living as well), in what respect are you worse off than then?*

"The answers to this inquiry defy systematic tabulation or condensation; so we present the reasons in nearly the exact words of the writers, the figures giving the number of persons coinciding upon each reason: —

"'Less pay,' 30; 'In all respects,' 25; 'Out of work,' 7; 'Afraid of coming to want,' 1; 'Less means for support,' 3; 'Can't afford to live so well,' 1; 'More family and less pay,' 5; 'Do not get paid promptly,' 1; 'Larger family,' 1; 'Can't buy what we need,' 1; 'Expense fifteen per cent. less, and my wages fifty per cent.,' 1; 'Have had to curtail generally,' 2; 'Less work,' 9; 'Less work, less pay,' 9; 'No spare money, or new clothing,' 1; 'Savings most gone,' 2; 'In actual want of necessaries of life,' 5; 'Board is not so good,' 2; 'Wages less, and cost of living not reduced in proportion,' 3; 'Lost money in savings bank,' 1; 'Times are hard,' 1; 'Worse off in mind and stomach,' 1; 'Have cut short the extras,' 2; 'Can't save anything,' 4; 'No meat, and less of every thing,' 2; 'No work, and credit gone,' 2; 'Worse off as regards house, food, and clothing,' 11; 'Unreasonably low wages,' 3; 'Can't pay my bills,' 1; 'Fewer clothes,' 2; 'Cheaper food,' 2; 'Lost my house,' 1; 'No meat, butter, or sugar,' 1; 'Less of every thing but food,' 1.

"9. c. *Have you been obliged to reduce your outlay for rent, food, clothing, and other necessities? or have you only been forced to deprive yourself of what might properly be called 'extras,' or luxuries?*

"To this question 120 answered that they have been obliged to reduce *all* expenses; 23 have made reductions in either food, or rent, or clothing; and 14 have dispensed with 'extras.' A factory operative, who has been in the business thirty years, says he is obliged to live on one meal a day in order to keep along." — Pages 109–10.

Here is the concurrent testimony of both employers and workmen that it is only for a small portion of the year that work can be found for much the larger part of those who get any employment; that the mills are running with a smaller number of hands than ever before; that wages will not permit of any further reduction, even to those having constant work, except at the cost of misery and starvation; that very few live as well as they did nine years ago; that in every way has the condition of the industrial classes become worse, even to the want of the barest necessaries of life, and the living on one meal a day. These statements are well worth the most careful study and comparison, not only with the condition of things nine

THE SOURCE OF PROSPERITY. 229

years ago, but with their condition as described by the Hon. Daniel Needham, in the first portion of this chapter. Nine years ago all our business interests were in the midst of the distress that had then been raging like a storm for full eight years, and had strewn our country with the wrecks of 25,405 trading houses, beside the multitude of those engaged in other occupations of whom no record can be obtained, all of which had thrown great numbers out of employment and largely reduced wages and incomes. But the condition described by Mr. Needham was the condition that existed in 1863, 1864, and 1865, when all the people were in active employment and reaping the sure rewards of their industry — before the storm of speculation and disaster that immediately followed the war had burst upon us. Why 1873–4 are chosen as the years to compare with 1878–9 can not be understood, unless it is to show that our state is still tending from bad to worse.

Then question 9. c. is a most extraordinary one. What are "extras," or "luxuries?" Are they carpets, fine furniture, fine ware, pianos, organs, ornaments, etc.? The production of all these things is a part, and a valuable part, of the industries of our country, that should be fostered and sustained. But if their use and consumption by the people are destroyed, how can these industries be supported? Are they to be deemed, in their use, as exclusively the right of millionaires and plutocrats? All these "extras" and "luxuries" are supposed to have an elevating and refining influence. Shall not the workingman and his family be surrounded by these influences?

Do not the true interests of society, industrially and socially, require that "extras" and "luxuries" shall be used and consumed by the workingman as well as by the millionaire? Shall not the makers and builders of these things have the benefit and pleasure of their use, as well as those who trade in and distribute them? Can not the users and consumers of these "extras" and "luxuries" do without them with less damage to themselves than can their manufacturers and dealers do without the custom and consumption of the masses of the people? Does not the general use or nonuse of "extras" and "luxuries" by the industrial classes mark the periods of prosperity or adversity? Shame to the official of Massachusetts who raises such questions, and by implication declares that the rich only may have refinements.

The great facts in the whole matter are, that eighteen and nineteen years ago, when all the people were employed and in receipt of wages at least double the amount of those now received, though the product of the laborer was then only about one third of that which is now produced by each workman, both employer and workman then prospered, and society made rapid progress in every useful development. But now, when the product of the labor of the workman is three times greater than it was at the close of the war, and wages are not half what they were then, neither employer nor workman prosper, and society makes no advance in useful development. Everything excepting food and rents is cheap, cheaper than ever before, and the masses are less able, far less able to now buy and use the cheap product, than they were formerly to buy and use the same product at three to five times the present cost.

Why is it?

Because, eighteen and nineteen years ago the masses, who are always the great consumers of all products, were rich, as compared with the present time. They were all employed and in receipt of good wages, and from their abundant means they bought and used freely and liberally. But now these same masses are in poverty. They are not more than half employed, and the wages received are so low that they can not buy and use enough to supply the commonest demands of existence. See the testimony of the workmen and employers above.

Eighteen and nineteen years ago the workman was well paid, and behind every product there stood a well fed, well clothed, well housed, and prosperous man or woman, able and ready to buy and use freely of the product of his or her own labor and the labor of others. But now the workman is but little employed and badly paid, and behind every cheap product stands the skeleton of want, half fed, half clothed, badly housed. Back of cheap products there stalk misery, degradation, drunkenness, prostitution, insanity, crime, and suicide, with men and women who can but very scantily buy and use of the work of their own hands or of that of others.

Eighteen and nineteen years ago the geese that laid our golden eggs were well fed and cared for. But now avarice has them in its power, and, under the instruction of modern political economists, they are starved and squeezed until there is only the skeleton left.

Inasmuch as the great market for all products must be found among the masses; and inasmuch as the masses are composed of the working people of society, in all and every occupation; and inasmuch as not only is all the wealth of the world the product of their labor, but, also, as it is in and by the use and consumption of these products by the working classes themselves that trade is created and a demand for distribution is made, which give to the nonproducer, or capitalist, the opportunity to obtain any portion of these products, or of the profits of their use and distribution, the smallest exercise of intelligent selfishness should teach them that it is to their direct and immediate interest that the masses should be enabled to buy and consume the greatest possible quantity of all of their own products; that the industrial goose should be well kept, well fed, that it may freely lay its golden eggs. These propositions are not hard to understand.

It must always be remembered that it is the labor of the workingman that produces everything, and that the laborers are also the great consumers. Hence it is that between these two points of production and consumption that the nonproducer and capitalist find their only opportunities for gain or profit. By taking the products from the hands of the producers, and distributing them among the consumers, they perform the service which yields to them their gains, and it is their only function. Consequently the highest interest of the capitalist requires that the masses should be in the most prosperous condition, to the end that their ability to consume may be in every way developed, and the volume and profits of trade be increased.

Here is where the capitalist finds it to his interest to employ manufacturers, and in the employment of a multitude to grow rich. Between the production of his workmen and the consumption of the products, whether consumed by his own operatives or by others, a trade is created, which the manufacturing capitalist holds and controls. All the products of his laborers passing through his hands to the consumers, gives him an opportunity for profit that is limited by only two conditions: first, the number he employs, and, secondly, the ability of his customers to buy and consume. If their ability is great their consumption will be liberal. If they are paupers, or but little better, their trade will be worthless. The surest measure by which the manufacturing capitalist can gauge the ability of the masses to buy and consume of the products he wishes to sell, is to study the condition of his own employés; he may be sure that others can not be very different, and that they represent the great bulk of his consumers.

Manifestly, then, when one half of the manufacturers, or workmen, are idle, not only one half of the producing power is lost, but one half the consuming power is undeveloped; and, consequently, the volume of trade is not more than one half what it might be. But there is still another bad feature in this connection. The nonemployment of large numbers of workmen creates a destructive competition among them, that will not only destroy their purchasing power, but will react to the destruction of all trade. This principle is now being fully illustrated in the late strikes and stagnation in trade.

A correct understanding of these principles will fully explain the maxim of Adam Smith's that "a man grows rich by employing a multitude of manufacturers." A man does not grow rich upon the products of the few, but of the many; and the trader, also, finds his profits in the trade of the multitude, and not in the occasional visitor.

And those other maxims of the great political economists should be noted, that "though the manufacturer has his wages advanced to him by his master, he, in reality, costs him no expense, the whole value of those wages being generally restored, together with a profit, in the improved value of the subject upon which his labor is bestowed;" and, "it was not by gold or by silver, but by labor, that all the wealth of the world was originally purchased." Here Adam Smith enforces the idea that it is labor only that enters into and remains fixed in any and all products. The money, or capital, which is used, is but an agent to facilitate the operations in the production, and for purposes of distribution. It never remains there fixed, nor is it destroyed nor consumed, but is always returned with a portion of the fruits of the labor which it has facilitated, and the distribution which it has made. Capital may very properly be deemed a fertilizer, which, judiciously used, makes labor more productive of the wealth which enriches the whole of society; but without the labor upon which to work it loses its value. This principle is most remarkably illustrated in the present condition of things; labor is but little employed and capital has largely depreciated in value.

Therefore the real bearings of this question of labor are not confined to the industrial classes, but vitally affect every interest and class of society. To be sure the workingmen appear prominently in the discussion, for the simple reason that they are the "mudsills" of society, and can not be eliminated, unless it is possible to build without a foundation, or from the top downwards.

"No society can surely be flourishing and happy, of which the greater part of the members are poor and miserable. It is but equity, besides, that those who feed, clothe, and lodge the whole body of the people, should have such a share of the produce of their own labor as to be themselves tolerably well fed, clothed, and lodged."

"The liberal reward of labor, therefore, as it is the necessary effect, so it is the natural symptom, of increasing national wealth. The scanty maintenance of the laboring poor, on the other hand, is the natural symptom that things are at a stand, and their starving condition that they are going fast backwards." — ADAM SMITH, *Wealth of Nations*.

Now the question is, shall the welfare of society be sacrificed to the gratification of blind, ignorant class prejudice and arrogance, or shall we be guided by the simple dictates of intelligent self interest, which, no doubt, will prove the wisest philanthropy?

If we adopt intelligent self interest for our guide, we can again restore prosperity to our country and people as quickly as it came upon us in the first years of the war of the rebellion, and that in the midst of profound peace, and make the prosperity permanent.

CHAPTER XIII.

THE RELATIONS OF TRADE TO THE EMPLOYMENTS OF THE PEOPLE.

OF the absolute dependence of all trade upon the labor and consumption of the masses of mankind abundant evidence has already been presented, and it might be extended indefinitely. But labor, in its primary state, is in no sense dependent on trade. In the economy of life they are not equal. It has been only in the developments of civilization that trade has been brought into existence, and has arrogated to itself the first position in society, seeking in every possible manner to degrade and destroy that which gave it life, and has ever been its sole support.

There are a few additional facts and considerations, in the present exaltation of trade and degradation of labor, that invite examination.

Notwithstanding the fact that mechanical forces have taken the place of muscle in all production, and man has, to an alarming extent, become an idler, he still remains the only consumer, and without his consumption production becomes a waste of force, and trade must cease; for it is between production and consumption that trade finds its use — in carrying from one to the other for the sole purpose of consumption. Machinery now doing at least nine tenths of the work of production, gives to man a far higher importance, as the consumer of these products, than he ever before attained. It is now solely as a consumer that he has become indispensably valuable. Without consumers all production would be absolutely valueless, and the importance of trade is enhanced in exact ratio with the increase of consumption. These are self evident facts that have an important bearing on social relations, and are of vital interest to trade.

In our country it is a patent fact that a large portion of the people are practically nonconsumers. As machinery has taken their place in production their consumption has fallen off and trade has become lessened and demoralized. Our over production is apparently enormous; and whilst we are sending our products to other lands for a market, we have millions at home suffering and perishing for want of the very necessaries of life that we are sending abroad from before them. This large exportation is a notable symptom and constant aggravation of the fundamental disease that affects society.

It is also well to see at what cost to the farmer, and other producers, these foreign markets are found. Four years ago Senator Blaine, from his place on the floor of the Senate, said that eighty million dollars per annum were paid to foreign ship owners for ocean carriage of our products to distant markets. But that is only one item of the cost paid by our farmers to get their corn and their wheat, their oats, pork, beef, cattle, butter and cheese, cotton, hay, and other products to foreign consumers. To our railroads, our canals, our steamers — all our inland transporters from the interior to the seaboard — to the commission merchant, the insurer, the speculator, the gambler, the multitudes of middlemen, at least three times as much is paid as to the ocean carriers, by the American producers, to reach foreign markets. In the interest of foreign trade the American farmers and producers pay a direct tax upon their products of fully four hundred million dollars per annum. A tax greater than the whole cost of our national government. The American farmer receives seventy cents a bushel for his wheat, and the English consumer pays one dollar and fifty cents for the same, the middlemen taking the margin. It is not difficult to see how and where the great railroad kings, with the whole class of middlemen, obtain their colossal fortunes.

These facts are enough to indicate the tendencies of present development. The number that might be added is inexhaustible. To achieve these results all the resources and devices of the age are taxed to their fullest extent. Mechanical forces and labor saving machinery, wherever possible, are made to take the place of muscle. Man's labor has been saved, that is, dispensed with, to such an extent as to make a large portion of mankind either partially or wholly idlers. Competition between the idle and the employed — between producers, carriers, merchants, and all engaged in any and every avocation by which subsistence is obtained — is driven to the verge of destruction.

The struggle for the extremest cheapness has become an universal mania. A superintendent of a

Boston institution for the shelter of poor working girls, says the insufficiency of wages paid to girls in that city is most disheartening. Because of low pay and the increased cost of living, more young women have gone astray during the past two years than has been known to be the case in a great many years before. This complaint finds an echo throughout the country. Degradation and crime in every form, of every texture, is the fabric that is woven of competition and cheapness. Poverty is everywhere, with a rapid concentration of all property, all the sources of subsistence, of comfort, and wealth into the hands of the few. Trade is in a chronic state of demoralization. Our annual failures are numbered by thousands; for the last ten years but once a little below five thousand, and ranging up to more than ten thousand per annum. Society and all its interests are the sport of gamblers, speculators, and monopolists.

It has been shown how these evils have grown upon us as the people have been forced into idleness — as their labor has been saved, or dispensed with — through the operation of the mechanical forces that have been so largely developed during the present century. That, as they have become idle, poverty, helplessness, and demoralization have spread in every direction, reaching up and permeating every fibre of trade and financial development. But every step that has been taken on the road that has led to the present condition has become an important indicator of both cause and cure.

The first thing to be done in seeking for remedies to cure the evils that have been pointed out is to obey the primal law of man's existence. In violating it we have brought all these evils upon ourselves.

When God thrust Adam from the garden of Eden he declared the law of his existence to be, that "in the sweat of thy face shalt thou eat bread all the days of thy life." When Jehovah with his finger wrote upon the tablets of stone, He indelibly inscribed, "six days shalt thou labor, and upon the seventh only shalt thou do no manner of work." The Divine Master taught his disciples the same lesson when he bade them to pray that day by day they might obtain their daily bread.

Here we have the Divine law, that it is only by daily labor that man can obtain the right to live, and all the blessings of life. This is the whole law in the case, and as certain in its effects as is the law that your finger will be burned if you hold it in the fire.

It goes without saying that all sound human economic laws are and must be in perfect harmony with the Divine, and that their violation must entail disaster and distress just so long and in exact degree with the extent of the violation. But in place of obeying this first of all laws, man is exerting every power of which he is possessed to violate it, to devise means whereby the masses shall not work; shall not eat bread in the sweat of the face; shall not labor on any day; shall not day by day receive their daily bread. The supreme effort has been to force the greatest possible number into idleness by altogether "saving" their labor, with the resulting demoralization and distress that is sure to come from any and every attempt to nullify or oppose fundamental human or Divine laws. The great effort which has enlisted all the energy and force of man, to devise means whereby he might be released from work — by which his labor might be saved — has filled the world with woe. God's law has been vindicated, and the folly of man's efforts to avoid its requirements amply demonstrated.

Manifestly, then, our only remedy for these great evils and tendencies in society is to be found in strictly and literally obeying the law.

It will be observed that there is no requirement that in any sense forbids man to lighten his labors. The law simply requires him to do such an amount of daily labor as will give him his daily bread. In the dispensations of Divine Economy there can be no doubt of a purpose that in human development a point should be reached where man should provide for all his physical requirements by that use of the forces of nature that will reduce his daily labors to the least possible amount, and at the same time that will enable him to partake most abundantly of all the blessings of life. But at no time and under no conditions can the universal requirement to labor be avoided without disaster. It is by universal labor only that permanent good can remain with any portion. Hence means must be devised whereby the law of man's existence may be strictly obeyed — the right and opportunity of all, day by day, to earn their daily bread — and the greatest good be obtained for all.

To do this effectively requires an intelligent understanding of man's requirements and of his powers. In the first place is presented the fact that all requirements for production, or labor, are found in the necessity of producing sufficient to supply society with food for body and mind, clothing, and shelter. These wants are the same that compelled Adam to labor, and since the beginning of time a new want has not been discovered. All the changes that have occurred in the long ages that have passed since man has been upon the earth, have been in the form and manner of the supply.

It has been shown that within the present century, since the time of our immediate fathers, our powers of production, in the supply of our physical wants, have increased more than ten fold. That being the case it follows as a logical conclusion that the concrete man should now be in the enjoyment of ten fold of the comfort and ease that our fathers could command. But the fact is, that as our powers have developed idleness has increased, and, consequently, poverty and distress have multiplied. Strikes have become more frequent and upon a larger scale, and their failures more significant. Wages, under the power of competition, have been steadily depressed, and the consumption and trade of the masses reduced.

In a purely commercial view we are ultimately thrown back upon the conclusion that it is in the condition of the masses of society that is found all the elements of successful trade or financial disaster. That it is in the consumption of the masses that is found the demand for production; and that to-day there is a more imperative demand that every man's power of consumption should be cultivated to the fullest extent than ever before. No man can throw into trade, through consumption, a greater amount than his income. If he receives but one dollar a day, or three hundred dollars a year, in wages, that is the exact amount of his contribution to trade. Assume that we have in the United States a productive, or laboring population of ten millions, and that their income is three hundred dollars a year each. In that case the contribution to trade from that source would be three billions. But suppose that their income should be three dollars a day, or, say, one thousand dollars a year. In that case their contributions to trade would be not less than ten billions, and more than three times greater than it is at present. The principle here stated governs the case.

In the days of our fathers, when every household became the focus for the production and manufacture of all that went into the consumption of the family — the food, the clothing, and the shelter — when everything was grown and manufactured by the very persons who would use and consume them, the conditions of trade were but little affected by the consumption of the masses. Then the farmer had but little use for money; buying and selling formed no part of his methods of obtaining a subsistence. He grew his grain for his own consumption, had it converted into flour or meal at the neighboring mill, paying toll in kind for the service. He grew his own wool and flax, made it into cloth in his own house; then into garments and put them upon his person and wore them. So he built his own dwelling, made his own tools of every kind, and used them. He was independent of trade. When he had occasion to make use of the services of the village, or neighboring blacksmith, or carpenter, or shoemaker, he was paid in the products of the farm. His minister and his doctor were also paid in the same way. These operations pervaded, as a rule, throughout the whole country. The only use that the farmer had for money was to pay his taxes, and other demands of government. In this manner was the great mass of the business of the country done, causing the least possible amount of trade, and in no sense dependent upon trade, as we now understand it, for its success.

In the larger towns and cities it was but little different, for the methods of barter and exchange, universal in the rural districts, were largely used in the greatest centers of population. But whatever trade there was, whatever use and demand existed for money, was confined almost wholly to the cities. There were the centers of governmental operations, but by no means were they the centers of production, manufacture, and consumption. Those operations were distributed throughout the country, among the masses of the rural districts, and were carried on almost wholly independent of trade and money. It was there that the great body of the population of the country was then fixed; and it was there that much the greater part of the industries of the country were exercised. At that time the cities, in weight of population and amount of productive manufacture, were quite insignificant as compared with that in the agricultural and rural districts.

But now, under the changed conditions of production and manufacture, trade and commerce of every nature are, in the fullest sense, altogether dependent upon the conditions and consumption of the masses of the people, because no one manufactures for himself solely, but every one, through trade, produces for the consumption of society and for the benefit of all.

Under these conditions the trader is as necessary to the welfare and prosperity of society as is the farmer or manufacturer. Through him must the exchanges be made that will place the varied products of industry within the reach of all. But the speculator, the gambler, the maker of "corners," still remain the curses of trade and leeches of society.

At the present time the farmer is as much dependent upon the operations of trade, for subsistence, as is the merchant himself. The farmer now sells his grain to one and buys his flour and meal of another. He sells his wool, and flax, and cotton, at one time; at another he buys his cloth, and often his ready made clothing. He sells his hogs and buys his pork; his cattle and buys his beef, his shoes, his plows, his tools of every nature, and pays cash for the services of the blacksmith and carpenter. Of all the operations that are now resorted to, to supply the wants of man, there are few that do not enter into trade for their consummation.

The man who attempts to understand the great changes that have taken place in the social condition of the people, within the memory of many now living, and does not take these facts into consideration, nor give them their due weight, is sure to fall into grievous errors, and becomes an unsafe counsellor. Now, when all production goes into the channels of trade, all the profits of the business of the merchant or trader, and of the transporter, is found, as it ever has been, between the producer and consumer, and is in exact ratio with the amount of the consumption, the producers themselves becoming the greatest consumers. The greater the amount that the producers are enabled to consume of their own products, the larger the bulk of trade, and the greater the profits. It is in the tolling of the products as they pass through the various hands between the producers and the consumers that is found the contributions that sustain all the classes of society that are not immediately engaged in productive pursuits, and serves to distribute the benefits of abundant production among all. As a consequence it follows that the greater the amount that is brought into consumption, the more liberal will be every class of contribution, and the greater the amount of comfort derived from their own products by the immediate producers themselves.

Therefore the greatest want of trade, as well as of society, is the adoption of a means that will bring all the now idle, and the partially employed, into constant employment, and thus not only make them active producers, but consumers also. The labor required to supply the wants of society must be distributed among all its members, that all may partake of its blessings; and the great advances that have been made in the use of mechanical forces in production must be directed to lessening the toils of the workingman, and the increase of his comfort. In this way the Divine purpose which has enabled man to chain the lightnings to his car, and to compel the coal and the iron of the earth's crust, and the vapors of its waters to do his bidding, and relieve his toil, will have been accomplished, and man will then have entered upon his true mission in obeying the commands of God, and in working upon those economic principles that are sure to contribute to his greatest welfare.

Having shown the idleness among our people, and the absolute necessity for all to be employed, that trade may prosper, it becomes a matter for serious consideration to determine what measures may be adopted to secure that end. Inasmuch as the only requirement that there can be for labor lies in the demand for reproduction that is created by the consumption of society, it follows that the labor required for the necessary reproduction must be distributed as widely and as generally as it is hoped may be the consumption. More than this, there stands the primal law of man's existence, his right and duty to labor, that he may eat and live, not as a beggar or criminal, but as a valuable member of the community, and in response to the requirements of society, which stands largely responsible for all its members.

As the immediate object to be attained is the distribution among all of the labor that is now performed by a portion only of the masses of society, we are happily helped in the suggestion made by the manufacturers in Massachusetts in response to inquiries from its bureau of labor, viz., that the hours of labor be reduced to six a day, in order that the mills may be run twelve hours a day, by two gangs of hands. The adoption of this suggestion will meet the whole requirement, and a little examination will show that those manufacturers would build better than they knew.

Let that principle be applied in all pursuits, and the result would be that at once there would be double the number of persons earning wages that there is now. For it would require just twice the number, working six hours a day, to supply the present demands of society than it does now when working twelve. There being twice the number earning wages, there would be double the number with incomes to invest in products for consumption. It is certain that wages would be increased, because the competition among workmen for employment would be destroyed, and instead there would at once be a competition among employers for workmen, compelling an increase in wages. Prices of commodities would also rise, and everything would advance in unison.

The great result would be that the doubling of the number of wage earning working men and women would at least double the number of consumers; whilst the advance in wages would have the effect of more than doubling the volume of trade and transportation and the profits arising therefrom.

We would no longer be compelled to seek foreign markets for our products, because our increased home consumption would require all that could be produced. The empty stomachs would be filled; the half naked backs would be warmly clothed; the barren, naked, cheerless dwellings, through the operations of trade, would be comfortably furnished; the naked floors would be covered; the wide staring windows would be curtained ; the fires of warmth and comfort would be kindled, and cheerful homes would take the place of what are now nothing less than dens of misery. In all these operations trade would be the active agent, reaping its rich rewards in place of the demoralization and disaster which now waits upon it in every direction. Thus would be repeated the economic operations of the war of the rebellion, divested of its horrible carnage of disease and death, and without the intervention of government as an employer, and the entailing of a mountain of debt.

But all efforts to achieve these great blessings would be altogether thrown away so long as our doors remain open, inviting competition from the outside world. The breaking down of the crushing competition among ourselves would be of no avail, if we permit it to come in from abroad. This is so self evident that it requires no more than the statement. Our first necessity is to so protect our own industries as to stimulate the production at home, on our own soil, of everything required to supply our own wants, in every case where the conditions of soil and climate are suitable. For instance, our yearly importations of sugar and molasses amount to a round one hundred million dollars, while we have soil and climate excellently adapted to its production in unlimited quantities. But the slaves of Cuba and the East Indies, and the coolies of the Sandwich Islands, can produce it at less cost to their masters than can our people and live. Thus the competition in trade, unrestricted, forces the introduction of the slave and coolie grown article, regardless of consequences to our own people.

The reply will be, that by the operation our people get their sugar and molasses cheaper.

Cheap sugar and molasses are not the vital wants of society; nor is cheapness the great want in any other thing. The primal requirement of the masses is that employment which is to be found only in the liberal supplying of their own necessities and comforts. The strife for cheapness has proved the national curse. Cheapness and poverty are inseparable, and are always found associated with idleness and competition. But constant employment, liberal compensation, and comfort, are the blessed trinity of true social and industrial economy.

As with sugar and molasses so with iron, with textiles, and many other things.

But a loud cry will go up that foreign commerce will be destroyed.

Well, what would be the harm done if it were destroyed? Has it ever proved an unmixed blessing to us? It certainly is not the chief want of man, and it would not be difficult to show that it has been far more of a curse than a blessing. But it would not destroy commerce; it would simply change its character. Whilst for every dollar lost to foreign commerce, there would be ten dollars added to home trade. This point has been sufficiently discussed in another chapter.

Both social and national prosperity is to be found only in the development of our own industries, and the employment of our own people. This can be best done by the full and complete adoption of all of the most effective and perfect devices for the use of mechanical forces and machinery. It is by the action of those forces and the powers of nature, where they can be controlled, that the greatest abundance of all that enters into the use and consumption of man may be produced with the least amount of physical toil. At the same time a perfection of product is achieved, in many things, that was not before attainable.

Hence, the development of mills, and factories, and workshops, completely furnished with the most perfect appliances of the age, are in the right direction. The fault has been, heretofore, in the abuse of their use. So with agricultural implements. They are all required in the full development of that industry. Those great machines that have been heretofore described as being in use on the bonanza farms, are by no means unavailable to the small farmer. When they shall have discovered that line fences are not necessary, but that their fields may be best cultivated when the greatest facility for passage from one farm to another is attained, and neighbors hold and cultivate their lands like friends rather than enemies, they will also learn that the great agricultural implements may be held in partnership, and be effectively worked by simple systems of cooperation.

CHAPTER XIV.

SIX HOUR LAW AND REASONS FOR ITS ENACTMENT.

MANIFESTLY a measure must be devised and adopted by which all shall share in the employments which give to society its sustenance and comfort. All having an equal and inalienable right to the labor by which the individual and society is sustained, the exercise of that right must be guaranteed and protected. This can be effectively done only by the organized action of society, in its national capacity — by law. Centuries, ages of individual action, uncontrolled by any action or rule of society that protected the weak from the natural aggressions of the strong, have resulted in the conditions that are now sweeping us so rapidly to destruction. Is it not time that a change should be made?

Without law, the concurrent action of ninety-nine in every hundred for relief, would amount to nothing against the "competition" of the one hundredth who should determine to follow his own selfish instincts in the way of what is called, in the slang of the period, "business." It is only in the passage, by Congress, of an Act, in character similar to the following, that real relief and improvement can be found.

n Act *to bring all the idle and the partially employed into constant work.*

Whereas, Idleness being the sum of all social evils, directly operating to destroy prosperity and create poverty, with all its attending miseries and crimes, it is the highest duty of organized society to use all necessary means to cause its removal, that industry and its comfortable fruits may be enjoyed by all; therefore,

Be it enacted by the Senate and House of Representatives of the United States of America, in Congress assembled, That six hours shall constitute and be deemed a legal day for work.

Sec. 2. That no action in any court of law, for compensation for work or labor done and performed, shall be recoverable where it is legally shown that any part of such account or demand is for work in excess of six hours a day; or where it is legally shown that the complainant did, at the time when, and for the party complained of, work in excess of six hours a day.

Sec. 3. Any incorporated company or association, doing business under operation of law, being legally convicted upon complaint of any person having knowledge of the offense, of working any of its employés for more than six hours in any one day, shall, for the first offense, forfeit and pay the sum of five hundred dollars, one half of the fine recovered to be paid to the complainant, and the other half to the order of the court; and for the second offense shall pay a fine of one thousand dollars and forfeit its charter.

Sec. 4. Every person and company, not incorporated, that shall, either as principal or agent, employ any person or persons for more than six hours in any one day, shall, upon conviction thereof, for each and every offense, forfeit and pay a fine equal to double the amount of wages made payable, and the costs of court; one half of all fines recovered to be paid to the complainant, and the other half to the order of the court. *Provided always*, That in all cases requiring extraordinary work in the protection of life or property, and in cases of house and body servants, the provisions and penalties of this Act shall not apply.

SEC. 5. The provisions of this Act shall apply only to those persons who are voluntary laborers or employés, either upon time or piece work. All persons who are forced to labor or work in pursuance of a sentence of any court, for crime or offense against the law, shall do so for at least ten hours on each and every working day.

SEC. 6. The provisions of this Act shall go into effect and be in force from and after six months from the date of its passage and approval by the President.

In connection with the above law a National Bureau of Labor should be created, the duties of which shall be the collection, from all parts of the country, of all the data necessary to guide the government in any future action, and especially for the following purposes, viz. : —

1st. That when, upon a careful and complete examination, in all parts of the country, it shall appear that all who are dependent upon their work or labor for subsistence are fully employed, and that there is not produced a sufficiency of the necessaries and comforts of life to meet the demands for home consumption, the hours of labor may be so lengthened, in all parts of the country, as to enable the required production to be made.

2nd. That when the examination shall show that all the demands of society, in home consumption, are fully met, and that any considerable number, needing work, are wholly idle, or but partially employed, causing competition that reduces wages, or in any other manner injuriously affects labor, the hours of work, throughout the country, may be so shortened as to bring all into regular and constant employment.

In the economy of life the necessity to labor grows out of the fact that man must work that he may live. Though nature, in its munificence, provides in the greatest fulness for the sustenance of all brute animal life, man is alone required to provide for himself. The earth is given to him that he may subdue it. It produces abundantly of grass, weeds, thorns, thistles, and wild fruits, well adapted to furnish food for the lower animals, but not for man. He must subdue the weeds, extirpate the thorns and the thistles that he may sow the seed and grow the grain that gives him bread.

Nature, from the storehouse of its providence, fitly and abundantly clothes all animal life, except man, with the raiment adapted to its requirements, localities, and seasons. But man is born into the world naked, and so remains if he does not clothe himself. He must grow or gather the wool, the flax, the grass, the cotton, the silk, the bark, the skins, the furs, the feathers, and whatever else may be used, and work and fashion the whole into material fit for garments, and make the same into the clothing that shall cover his body.

The Divine Master declared that the foxes have holes, and the birds have nests, but that the Son of Man hath not where to lay His head. A literal truth that describes the condition of the whole human family, except where the members thereof, through the operation of labor, have built themselves dwellings. For this the earth is mined and quarried, the forests are felled and fashioned into lumber, the soil is formed into bricks, the natural ores are converted into metals and wrought into building material and tools, and dwellings are constructed by and through the operation of labor, and by that alone. By it man is fed; by it he is clothed; and by it he is housed. By labor he is enriched with all the necessaries, comforts, and luxuries of life; but without labor the condition of man becomes worse than that of the brute.

In these conditions lies the only necessity that exists for man to work. They are the conditions under which man has existed from the very first, and they are the same that will continue to the end. There is no escaping the Divine fiat, that "In the sweat of thy face shalt thou eat bread till thou return unto the ground." Hence we see the imperative necessity that exists for a way to be devised by which all shall work that all may live.

It has been shown that, in our country, whilst an abundance is produced for the comfort of the whole people, it is done by the labor of a portion only, with the resulting evils of great idleness and consequent distress, whilst large amounts of the general product are sent out of the country to be consumed abroad. And it has also been shown that the only demand that can possibly exist for work is in the supply of our own society with the three great necessaries of life, and its comforts and luxuries.

To a great extent these are fixed factors. Our statisticians will tell you, approximately, the amount of food required for a given population; the number of dwellings when the number of families is known; and the amount of clothing, and the labor required to produce these things. They all come within the realm of calculation. It is labor that provides all the necessaries, comforts, and luxuries of life, and data may be collected to estimate the amount that will be required of each individual to provide for all these requirements when a proper system comes into operation, and the study of labor with its relations to society takes the place its importance demands. But now we have to do with things as they are, and leave speculations to be worked out by those who may follow.

At present we find that fully one half of our productive power is practically unemployed, and that distress is universally prevalent. The distress among the employed being only a little less than it is among the idle. We also find that one of the most marked characteristics of the present state is a crushing, killing competition among all producers, professions, trades, and traders, to obtain business and the means of living, by cheaper production, less compensation, less wages, and smaller profits, until the point is reached that threatens universal disaster, having long passed the point of general distress.

The immediate and dominant necessity is to break down this competition. The only way in which this can be done is to remove the cause. The cause is found in the fact that a large portion of the people are absolutely without the means of subsistence, and to get that they are compelled to compete with and underwork their fellows. The movement that commenced at the foundation of society widens and rises until all classes are involved, and the condition is reached under which we are suffering.

Therefore we are compelled, first, to ascertain how this competition at the foundation of society, among the workers and laborers, from the street scavenger upwards, may be removed. This reduces the matter to a very simple proposition, easily understood, and a result readily effected. Where there is but a single loaf, with two struggling for it, and equally necessitous, the struggle may be at once ended, and both quieted, by a division of it between them. Especially so when the divided loaf would give each an abundance. So with the labor loaf; there is abundance for all. Divide it; it will satisfy all.

The means for this division are as simple as the proposition itself. Those who labor now do so for from ten to twelve hours a day throughout the country. There are, certainly, cases and classes where the time of labor is as much as fifteen and even eighteen hours a day; and others that go as low as eight or six hours. But the mean is not far from eleven hours. An equal division of this time would be five and one half hours a day. But the great manufacturers of Massachusetts, through their Bureau of Statistics of Labor, propose a reduction of the hours of labor to six, provided it is a national movement. Following are three of the propositions, all from the great textile interest. See Tenth Annual Report, for 1879.

(e) "You can say we shall not work certain persons more than so many hours per day or week, but if we can dispose of our goods at a profit, and of all we can make, nothing can hinder us from employing two sets of hands, and thus, in our judgment, no curtailing of production can be brought about by simply reducing hours of labor, while there is no power to stop machinery."—Page 157.

(*f*) "Nor would it be impracticable to reduce the time to six hours, and this reduction would be preferable; for we could then run our mills eleven or twelve hours per day by employing two sets of operatives."—Page 158.

(*m*) "If the agitation is kept up for still shorter hours, I would favor it, and place it at six hours per day. We could then work two gangs per day, and get something like a fair production from machinery."—Page 162.

The Chief of the Bureau, Hon. Carroll D. Dwight, comments as follows:—

"In addition to written statements, we have conversed with a large number of proprietors; and, while for the most part they are willing to adhere to the requirements of the law of 1874, they strenuously oppose any further reduction unless to six hours per day; and thus they would practically demonstrate the wisdom or unwisdom of the theory that the true solution for over production lies in less hours of labor. We have no faith in that theory as a solution for over production; for, under a six hour rule, two sets of hands would be employed. Lessened hours of labor will come, must come, as the absolute outgrowth of the effects of machinery; and, could the regulation for the legal reduction be national, our manufacturers would not object."—Page 163.

It will be observed that the manufacturers, as also the Chief of the Bureau, look at the proposition for a reduction of the hours of labor as affecting solely the question of over production. But the real fact is, the matter does not touch the question of over production, which really does not exist, but rather of under home consumption; and even that but incidentally; neither of which being assigned a place among the reasons for a reduction to six hours.

The one great and controlling reason for shortening the hours of labor is, that the number of persons who are now employed may be doubled, either by working two sets of hands or by the building of new mills; the additional number who are given employment to be taken out of the ranks of those who are now idle, or but partially employed, that double the number of workmen and women may enter into the receipt of wages, and thus increase the number of consumers, the amount of consumption, and demand for additional production. These are the things sought for. But more of this farther on, first taking up some other matters.

Therefore the next proposition to consider is that of the necessity of national action. Upon this point the following testimony is also taken from the Tenth Annual Report, 1879. A furniture manufacturer, in answer to the circular of inquiries from the Chief of the Bureau, touching the hours of labor, writes: —

"The reduction of the hours of labor, in our branch of industry, would meet our approval provided the reduction should at the same time extend throughout the country. We think it would be for the interest of all, both employer and employé, inasmuch as it would give employment to a larger number to do the same work, and, by so doing, give a greater circulation to capital. The goods would cost more to make; but the employé, being at work, would spend his wages freely, as is the case with most laboring men, and, by this cause business to revive. Our wish is to reduce the hours of labor, but not in this State alone, for, in so doing it would give the manufacturers in other States the advantage of having their goods cost less, and thus be able to undersell us." — Page 152.

A paper manufacturer says : —

(*a*) "If ten or more hours is the legal day's work in our neighboring States, Massachusetts should not fix a less number." — Page 153.

A manufacturer of rubber goods writes : —

(*a*) "If Massachusetts is to compete successfully with other States and foreign countries in the manufacture of various fabrics, restrictions upon the hours of daily labor must *all* be removed, till *all* other States and countries adopt the same." — Page 154.

A producer of straw goods replies : —

(*a*) "A reduction in the hours of labor in our business would be decidedly against us, as the competition would be large against us from other States." — Page 155.

The statements of eight textile manufacturers are as follows : —

(*b*) "Unless we are allowed to run our machinery the same number of hours per day as manufacturers in other States, I do not see how it will be possible for us to compete with them. . . . . . If the hours of labor in this State are reduced still lower than in other States, it must compel manufacturers to reduce wages, run at a loss, or to shut down." — Page 156.

(*c*) "Manufacturers in this State can not pay higher wages for the hours of actual work than are paid by their competitors in other States; and a reduction of hours, at the same wages per hour, would increase the cost of goods." — Page 157.

(*d*) "Such a reduction would tend to throw the development of our industry into other States, which are now more favorably situated than we are, both by location and legal enactments for its operation." — Page 157.

(e) "Taking the interest as a whole in the United States, it would appear that if a general law could be made to extend to all the States, affecting all alike, reducing the hours of daily labor, such general interests would, in our opinion, thereby be promoted. . . . . . We believe shorter hours of labor would be better for the physical well being of the operatives, and we shall be glad to see such a limitation when it can be made general the country over. . . . . . We protest, however, against partial limitation, applying only to our State." — Pages 157–8.

(f) "It would be impracticable to run our mills nine and two tenths hours per day, and produce the same financial results as is produced by the mills outside of Massachusetts, which run eleven hours or more. . . . . . My mill has run ten hours per day, and the Nashua mill eleven hours per day. . . . . . It is thus evident that the manufacturers of Massachusetts suffer a direct disadvantage in their competition with those of other New England States of ten per cent. on the amount of their pay rolls. This I believe to be true as compared with all the other New England States." — Page 158.

(h) "By the Act of the legislature of 1874, the hours of labor for all females, and males under eighteen years of age, were reduced to ten per day, or sixty per week. This law has been passed by no other New England State; and the consequence is, that the cotton manufacturers of Massachusetts are to-day, with difficulty, able to compete with the other New England States, on account of the increased cost of manufacture, caused by the lessened production." — Page 160–61.

(m) "With regard to a further reduction in time, I would say that the present time of sixty hours per week is long enough, provided our competitors in Rhode Island, Connecticut, and New Hampshire work the same hours; but, as they work sixty-six hours per week, the result is operating disastrously for Massachusetts." — Page 162.

Here is abundant testimony showing that any legislative action by any one State, or any portion of the States, reducing the hours of daily labor, must prove disastrous, because of the competition that would arise between the manufacturers in the States with long hours, and those with short, resulting in the destruction of the industries of the latter. If attempted the power of competition would be brought into action with the most deadly effect. It must be evident to all that such would be the inevitable result.

Consequently, the necessity for national action, if any, being determined, we are brought to the consideration of the question, Has Congress, under the Constitution, power to legislate in this matter?

Here there is sure to be a conflict of opinion. But I fail to discover on what ground that right can be either consistently or constitutionally denied. Section 8, Chapter I, of the Constitution, declares that Congress shall have the power, among other things, "to pay the debts and provide for the common defense and general welfare of the United States." I am well aware that some take the position that the "general welfare" clause is a provision of limitation and restriction. If Congress is not permitted to "provide for the . . . . . general welfare of the United States," by the same process of interpretation it has no right nor power "to pay the debts and provide for the common defense." These three distinct powers are clearly given in one sentence, and covered by one and the same provision; they are all equally affirmative or negative; they must stand or fall together. The only question that can possibly arise under these general powers are as to what are "the debts," what are the conditions that require provision "for the common defense," and its nature; and what constitutes "the general welfare." In all these matters Congress is the sole judge, and from its judgment there is no appeal, except to the people through the ballot box. Most certainly no court has jurisdiction in the case.

But the fact is, there is not a limitation or restriction in the whole section. The limitations and restrictions are found in section 9, of the same chapter, and there is not one, in the whole number, nor do the whole body, in any particular, nor in general spirit, restrict Congress in any action which it may deem proper to be taken in this matter. Congress long since took action for the welfare of sailors, and for the mercantile and banking interests. Has it not equal power to make provision for the welfare of the whole of the industrial classes as for the mariners, or for the trading and banking interests? It certainly appears that the affirmative must be true.

Therefore it is clear that, under the Constitution, Congress has ample power in the premises. But even if, under the power which capital and monopoly may wield, the Supreme Court should see fit to attempt to nullify the action of Congress by declaring the six hour law unconstitutional, a thing most unlikely, there is still a higher power for appeal, before which courts and congresses must bow — the people — who, when necessary, may amend the Constitution itself, to meet necessary requirements. Abraham Lincoln formulated and declared the fundamental truth, that our government is a government of the people, by the people, and for the people. Therefore, when the people speak, under the forms provided by law, the voice will be heard and made effective. In this particular our people occupy a vantage ground possessed by no other—they are the high court of appeal, in which all have an equal voice.

There is only one other point, in this connection, remaining to be discussed:—Would governmental action, in the effort to remove idleness from out the nation, and give remunerative employment to all, be a measure contributing to the "general welfare of the United States?"

There are some who hasten to put themselves on record against any such measure. In the answers made by the manufacturers, to questions from the Chief of the Massachusetts Labor Bureau, heretofore quoted from, are found the following. A shoemaker writes:—

(d) "I am not able to see how any legislation can have any effect to benefit the operative. What business men can not accomplish, actuated by self interest, the State had better let alone. . . . . . Of course an enlightened self interest should induce capitalists and employers to do whatever they can to permanently improve the condition of the laboring classes, so called."—Pages 149–50.

A chair manufacturer:—

"We see no way to adjust this matter of short hours, except by the mutual agreement of the employer and employed. Legislation never can do it. There are too many peculiar circumstances connected with each line of manufacturing to be adjusted by a legislative body."—Page 151.

A paper manufacturer:—

(b) "We do not see how the hours of labor in our manufacture could be fixed by law to the advantage of employer or employé."—Page 153.

A manufacturer of rubber goods : —

(*a*) "Moral influences and forces must be left to work out questions relating to the welfare of the employed, rather than legislation affecting the time they shall labor, or price they shall receive." — Page 154.

A textile manufacturer writes : —

(*h*) "My opinion is, that legislative interference in regard to the hours of labor is unwarranted and uncalled for, and can only bring further distress upon the laboring classes, ... and, to my mind, legislative interference will not only increase their burdens, but be a direct blow to their rights and liberties." — Pages 160-61.

Such are the arguments that are used by those opposed to legislation in the matter of labor. One writes that it is a matter to be settled by the self interest [selfishness ?] of "business men," just as if the whole difficulty had not grown to its present magnitude under the fostering care of this very quality of "self interest." Another says that he can not see how to adjust this matter except by mutual agreement; a thing which has obtained from the first to the present time. One party agreeing to work any number of hours that can be legally demanded, and for any wages that may be offered, to save the family from starvation; whilst the other party is sure to demand the largest number of hours that the law will allow, or nature can endure, and the least compensation that can be imposed for the work done. This is the only kind of mutuality that is as yet discoverable or proposed.

Another writes that "moral influences and forces

must be left to work out questions relating to the welfare of the employed." These are not questions of simple morality, nor primarily so, but of material subsistence; as is the manufacturer's bank account a matter of finance, but not of Christianity. The workingman can not feed his wife and family upon good advice, tracts, and homilies, however abundant they may be, or excellent their quality. There is far more of nourishment to be obtained from the crumbs that fall from the rich man's table than from the great loaves of "moral influences and forces" so liberally distributed.

Another believes that "legislative interference will increase the burdens and be a direct blow to the rights and liberties of the laboring classes." Inasmuch as the laboring classes form a large majority of the people, and that whatever legislation is obtained will be in response to their demand, any little inconveniences of that kind may safely be left to work out their natural results. As the increase of burdens and loss of rights and liberties will be confined to the laboring class, it is difficult to see what call is made upon the employers to protect them from these anticipated evils. It certainly is an unexpected exhibition of remarkable philanthropy on their part.

Such are the reasons and arguments offered in opposition to legislation in behalf of the working classes. Arguments that will not bear the slightest examination. Indeed, every fact that has been brought to the surface in the great development of our present economic and social conditions, point to the absolute necessity that exists for some organized action that must be taken by society for the protection of the foundation upon which it rests. This means law, pure law and nothing more nor less. Anything else would be anarchy, dire confusion, of which we have already too much. Without the strong controlling force that can be found only in law, the spirit of competition and desire for monopoly which has so long ruled only to ruin, can not be controlled. Therefore we must resort to law, or allow things to drift on in the current now sweeping to destruction.

The effect of the enactment of this law will be multifarious and wide reaching. There is hardly a condition in life that would not, by it, be modified or revolutionized. The first effect would be to take the idle out of idleness and put them into remunerative employment. The destruction of the competition that now exists would directly operate to the increase of wages, an increased demand for production, to meet the increased consumption, and the general prosperity that would be developed in every direction. But these points have been sufficiently discussed in other chapters.

The next most important effect would be, that through it the great land monopolies and machine cultivation of bonanza farms, without population or family occupations, would be destroyed, for want of a large body of idle or half employed labor to draw upon.

When it is said that it was the great landed aristocracy that destroyed Rome, but half the story is told. Pliny's words, "latifundia perdidere Italiam," tell but half the truth. Without conditions existing that enabled the great Roman landlords to control the proletariat and their slaves, so as to compel them to cultivate and manage their large estates in a manner that would destroy and swallow up the small landholders, and thereby to practically make the whole people slaves, they would have been powerless, and there would have been no great estates. This is the dominant factor that is left out of the discussion of these matters by economists of the feudal stamp. Without a large amount of idle or half employed cheap labor, or slaves, that can be used at the pleasure or convenience of the great proprietors, there would be no great estates, nor swallowing of small landholders. The effective weapon of destruction, in the hands of the plutocrat, is competitive idleness; without that he is powerless. Indeed, he would cease to exist. But with the Romans their slaves and the proletariat became the club with which they beat down the smaller and weaker landholders, and thus they were enabled to rule and ruin. It was with them as with us, a mad consuming competition; the strong against the weak; the weak went down, and the real strength of Rome was buried with them.

By this means have the great landed interests controlled in all ages and among all peoples. So it is in Europe to-day; so it was in the Southern States, before the rebellion, when the negro was the slave club, whilst in the Northern States the large landholdings were practically unknown. And so it is now throughout our whole country, under the plutocratic competition and monopoly that are making practical slaves of our whole people.

But by the operation of the six hour law the great

mass of half employed or fully idle laborers, who form the force from which the bonanza farmers draw their supply of labor, will disappear. They will become fully employed, where their wages will be constant and remunerative, and the necessity for tramping over the country to find an occasional day's or week's work, will have ended. At seed time, when the bonanza farmer would need a body of laborers to appear as formerly, and prepare his ground and sow his fields, they will not show up; and at harvest, if it is ever reached, the harvesters who formerly did that work will be otherwise engaged, and there will be none to take their places. The bonanza farmers, like all other employers, will be limited to the number of laborers that find constant employment upon their estates. The transient employé will have disappeared.

Thus those large estates will become unmanageable, unprofitable, and be broken up. Instead of competing with the small farmer as at present, and driving him out of the field, the bonanza farm will inevitably crumble to pieces, and be divided more rapidly into small holdings than they have developed into their present magnitude, and will become the homes of a strong and thriving people. Every large estate that thus disappears will be the removal of an element of weakness from out of the nation; and every small holding that becomes so established will be an addition to the strength of society. In this grand break up and reformation the opportunity for a change in the condition of the tenant farmer will be sure to appear, for there can be no very general improvement in the condition of these great interests without beneficially acting upon all. But in their case, to make the change complete, and to best conserve the general welfare, special legislation will be required; such as will, also, affect the whole landed interest of the nation, to the discussion of which another chapter is devoted.

That these effects will follow the enactment of the six hour law may be counted as certain as that day follows night. And in no other way can these things be accomplished. The whole movement may be effected without a clash. Indeed, no opportunities will be presented for collisions of any nature; nor even for bitterness. There will be no confiscations, no arbitrary exercise of power. It will be simply, that under the operation of law, bearing equally on all, the people will go into regular and remunerative employment, which will necessarily compel a radical change in all business operations that depend upon a half employed and idle community for success.

But the law here proposed can not go into operation without encountering some real difficulties, and more that are purely imaginary. Of the imaginary difficulties the one most sure to be encountered, and at the same time the most groundless as well as thoughtless, is the objection which declares that the hours of labor must not be shortened because it will give to laborers more time to spend in saloons and all manner of dissipations. These objectors forget that under present conditions one half of those who should be at work, for want of employment, may now pass their whole time in saloons and dissipation; whilst those who have constant work are driven by the exhausting toil of their long hours of labor to the saloons and drink as the only accessible relief from the monotonous slavery of their lives. Ten to twelve, and even eighteen hours of work a day in shop, factory, or field, for six months in the year, drives the laborer out of bed whilst it is yet dark, to a hasty breakfast, then to toil till it is again dark, and into another night before the supper can be taken. In the morning the father leaves his children still in bed, and at night, when he gets home, they are again, or should be, in bed. He does not see enough of his family by daylight to become really acquainted with its members. In the long days of summer the laborer has greater opportunities to see his children. The wife is as much a slave as the husband and father. The dwelling is a home of poverty and destitution, without a single comfort or attraction of any kind. The only wonder is that saloons do not multiply more rapidly, and that intemperance is not more prevalent. At a great temperance gathering at Liverpool recently, Cardinal Manning spoke of wretched homes being the greatest temptation to drink. He went to the very heart of the whole matter. Out of the two conditions of idleness on the one hand and excessive toil on the other have grown the great evils of poverty and intemperance with which we are now cursed. There can be no hope of improvement till the causes which produced these evils have been removed. The moral condition and family relations of the workingman can not be improved so long as he is a slave to toil for the full time that he is out of bed. He must have time for rest and improvement, as well as means to make his home comfortable. The condition of the idle man, in everything that relates to improvement, is worse than that of the unresting toiler.

With these facts, apparent to everyone who will give them a moment's thought, I ask, which is most desirable, the continuance of the conditions of extreme toil on the one hand, and idleness on the other, with the results which are now everywhere seen around us, or the distribution of the work to be done among all, in such manner that everyone may have regular employment, with abundant time for rest, recreation, and improvement, and the means of making homes that are comfortable? These are matters not to be dismissed with a curt word and a sneer, but challenge earnest attention.

The first and most considerable real difficulty is, that much the greater portion of the unemployed labor of the country is unskilled. This fact will be seized upon by the opponents of the measure, and be magnified and distorted in every possible form. Yet, though it be a real difficulty, it will not diminish by procrastination. It must be met and overcome. It certainly is not insuperable. Under the present system of almost universal production by machinery, the first and great thing to learn by the unskilled is the method of controlling or attending upon a single machine, which may be more or less perfectly accomplished in a few weeks. The acquiring the management of a machine, in its constant repetition of the same operations, within a limited range, is widely different from what the learning of a trade was fifty years ago, where everything was wrought by hand. But whatever the difficulties may be, they must be overcome. The existence of the great mass of unskilled labor that we now have, is the inevitable result of the operations of society, under present developments, and society can not escape the consequences. Therefore, the quicker the difficulty is met, and unskilled labor is converted into that which is skilled, the better it will be for all.

Another difficulty will be found in the fact that for the last eighteen years we have been educating a large body of tramps — we may safely say, armies of them — who have no habits of industry nor love for work. Vagabondage has so long been their habit that they have learned to love it. Their condition must be changed, cost what it may. It is another of the penalties that society must pay for its transgressions. The tramp, also, is an inevitable growth out of present conditions. But the difficulty will not prove so great as many will seek to make it appear. The shortened hours of labor under the law, and the advance in wages that is sure to follow, will have a powerful influence on the tramp, however fixed his habits. The task of educating that class to habits of industry, under the new conditions, will not be as great as it now is to control and provide for them under the present state of things. The wholesome application of a stringent vagrant law would also operate beneficially in the cases of the otherwise incorrigible. They would not be long in learning that six hours of free labor, each day, will be far easier than ten hours of enforced toil.

The hope of constant employment, with shortened

hours and liberal compensation, will develop a mass of anxious, competent, intelligent applicants for work, old and young, male and female, that will pull off the scales from many eyes that will not now see the great desire which everywhere exists for work that is not slavery, and a compensation that will buy comfort.

These two classes of difficulties, real and imaginary, are all that merit discussion, and they would be overcome in the first year of the operation of the six hour law.

Having secured to our people the blessings that are sure to come out of the proposed change, it is a matter for grave consideration whether it be desirable to longer keep our doors wide open, and fill our country with the poor of Europe. Is it not a duty that we owe to our children to check the great influx from abroad, and save to them the room for expansion that is being so rapidly curtailed by the alien? It certainly appears that when we have shown to the world how a nation may become prosperous from the development of its own industries, and the proper division of its labor, we shall have rendered to humanity the greatest service that can be expected from us, and that America might very properly be preserved for Americans.

But there is another matter that should be considered in this connection; and that is the one so earnestly dwelt upon by Herbert Spencer in his last utterances before returning to his native land. He named it the *Gospel of Relaxation*.

CHAPTER XV.

THE GOSPEL OF RELAXATION.

[BY HERBERT SPENCER.]

HERBERT SPENCER, at the reception which was tendered to him, in New York, on the evening preceding his departure for England, made some most timely remarks to the gentlemen who were his entertainers. They were some of the most widely known men of our country, representing the learned professions, merchants, and financial interests; but not a member of the great body of the people was present. Therefore it is possible that no part of what he said was intended to pass over the heads of his immediate listeners, and to reach the great audience of the masses. But his criticisms and suggestions were so perfectly in line with the objects sought in this volume, that I can not forbear the pleasure of transferring them to these pages. He said: —

"Already in some remarks drawn from me, respecting American affairs and American character, I have passed criticisms which have been accepted far more good naturedly than I could reasonably have expected; and it seems strange that I should now again propose to transgress. However, the fault I have to comment upon is one which most will scarcely regard as a fault. It seems to me that in one respect Americans have diverged too widely from savages. I do not mean to say that they are in general unduly civilized. Throughout large parts of the population, even in long settled regions, there is no excess of those virtues needed for the maintenance of social harmony. Especially out in the West, man's dealings do not yet betray too much of the 'sweetness and light' which we are told distinguish the cultured man from the barbarian. Nevertheless there is a sense in which my assertion is true. You know that the primitive man lacks power of application. Spurred by hunger, by danger, by revenge, he can exert himself energetically for a time; but his energy is spasmodic. Monotonous daily toil is impossible to him. It is otherwise with the more developed man. The stern discipline of social life has gradually increased the aptitude for persistent industry; until, among us, and still more among you, work has become with many a passion. This contrast of nature has another aspect. The savage thinks only of present satisfactions, and leaves future satisfactions uncared for. Contrariwise, the American, eagerly pursuing a future good, almost ignores what good the passing day offers him; and, when the future good is gained, he neglects that while striving for some still remoter good.

"What I have seen and heard during my stay among you has forced on me the belief that this slow change from habitual inertness to persistent activity has reached an extreme from which there must begin a counterchange — a reaction. Everywhere I have been struck with the number of faces which told in strong lines of the burdens that had to be borne. I have been struck, too, with the large proportion of gray haired men; and inquiries have brought out the fact that with you the hair commonly begins to turn some ten years earlier than with us. Moreover, in every circle I have met men who had themselves suffered from nervous collapse, due to stress of business; or named friends who had either killed themselves by overwork, or had been permanently incapacitated, or had wasted long periods in endeavors to recover health. I do but echo the opinion of all the observant persons I have spoken to, that immense injury is being done by this high pressure life — the physique is being undermined. That subtle thinker and poet whom you have lately had to mourn, Emerson, says, in his essay on the gentleman, that the first requisite is that he shall be a good animal. The requisite is a general one — it extends to the man, to the father, to the citizen. We hear a great deal about the 'vile body;' and many are encouraged by the phrase to transgress the laws of health. But nature quietly suppresses those who treat thus disrespectfully one of her highest products, and leaves the world to be peopled by the descendants of those who are not so foolish.

"Beyond these immediate mischiefs there are remoter mischiefs. Exclusive devotion to work has the result that amusements cease to please; and, when relaxation becomes imperative, life becomes dreary from lack of its sole interest — the interest in business. The remark current in England that, when the American travels, his aim is to do the greatest amount of sight seeing in the shortest time, I find current here also. It is recognized that the satisfaction of getting on devours nearly all other satisfactions. When recently at Niagara, which gave us a whole week's pleasure, I learned from the landlord of the hotel that most Americans come one day and go away the next. Old Froissart, who said of the English of his day, that 'they take their pleasures sadly, after their fashion,' would, doubtless, if he lived now, say of the Americans that they take their pleasures hurriedly, after their fashion. In large measure, with us, and still more with you, there is not that abandonment to the moment which is requisite for full enjoyment; and this abandonment is prevented by the ever present sense of multitudinous responsibilities. So that, beyond the serious physical mischief caused by overwork, there is the further mischief that it destroys what value there would otherwise be in the leisure part of life.

"Nor do these evils end here. There is the injury to posterity. Damaged constitutions reappear in children, and entail on them far more of ill than great fortunes yield them of good. When life has been duly rationalized by science, it will be seen that among a man's duties, care of the body is imperative, not only out of regard for personal welfare, but also out of regard for descendants. His constitution will be considered as an entailed estate, which he ought to pass on uninjured, if not improved, to those who follow; and it will be held that millions bequeathed by him will not compensate for feeble health and decreased ability to enjoy life. Once more, there is the injury to fellow citizens, taking the shape of undue disregard of competitors. I hear that a great trader among you deliberately endeavored to crush out everyone whose business competed with his own; and manifestly the man who, making himself a slave to accumulation, absorbs an inordinate share of the trade or profession he is engaged in, makes life harder for all others engaged in it, and excludes from it many who might otherwise gain competencies. Thus, besides the egoistic motive, there are two altruistic motives which should deter from this excess in work.

"The truth is, there needs a revised ideal of life. Look back through the past, or look abroad through the present, and we find that the ideal of life is variable, and depends on social conditions. Everyone knows that to be a successful warrior was the highest aim among all ancient peoples of note, as it is still among many barbarous peoples. When we remember that in the Norseman's heaven the time was to be passed in daily battles, with magical healing of wounds, we see how deeply rooted may become the conception that fighting is man's proper business, and that industry is fit only for slaves and people of low degree. That is to say, when the chronic struggles of races necessitate perpetual wars, there is evolved an ideal of life adapted to the requirements. We have changed all that in modern civilized societies, especially in England, and still more in America. With the decline of militant activity, and the growth of industrial activity, the occupations once disgraceful have become honorable. The duty to work has taken the place of the duty to fight; and in the one case, as in the other, the ideal of life has become so well established that scarcely any dream of questioning it. Practically, business has been substituted for war as the purpose of existence.

"Is this modern ideal to survive throughout the future? I think not. While all other things undergo continuous change, it is impossible that ideals should remain fixed. The ancient ideal was appropriate to the ages of conquest by man over man, and spread of the strongest races. The modern ideal is appropriate to ages in which conquest of the earth and subjection of the powers of nature to human use is the predominant need. But hereafter, when both these ends have in the main been achieved, the ideal formed will probably differ considerably from the present one. May we not foresee the nature of the difference? I think we may. Some twenty years ago, a good friend of mine, and a good friend of yours, too, though you never saw him, John Stuart Mill, delivered at St. Andrew's an inaugural address on the occasion of his appointment to the Lord Rectorship. It contained much to be admired, as did all he wrote. There ran through it, however, the tacit assumption that life is for learning and working. I felt at the time that I should have liked to take up the opposite thesis. I should have liked to contend that life is not for learning, nor is life for working, but learning and working are for life. The primary use of knowledge is for such guidance of conduct, under all circumstances, as shall make living complete. All other uses of knowledge are secondary. It scarcely needs saying that the primary use of work is that of supplying the materials and aids to living completely; and that any other uses of work are secondary. But in men's conceptions the secondary has, in great measure, usurped the place of the primary. The apostle of culture as it is commonly conceived, Mr. Matthew Arnold, makes little or no reference to the fact that the first use of knowledge is the right ordering of all actions; and Mr. Carlyle, who is a good exponent of current ideas about work, insists on its virtues for quite other reasons than that it achieves sustentation. We may trace everywhere in human affairs a tendency to transform the means into the end. All see that the miser does this when, making the accumulation of money his sole satisfaction, he forgets that money is of value only to purchase satisfactions. But it is less commonly seen that the like is true of the work by which the money is accumulated — that industry, too, bodily or mental, is but a means, and that it is as irrational to pursue it to the exclusion of that complete living it subserves as it is for the miser to accumulate money and make no use of it. Hereafter, when this age of active material progress has yielded mankind its benefits, there will, I think, come a better adjustment of labor and enjoyment. Among reasons for thinking this, there is the reason that the process of evolution throughout the world at large brings an increasing surplus of energies that are not absorbed in fulfilling material needs, and points to a still larger surplus for humanity of the future. And there are other reasons, which I must pass over. In brief, I may say that we have had somewhat too much of 'the gospel of work.' It is time to preach the gospel of relaxation.

"This is a very unconventional after dinner speech. Especially it will be thought strange that in returning thanks I should deliver something very much like a homily. But I have thought that I could not better convey my thanks than by the expression of a sympathy which issues in a fear. If, as I gather, this intemperance in work affects more especially the Anglo American part of the population — if there results an undermining of the physique, not only in adults, but also in the young, who, as I learn from your daily journals, are also being injured by overwork — if the ultimate consequence should be a dwindling away of those among you who are the inheritors of free institutions and best adapted to them; then there will come a further difficulty in the working out of that great future which lies before the American nation. To my anxiety on this account you must please ascribe the unusual character of my remarks."

If what Mr. Spencer had seen and heard among the class in which he had moved, and to whom he was talking, had forced on him the belief that their persistent activity had reached an extreme from which there must begin a counterchange — a reaction; if everywhere he had been struck with the number of faces which told in strong lines of the burdens that had to be borne; if among that class he had also been struck with the large proportion of gray haired men;

if his inquiries had brought out the fact that with them the hair commonly began to turn some ten years earlier than with his own people; if, in every circle that he had moved in he had met men who had suffered from nervous collapse, due to stress of business, or been informed of others who had killed themselves by overwork, or been incapacitated, or had wasted long periods in endeavors to recover health; if he but echoed the opinion of all observant persons to whom he had spoken, that immense injury is being done by this high pressure life — that the physique is being undermined; and if, among the classes there represented — the wealthy, those who had abundance, and enjoyed to an unlimited extent all the comforts of life, there were still such dismal signs of overwork and care, what are the signs that must mark the condition of those who were there unrepresented — the poor, the daily laborer, the mechanic; those who have not one of the comforts of life, hardly the necessaries?

The answer to the foregoing question is best made by the following report of vital statistics quoted from the daily press: —

"Investigations made in Germany concerning the vitality of children under various methods of feeding exhibit some curious results. Thus, of 100 children nursed by their mothers only 18.2 died during the first year; of those nursed by wet nurses, 20.33 died; of those artificially fed, 60 died, and of those brought up in institutions, 80 died to the 100. Again, taking 1,000 well to do persons and 1,000 poor persons, there remained of the prosperous after five years 943, while of the poor only 655 remained alive; after fifty years there remained of the prosperous 557, and only 283 of the poor; at 70 years of age there remained of the prosperous 235, and but 65 of the poor. The total average length of life among the well off class was found to be 50 years, as against 32 among the poor."

Here is the clearest evidence that if burdens and overwork had marked with strong lines many of the faces of the class that Mr. Spencer addressed, and incapacitated and killed others, that overwork and burdens had been doubly injurious and twice as mortal among the great masses upon the outside. To these great masses, also, must the "Gospel of Relaxation" be preached; and in the principles of the six hour law is found the only method by which that preaching can be made effective. It is to be reached only by destroying that spirit of destructive competition referred to by Mr. Spencer, in the case of the "great trader" who "deliberately endeavored to crush out everyone whose business competed with his own," up and down, through all classes, to the utmost limit.

In that one little effort Herbert Spencer deftly held up to view the consuming greed that is wasting the vitality of our whole people, for which he should ever be held in the most grateful remembrance.

CHAPTER XVI.

GENERAL EFFECTS OF THE MECHANICAL CHANGES OF THE PAST FIFTY YEARS, AND OF INDUSTRIAL REDISTRIBUTION IN THE FUTURE.

THE real effect which the general use of machinery in all industries has wrought upon the social condition of our people, is not to be satisfactorily measured or appreciated in the changes which occur from year to year, but, far better, from decade to decade; and, better still, from half century to half century.

That during the past fifty years there has been, in the invention, improvement, and use of machinery, an enormous increase in man's power to provide for his necessities and comforts; and that, at the same time, there has been an alarming development of extreme want and pauperism can not be successfully denied.

Fifty years ago the bonanza farm was unknown. Then there were no huge tracts of our best lands cultivated without a family rooftree upon its whole extent — without woman or child, or other indication of a home; where for a portion of the year were to be found laborers only, under the eye of an overseer, himself a hireling, with cattle and machinery; and where, for the remainder of the twelve months the human cattle were not permitted to remain, but were driven forth, and the quadrupeds only, with the machinery, were kept and housed and cared for by the least number of laborers that were able to do the work. But these monster estates are now numbered by tens of thousands.

Fifty years ago, in our country, that crushing relict of feudalism — the tenant farm — was little known to us except as we learned of it in Europe. But now we have them in millions, worked and held under conditions that make the tenant farmers in England appear as princes when compared with the tenant farmers in our boasted land of comfort and plenty.

Fifty years ago there were no large sections of our cities and towns given up to and crowded with tenement houses, with a family to every room, whether light or dark, in garret or in cellar, with hundreds of men, women, and children in every house, living in a state of wretchedness that beggars description. But it is so at this time.

Fifty years ago there were no armies of able bodied, healthy men and women, skilled in the arts, professions, and trades — many of them temperate and cultured — wandering all over the face of our country, vainly seeking work, begging food and clothing, sleeping where they can, and the next day continuing their vain hunt. But we have them now.

Fifty years ago there was not an enforced idleness amounting to fully one half the working force of our people. But there is to-day.

Fifty years ago one half of our workmen were not

employed to the extent of their physical endurance, at compensations that barely sustained life, whilst the other half got but little or nothing to do, and lived God only knows how. But it is the case at this time.

Fifty years ago we had the poor with us, as we ever shall have, but not as we have them to-day. Then the poor consisted of the halt and the blind, the aged and the infirm, the widow and the fatherless. Then the healthy and able bodied never went hungry and cold because work could not be found to pay for food and clothing. But to-day there are multitudes of the most healthy, the most able bodied, the most skilled, the most cultured, who are compelled to accept their food, if they get any, from the hands of charity, and their bed upon the bare bosom of mother earth, or the stone floor of the station house.

Fifty years ago the beggar, in town or city, was a rare visitor, and in the country he was not to be found. But to-day he is everywhere.

And it is a notable fact that intemperance, ignorance, insanity, and crime keep even pace with the development of all the evils that are here enumerated.

Neither did these things exist forty years ago as they do to-day, nor thirty, nor twenty, nor fifteen, nor ten, but have been steadily growing upon us for the last half century, or more, with one notable reaction, since which time the development and growth of these evils have been appalling, and challenge the earnest thought and careful examination of all.

Who does not know that during the last fifty years there has been an enormous increase in pauperism and crime? And, at the same time, that there has been a corresponding increase and concentration of wealth in the hands of the few?

Now the fact stands out bold and distinct, that in the midst of a greater abundance than the world ever before saw, with a greater productive power than man has ever before known, there never before was so great an amount of idleness and destitution. One half of the world in slavery, the other half in idleness, and all in misery because of these two conditions.

But here comes an alternative proposition from the manufacturers, through the Massachusetts Labor Bureau, to reduce the hours of labor to six per day, to the end that they may run their mills, factories, and workshops twelve hours per day, by the use of double gangs, or two sets of hands.

What would be the effect, if it were done?

Evidently the first would be to require double the number of hands that are now employed; because there still must be produced sufficient to supply society with all the necessaries and comforts of life, and this would require double the number of operatives working six hours a day, that it would when working twelve.

This demand for additional hands would create a competition among employers for those who would work, and this would inevitably cause an advance in wages. Adam Smith says that:—

"When in any country a demand for those who live by wages —laborers, journeymen, servants of every kind—is continually increasing; when every year furnishes employment for a greater number than had been employed the year before, the workmen have no occasion to combine in order to raise their wages. The scarcity of hands occasions a competition among masters, who bid against one another, and thus voluntarily break through the natural combination of masters not to raise wages.

"But it would be otherwise in a country where the fund destined for the maintenance of labor was sensibly decaying. Every year the demand for servants and laborers would, in all the different classes of employment, be less than it had been the year before. Many who had been in the superior classes, not being able to find employment in their own business, would be glad to seek it in the lowest. The lowest class being not only overstocked with its own workmen, but with the overflowings of all the other classes, the competition for employment would be so great in it as to reduce the wages of labor to the most miserable and scanty subsistence of the laborers. Many would not be able to find employment even upon these hard terms, but would either starve, or be driven to seek a subsistence, either by begging, or by the perpetration of the greatest enormities." — *Wealth of Nations.*

Here are clearly defined the conditions that certainly follow the full and the partial employment of "those who live by wages." A demand for workmen and advance in wages would have the direct and immediate effect of putting into the hands of the great body of the people a largely increased amount of funds; first, because of the additional number that had been brought into employment; and, secondly, because of the advance in compensation, caused by competition among employers to obtain operatives.

The market for home consumption would at once be fully doubled by the increased normal consumption of the people, before whom all our present surplus would quickly disappear, creating greatly increased demands for reproduction and stimulating every industry, as did the bringing of all into employment at the opening of the war of the rebellion. These causes and effects, in the law of economics, follow with the utmost certainty, the converse of which we have abundantly demonstrated during the past seventeen years. The industrial operations of the war of the rebellion, from 1861 to 1865, when the increased demand for operatives, either in the armies or in the abnormal industries, which were followed by all the effects already pointed out, fully illustrate the law that governs in these matters. It needs no further argument on my part to prove that every dollar that goes into the hands of the wage receivers is immediately turned into trade, and goes back again to the fund from which it started, with a large per centage of the value of the products which it has helped to circulate. And, manifestly, this demand for consumption and reproduction would be limited and restricted only by the amount of wages or compensation received by the operatives, up to the limit of the most liberal consumption; thus creating and sustaining a largely increased demand for reproduction and distribution, and prosperity with all. These would be the general effects.

In agriculture it would have the direct and immediate result of restoring the small farmer to that condition of independence and security that would insure the return to the farm of the multitudes now vainly seeking employment elsewhere, and at the same time put an effective stop to great capitalists and corporations obtaining and working large bodies of land, by means of machinery and hirelings, in the manner that has been described. It would compel the division into small tracts of the large farms already created, each and all of which would be occupied by a family that would surround itself with all the improvements its means could command, and fill the country with independent homes.

The large farmer, capitalist, and corporation that depended on occasional labor for the work necessary to the successful use of machines and animals on their farms, would, in the first place, at seed time and harvest, be unable to find a great amount of unemployed labor, ready to take any work that might be offered, however short the time required or small the compensation; and when hands could be found, they would be limited to six hours of work per day. If more work should be required, more hands must be obtained. But the small farmer, doing his work within his own family, would not be affected by any of these disabilities. He would govern his own time for work by the necessities of the occasion, making it longer or shorter, as might be required, whether it were twelve hours per day or but one. And in those operations requiring the use of the great agricultural machines that so materially facilitate and lighten the work of the farm, cooperation and joint ownership could be most advantageously adopted; or the reaping, thrashing, etc., as now often done by specialists, who own the machines, may be more generally adopted; thus giving to the small farmer of to-day the full benefit of all the improvements that have been made in agricultural implements, and immeasurably advancing his condition above that of the farmers of our fathers' time. Under these conditions the small farmer would have that percentage of labor in his favor that would amply secure him from all harmful competition by large capitalists and corporations ; and, on an average, every quarter section of land would be occupied as a homestead that would receive the full benefit of all the improvements that could be put upon it. Thus continually advancing the general condition of the people and increasing the wealth of the country.

The railroads would have not only the large amounts of produce to carry to market that they now enjoy, but would also have large return freights, for the supply of the numerous families occupying the farms of the country. And more than this : there would be created a large local and distant passenger travel, now so conspicuously wanting, sustained by both the increased population and their improved condition, the absence of which, at this time, in the agricultural sections, is one of the most serious matters that affect those interests. Excepting that of the farmers, no interest in our whole country, especially in the great West, would be so largely and so beneficially affected by the redistribution of labor that the adoption of this proposition would bring about, as that of the railroads. It is not in unpopulated regions, nor among tramps and beggars that those great interests find favorable conditions. In the general prosperity of the people do they find their best requirements ; and in the agricultural sections it is by the numerous small farms and prosperous homes that their success is assured ; whilst large tracts, however well cultivated, without homes or fixed population, afford but meager support to any great interest.

But long before this point has been reached in the discussion the voices of the capitalists and the employers are heard, crying out, "What, shall the laborer be paid the same for working six hours as he has been for working ten?"

Wait a moment, gentlemen. Let us understand what is understood by that question, and what considerations are involved. For what do you pay wages to laborers and workingmen? Do you pay them for the time they occupy or for the amount of work they do? When you pay them for a day's work is it not because they are supposed to have produced something? If of two men working side by side, upon the same work, one is producing only one half as much as the other, do you pay them both the same amount for their day's service, except upon compulsion? Is not the work of one of these men of twice the value to yourself and to society than is that of the other? Is not the service of the man who makes two pairs of shoes in a given time of more value to the employer and society than he who can make but one pair of like quality in the same period? If, to-day, the shoemaker can make two pairs of shoes, where yesterday he could make but one, is not the service of to-day of double the value of that of yesterday?

These questions carry their own answers. Whether men are employed by piece or time work the compensation is popularly supposed to be gauged by the amount of work done or real service rendered, and not by the mere time occupied. At any rate it should be so, say one and all, and any other rule is grossly unjust, to call it by the mildest of terms.

A pair of shoes is of the same value to the individual and to society, in their wear and use, whether made by one man or by two; or whether made yesterday or to-day; and worth the same compensation, either in kind or in money, which is only the representative of that which we call kind. So is a bushel of wheat, or a sack of potatoes, or a yard of cloth. It is the product that bears the intrinsic value, in ministering to the wants and comforts of society and to the volume of trade, and in exact proportion to its use, only, does it perform those functions. Manifestly, then, the only standard by which the value of wages can be measured is by the product, and in proportion to that amount should it be compensated.

But what are the facts in this relation? A careful examination will show that the workingmen are compensated in inverse ratio to the amount of product produced or real service rendered. Eighteen years ago 24,151 persons were paid a greater amount for producing 175,875,934 yards of cotton cloth than were 31,707 persons ten years afterwards for the production of 874,780,874 yards, or nearly five times greater product. So in boots and shoes. In 1865, 52,821 persons were paid at least three times as much for making 31,870,581 pairs as was paid to 48,090 persons in 1875 for making 59,762,866 pairs. So in woolen goods; so in building; so in agriculture; so in everything.

Ever since machinery came into use in general production there has been a constant, but gradual, decrease in the amount paid to labor for a given quantity of any production, and in the amount of labor employed, until the general condition has been reached that is stated in the first portion of this chapter. A competition has been developed that in no way tends to the elevation of the masses, or improvement in their condition. On the contrary the whole effort has been to cheapen labor — to make it of less necessity, of less value — to give it less power in the struggle for subsistence — to create a competition that never ceases its grinding of the labor of man to a lower level. In the interest of what Adam Smith terms the "mercantile system" the sole end and aim of all effort appears to be to sacrifice every interest to cheap production, that the merchant may be enabled to "buy cheap and sell dear" — to build up trade — to extend commerce — that the whole world may, either as cheap producers or dear purchasers, or as both, pay tribute to trade — and to trade only.

To the mercantile class it seems that the only value of the workingman is in producing the greatest possible amount at so cheap a rate that it may be bought and sold, at home or abroad, so as to yield the greatest possible margin of profit to the merchant. The effect that this system may have on the producer is a matter of the utmost indifference. And of equal indifference appears to be the ultimate effect that these operations may have upon trade itself and society in general. The supreme effort, to subserve which all the powers of society appear to be directed, is the production of every product primarily for mercantile uses, that the merchant may obtain a profit. In this effort is found enlisted the whole power and influence of the daily and periodical press. It shapes our legislation and controls our governmental policy, both domestic and foreign. All other interests and persons are compelled to yield to the apparently paramount importance of trade and the trader.

The present competition practically teaches that society exists and is organized for the sole purpose of buying and selling, and that the most successful trader — he who can buy the cheapest and sell the dearest — is the person most to be honored. The tendency of present feudo-economic teachings and practices is not to the advancement, but to the demoralization, of society in general.

But at the time when the most liberal compensation was paid to workingmen for the product produced, or service rendered, society was in its most prosperous condition and all enterprises flourished. Then it was that the merchant or trader really made his greatest gains; because, being dependent upon the masses for the sale and use of his goods and wares, they were then in condition to buy and consume most liberally. More than this: the workman who receives two dollars per day can better afford to pay to his merchant ten per cent. profit upon the goods bought and consumed, than can he who receives but one dollar a day pay five per cent.; for the reason that in the one case, after paying the merchant's ten per cent. profit on the subsistence purchased, there yet remains one dollar and eighty cents for the workman's support; but in the other, after paying the five per cent. of profit, there remains to him but ninety-five cents for his sustenance. Thus it is seen that the well paid workingman not only greatly adds to the volume of trade over and above him that is poorly paid, but also pays double the profit. The business experience of our country within the past twenty-five years amply illustrates these principles. Perhaps they will be better understood when the manufacturers, traders, and capitalists of society can be made to understand the selfevident truth uttered by Adam Smith, that the great masses — "servants, laborers, and workmen of different kinds make up far the greater part of a great political society" — and that "no society can surely be flourishing and happy of which the greater part of the members are poor and miserable."

During the last twenty-five years the workingman's power of production has been increased at least four fold. That being the case it necessarily follows that his condition should be proportionately improved. When the powers of an individual or of society are so developed as to increase his or its means of subsistence or comfort, it follows that no useful result is reached if that individual or society does not receive a corresponding benefit, either in the greater abundance of subsistence and increase in comfort, or in lessening the amount of toil or labor required in their production, or in both. But during this period the workingman's compensation has not increased either in kind or in its representative — his subsistence has not become more abundant nor his comfort greater, except for a short season, and now his condition is worse than ever, as is evidenced by the universal distress and the hosts without any means of sustenance.

Therefore, to the question, "What, shall the laborer be paid the same for working six hours as he has been for working ten?" I answer, Yes, a thousand times yes, if the product of the six hours of to-day be equal to the ten hours of yesterday; because it is the only way in which society can receive any benefit from its increased power of production, or the workman obtain a greater amount of subsistence or enlargement of comfort. It would be only practically allowing to the farmer the natural benefit that should be derived from his ability to grow two bushels of wheat where before he could raise but one; or the shoemaker two pairs of shoes where previously he could make but a single pair. It would be illustrating the benefit of making two spears of grass grow where but one grew before, when the grower's condition was just that much improved.

It is evident that something must be done whereby the workingmen and society shall be restored to their condition of past prosperity, and receive a benefit from every new development of power, instead of being forced to greater privation. If, to-day, by six hours of work as great an amount can be produced for the comfort and sustenance of society as could yesterday be done in ten, then every principle of social development and sound business policy demand the adoption of the six hours, and it must be done, to the end that the idle may be brought into employment. These matters are simply questions of fact as to power of production, sustenance, and comfort, and rest solely on the employment of the people.

On purely economic grounds the principle involved in the six hour proposition must be adopted. Our power of production, within the last quarter of a century, has increased at least four fold. The simplest economic law demands that the consumption in society — among the masses where the increased production has developed — shall keep pace with it, or be compensated in some other form. But it has not. Individual consumption has actually fallen off — there has been no compensation in any form. The increased production, in great part, has been sent abroad, leaving many of our own people destitute — hungry and naked — and sold to foreigners at prices that represent the distress of our industrial classes, and at the same time destroys the productive industries of the people who buy.

Within the last half century our power of general production has increased at least ten fold. Has the comfort of the masses of the people increased in like degree? Let our crowded cities, our tenement houses with their squalor and horrible mortality, our abandoned farms and ruined homes of the people, our half employed and idle multitudes, our legions of beggars and armies of tramps, our poverty, distress, and crime of every nature, with the steady concentration and growth of wealth and luxury in the hands of the few — all of which, with us, are the result of the "beneficent competition" of the last half century — answer the question.

To the dullest apprehension these facts and principles should be selfevident. But generations of false teachings, fallacies, and indifference are stubborn obstacles to encounter.

One interest, and one only, in our whole country, would be even apparently injured by the six hour rule; and that would be the interest that would monopolize the great farming lands of the country and destroy the small farm interests. But the destruction of these great monopolies, in the manner suggested, would not only be an immediate and positive gain to society, but would save our country from the revolution of violence which the present tendencies are sure to bring.

The tenement houses in our towns and cities have grown out of the necessities of two causes, working in the same direction. First, in the necessity of the workingman living near the work by which he is subsisted, because the long hours he is employed, if at all, will not permit the loss of time required in traveling long distances; and, secondly, because the compensation he receives for his work will not permit of either the payment of anything more than the cheapest rents, nor the expense of railroad travel to places more distant, where rents are cheaper. However great the evils of these houses, they can not be lessened before the causes which produced them are removed. In this case, also, the adoption of the six hour rule would afford immediate and direct relief, in several ways. In the first place, the doubling of the number of operatives, by employing double gangs, in all occupations, would set their idle occupants at work, and give them greater means of subsistence. The shortening of the hours of work would give them the time to travel long distances to and from their homes; and the increase of wages would give the means to pay the expenses of the travel. In this way the tenement house evil may be radically cured. This remedy will also work to the direct benefit of the railroad interest, in furnishing a large amount of travel and business to suburban homes, and value to outside lands and rents. By this means one of the greatest evils that afflict society may be thoroughly and permanently removed, to the benefit of all, and without cost to any, except the owners of the tenement houses.

Under the operation of the six hour rule the tramps would quickly disappear. The small farms and the various industries of the country would absorb them all; and instead of being the itinerant pests of society, they would become valuable members of the social and political community — producing, consuming, and adding their equal share to the wealth of society.

This bringing of all into the industries of the country — this giving of employment to the idle — having secured to the small farmer the fullest opportunity for life and its enjoyments; having relieved the tenement houses of the cities and towns; and brought the tramp into useful and profitable occupation, it may with confidence be expected that again would the poor be limited to the halt and the blind, the aged and the infirm, the widow and the fatherless — those whom the Master declared we should always have with us; and the beggar would again become a stranger.

With the strength that society would gain by these great changes there can be little doubt that the demon of intemperance may be successfully attacked, and ultimately wiped out. The great causes of its general prevalence having been removed, the evil itself might be destroyed.

And in education, with renewed prosperity and

added strength in the people, there would most certainly be an advance.

These are some of the immediate and most direct benefits which society would derive from the adoption of this proposition, in bringing all into employment. With the most earnest desire to discover what would be the evils that would grow out of the adoption of these measures I have not been able to find even one. And in the matter of cost, or loss, which would at once arise in the minds of many, in every case the material compensation that would immediately follow would immeasurably more than repay for all.

In discussing this matter, as applied to employments, I have made special use of the facts in the development of agriculture to illustrate the operation of the measure proposed, for the reason that it is the occupation that lies at the base of the world's pyramid of industry. But the facts in any and every other employment wherein machinery is used may also be taken for illustration, though it may be that the effects may not so easily be made apparent.

And in trade, especially the retail trade, there is the most pressing necessity for the application of the proposed measure. It is notorious that a few great establishments are surely swallowing up and destroying the small ones. Here, also, the small trader can not compete with his gigantic neighbor. This is not to the interest of society, whatever it may be to the great merchant.

Would it be to the interest of society that half a dozen establishments, in one city, should do all the retail business, in any line, in place of an hundred?

Or that one should do it all in place of ten? The tendency, at the present time, is to one against a hundred, under the influence and power of precisely the same forces as are destroying the small farmers and fattening the nonresident plutocrats, and must be met with the same remedy. In any and all cases the adoption of the propositions from the manufacturers of Massachusetts will be ample to protect society and the workingman against the crushing weight of capital; because capital, without the uncontrolled, slavish use of labor, — that great fund which supplies every nation "with all the necessaries and conveniences of life," — is powerless for injury to the industries of mankind.

With the adoption of their propositions machinery would at once fill its proper function, in conferring upon mankind the great blessings of reduction in toil, and at the same time vastly increased production and use of the necessaries, comforts, and wealth of society.

Society is a vast and complex social machine, the force or motive power which runs it being labor only, but without regulator or governor of any kind. Every speculator, gambler, monopolist, and manufacturer uses and consumes the labor of the machine as caprice or self interest dictates. The result is, that the machine is always out of order and needing repairs. It becomes the toy or plaything of anyone who has the capital to make it so. "Crises" follow "booms;" "strikes" succeed "compromises;" "lockouts" are on the heels of "amicable arrangements;" "failures" and "hard times" are but a little behind "flush times" and "prosperity." There is constant friction and war of jarring interests. But through it all the arts of the speculator and gambler are not remitted; the monopolist and plutocrat gain in wealth and power, whilst the producer and laborer just as surely are losing their hold upon the means of life, and are becoming more and more the slaves of capital. The social machine, without a regulator can not run smoothly; its irregularities must increase; the disasters must multiply as the power develops, and become more and more subject to the evil influences which now control it, until, like every social machine that has preceded it, and every mechanical machine that ever was driven by an inconstant power, without means to regulate it, it will destroy itself. There is not a mechanic living who can not understand these principles. Our popular political economists and social gamblers, only, are opposed to all apparatus or means for regulation. Any mechanic will say that the first requisite for the successful working of a machine is a means by which the use of the power which runs it may be regulated; that being found, all its workings may be made as smooth and even as may be desired, with any power that may be required. By the adoption of the six hour law as the regulator, impartially applied and firmly administered, all the disorders and irregularities that attend the working of our unregulated social machine, at this time, will be removed, and order will take the place now held by chaos. The speculator, the gambler, and the monopolist will lose their hold of the great social power, and it will cease to be their sport.

Labor would be made attractive — a pleasure — when every day should also bring with it the time for rest, social intercourse, home employments and pleasures, with mental and physical development. Under these influences every interest in society which tended to improve its condition, would be developed and prosper. Schools, churches, libraries, lectures, and all healthy amusements, social recreations, picknics, excursions, and out of doors family enjoyments, conducive to health and strength, would be developed, for the simple reason that society would every day have the time that could be so employed. Whilst the nightly revels in dens of debauchery and drunkenness, and the neglect of all the ties of family and home, would be continually lessened and gradually broken up, because there would be time for something better; and the tone of that society which reaches down into the slums would be touched and beneficially acted upon by the improvement in that which lies above.

But to tell the workless that they must find something else to do — that new industries must be created — that men must abandon old and seek new occupations — is to repeat the words of the Egyptian taskmasters to the children of Israel, "Go ye, get you straw where ye can find it," when they knew that no straw was to be had — no, not even stubble. If we in the end escape the retribution that fell upon the people of Egypt, it will not be because of the wisdom of such counselors.

CHAPTER XVII.

TENTH ANNUAL REPORT, BUREAU OF STATISTICS, FOR THE STATE OF MASSACHUSETTS.

MASSACHUSETTS is largely in advance of any other State in the collection of valuable labor statistics, and their publication. But, unfortunately, the facts gathered do not appear to be of any special value in assisting its Chief to a proper understanding of their bearing upon the social and industrial problems now so pressing. Indeed, many of the facts are so tortured as to be made to support the grossest fallacies. The Tenth Annual Report, of January 22, 1879, is preëminently of that character, and presents with much plausibility several typical fallacies that merit attention, because of their general bearing. It is an extraordinary document, both from the conclusions to which it comes as to the amount of unemployed labor, or idleness, in that State and the Nation, and the methods by which its conclusions are reached. Its conclusions are, as stated on page 11, in what is there called, "The Investigation of November, 1878," that 23,000 males and females at that time represented the unemployed in that State, against 28,508 males and females in June, 1878, being "those only who really want employment." "On this basis there would be 460,000 unemployed able bodied men and women in the United States, ordinarily having work and now out of employment."

No doubt the very thing was intended that has resulted from these statements — a general belief that the numbers reported in the special report of June, 1878, and the November Investigation, truly represented the idleness in that State and the Nation at those two periods. It has been so received and republished throughout our country.

But there are two unknown quantities in these statements; that of June, 1878, is represented in the qualification of "those only who really want employment." The report gives us no idea of the number of skilled and unskilled workmen, then out of work, who did not "really want employment;" nor of the inquisition nor inquisitors who ascertained this vital fact. The qualification of November, 1878, is in the words, "ordinarily having work." Here, also, we are left in the dark, not knowing what is meant by "ordinarily having work," nor the manner, time, nor persons, in which, when, or by whom this fact was ascertained. Is it possible that these two unknown quantities were designedly left as points upon which to quibble and pettifog, and render these reports of no possible value? Can it be that the persons who get but a week, or a month, or six months of work in a year, are to be considered as "employed?"

The vital conclusions arrived at are, that 460,000 men and women now represent the amount of unemployed skilled and unskilled labor in the United

States, and 23,000 the number in that State. This is one per cent. of idleness for the whole population of the United States, or very nearly one and one third per cent. for that State ; or, three per cent. of the skilled and unskilled workpeople of the United States, and nearly four per cent. of the same classes in Massachusetts. This calculation is made upon the fact that something more than one third of the total population belong to the working classes, as shown by the report under review, and the United States census.

There is not an intelligent man or woman in our country who does not know that this showing is not true. Every ascertained fact in possession of the Massachusetts Bureau of Statistics proves that it is false. In spite of the two unknown quantities left open to quibbling, it is notorious that three in a hundred do not represent the unemployed men and women of our country "who really want work," or "ordinarily having work," but who are now without it.

On page 9, of this report, in the apparent effort to belittle the amount of national idleness, I find this statement : —

"The absurdity of the 3,000,000 statement is readily seen when it is known that there are but about 10,000,000 people in the country engaged in productive industries."

The census of 1860 gives 8,287,043 as the number of persons engaged in the industries of our country at that time ; the census of 1870 gives 12,505,923 for that period ; and now, with a population of over 50,000,000, as given in the census of 1880, with the same rate of increase as in the preceding decade, the number can not be less than 17,000,000 who belong to the productive classes and who should be at work. Consequently if there are but 10,000,000 at present engaged in the productive industries, there must be 7,000,000 who are not engaged. Does not that Bureau know that within the last twenty years we have had a large increase in our total population, and necessarily of those who do or should belong to the industrial classes?

From page 12, I quote: —

"Attempts have been made to convince the public that the June report and the census of 1875, taken and reported by this Bureau, were at great variance. And from the census returns the assertion has been made that there must now be nearly 200,000 *persons* out of employment in this State," *et seq.*

I filed with the Hewitt Labor Committee, in August, 1878, a statement, based upon the facts found in the Compendium of the Census of Massachusetts for 1875, published in 1877, showing that 92,042 persons, belonging to the industries therein enumerated (not any portion of the 638,661 contained in the first statement on page 85, Compendium), were unemployed and unaccounted for in 1875. The correctness of that statement has not yet been challenged.

In the paper which I read before the American Social Science Association, in May, 1878, upon the same authority, but in a different view of the matter, I showed that there was an idleness of not less than 97,975 persons. Those figures were made on a portion, only, of the factors in the case, and fall short of showing the actual amount of idleness. Yet the Bureau was swift to make up and issue its June report, with its unknown quantity. But I now emphatically say, that the idleness of 200,000 persons falls far short of representing the real idleness in that State, and that every *ascertained fact*, in possession of that Bureau of Statistics, proves it. I take it for granted that the Chief of the Bureau must know the facts, and their full significance, as reported by his own office, and therefore I say he must know that what I here state is true.

On pages 270-276, Compendium of 1875, is a table showing the average number of days employed in a year, in 262 occupations and subdivisions of occupations, which amount to 229 days and a fraction, showing a loss of one fourth of the working time. One fourth of the working time of the 584,690 persons who "belong to the skilled and unskilled laborers" of that State, amounts to the full time of 146,172 persons. This is only one out of many factors I might cite, but is enough to show the deceitful character of those two reports from that Bureau. I know that the table here referred to does not agree with the figures given in gross on pages 144-45 of the last report. I am under no obligation to reconcile the two reports, and much prefer the statement of items in the Compendium.

The Chief must know that the number of the industrial classes had been largely increased during the previous four years, first, as reported by himself, "from a class not furnishing competitors four years ago . . . . . simply dependents . . . . . numbering in all 56,117. From this class there have been large numbers of recruits to the ranks of labor." See page

10. And, secondly, from the normal increase of population, being a little more than two per cent per annum, or say 50,000 persons. This, notwithstanding the table on page 10, showing the rates of births and deaths. As this question relates simply to the development from the anteindustrial age into that of the industrial, by the lapse of time, it is difficult to see what immediate effect the neglect or refusal of children to be now born can have upon the age development of those now approaching man·or womanhood.

Another fact must be well known in the office of the Bureau of Statistics, for it is clearly shown by its ascertained facts, and that is, that notwithstanding the enormous increase in the products of that State, since 1865, there has been a very large per centage of decrease in the amount of manual labor actually employed, and that, consequently, all the additions that have since been made to what should be the ranks of labor, are just that much addition to the existing amount of idleness.

In Parts IV and V of the report much space is given to correspondence with employers and employés — some of which has been transferred to these pages — with the almost unanimous agreement upon the matters of uncertain and partial employment, and wages that will not permit of further reduction and sustain life, even where the employment is most continuous and best paid. If there is a great want of coherency, or that which is practical, in these answers, it is not because of the neglect of any useful lessons in political economy that have been by that Bureau wasted upon the people.

In Part V the matter of the reduction of the hours of labor is discussed, with tables and correspondence. If the alleged facts in the report, that the idleness in the country, among the industrial classes, does not exceed three per cent., be correct, all this discussion is inconsequential. No reduction can be made — indeed, no reduction is required — because, practically, there is no idleness; or, at most, but three per cent. To successfully reduce from ten hours to eight, there must be an idleness of twenty per cent., "seeking employment," to meet the additional demand. Why does not that Bureau, upon this ground, stop the discussion at once? Yet it not only tolerates, but invites a still wider discussion. It goes much farther, and seriously considers the propositions from the textile manufacturers to reduce the hours of labor to six, as quoted in the chapter on the Six Hour Law. The propositions are no doubt seriously made, and reasons are given for the proposed reduction. But to do it requires an idleness of fifty per cent. among the skilled and unskilled work people of society, "who really want work," of which neither the manufacturers nor the Chief of the Bureau express a doubt, nor of the practicability of doing for want of operatives.

All the facts that have been discovered in this examination go to show that the real amount of idleness in this country must be in excess of fifty per cent. of those who are dependent upon labor for subsistence. The following suggestive factors are recommended for consideration: —

First. — There is the great amount of muscular labor that has been displaced by machinery within the last fifty years, equal to at least nine tenths of that previously required to produce the subsistence demanded by society.

Second. — There is the fact that at the close of the war of the rebellion at least two fifths of the then working force of the North, and probably of the South also, were thrown upon the country, where there was no demand for their employment — where they were not wanted; and that the only work they have obtained, since that time, has been by compelling a division with those then and since employed.

Third. — Another important point is, that since the close of the war machinery has been so greatly improved that more than one half of the number then required have been dispensed with. In this manner has the ratio of idleness been steadily and constantly increased.

Fourth. — Then there are the operations on the bonanza farms, where, from three to six weeks in each year, are found from two to three hundred laborers, and for five months only from five to ten.

Here are four indisputable factors, out of many others that might be given, that sufficiently prove that the idleness must largely exceed fifty per cent. of the working force of the country. The facts upon these points are given in this volume, and are unimpeachable. It is a simple arithmetical problem, not a sentiment of desire or repugnance. Sentiment does not enter into the matter. There stand the facts, however disagreeable they may be, and ignorant denial will not change them. Take your pencils, dear readers, and work out the problem. It will prove a useful study for those who will take it up. The only change that the factors are subject to are their steady development in the direction in which they have been moving for the last half century.

The only direction in which there has been an absorption from the great mass of practical idlers, has been toward trade, which has enormously developed, and other unproductive pursuits, that have absorbed literally their millions (see pages 192–3), until those interests have become as demoralized as the productive industries, and still the idleness is not diminished. There is not a manufacturer in that State who does not know that he can double the number of his employés whenever he requires them and will pay living wages; a fact as well known in the Bureau of Statistics as in any mill, workshop, or factory in that State. And yet this same Bureau would make the world believe that three per cent. represents the idleness in our country. The idea that doubling the number of hands employed might also double the number of persons who would thus find the means to buy and consume their products, has not yet dawned on the minds of the manufacturers, nor of the political economists in that Bureau. And it is also possible that the application of the six hour rule might help them to an understanding of the principle laid down by Adam Smith, that the manufacturer finds his wealth in the multitude of hands he employs.

Attention is drawn to these points to show how utterly worthless and deceitful have been the attempts to belittle the idleness in that State and in our country. The only answer required by the statement found on page 13, "that all attempts to disprove the June and November reports by figures from the census simply deceive the public," is, that either the June and November reports do deceive the public, or the Massachusetts Census Reports, for 1875, are false. It is not necessary here to determine which. Still it may be said that the ascertained facts in the census report appear to agree with all that I have been able to gather, and that there can be no doubt that the June and November reports have done the service designed — and, possibly, some not anticipated.

But it is yet to be seen that it is for the interest or honor of the Commonwealth of Massachusetts, or any portion of its people, that one of its important bureaux should use the large funds it receives, and the power and influence it possesses, to give currency to reports of the character they are here shown to be. What is wanted is a clear and accurate statement of the real condition of the employments and idleness of the people, without reservations, unknown quantities, or quibbles. This information that Bureau can give, and nothing less can be either satisfactory or really useful.

There are other matters in the Tenth Annual Report as fallacious as that regarding the amount of idleness in the Commonwealth; and particularly so is that which relates to the mechanical industries of the State and the Nation, In part II, page 24, in treating of Convict Labor, is found the following statement:—

"In this connection it should be remembered that the products of the mechanical industries of the United States amount to over *five thousand million* dollars annually."

And on page 25, the following:—

"The examination of the boot and shoe interest will enable the legislature to see more clearly the relation of the statistics presented to other facts gathered during the investigation. This industry is taken for illustration, because it is the largest in the State, the product being $90,000,000 per annum."

Both of these statements are grossly erroneous — inexcusably so — and tend directly to foster the most fatal delusions. The mechanical industries of the United States hardly reach two thousand million dollars annually, in place of five thousand millions; nor do the industries of that State, which enter into the immediate production of boots and shoes, equal $25,000,000, in place of the $90,000,000 claimed.

No doubt there have been sold in Massachusetts boots and shoes to the amount of $90,000,000; but of the industries that went into their production that State furnished but a small part; only about one fifth. The hides of which the leather was made were the product of the industries of Texas, and other distant States — of Mexico, South America, Europe, Asia, and Africa. The industries which converted the hides into leather were those of Maine, and other States in the Union, as well as of foreign countries. Neither of these employments are part or portion of the manufacture of boots and shoes, as generally understood, nor as classified in the Labor Bureau Reports. So, also, of the thread, cloth, pegs, paper, buttons, etc., which enter into the composition of the finished product. Some of these industries have their separate and distinct headings and columns in the Massachusetts and other reports, and show large valuations, equally fallacious ; because they, as reported, include industries that have been developed under other classifications, and in other places ; as does the manufacture of boots and shoes, as there reported, include the industries of cattle and sheep raising, butchering, curing of hides, tanning and currying, making of cloth, thread, pegs, paper, buttons, etc., with transportation by sea and land, handling and storage; whilst, in reality, not one of these employments is any portion of the art of making boots and shoes, or enters into the manipulations of the boot and shoe manufacturers, any more than do the growing of the wheat, or manufacture of the flour, that comes from the West, become a part of the industries of Massachusetts, because it is handled, or resacked, or repacked, and shipped to Europe from the port of Boston.

When the leather, and other manufactured or prepared articles that enter into the make up of boots and shoes, are placed in the hands of the manufacturers, then that industry commences, and not before; and is continued until the finished product goes into the hands of the wholesale or retail trader. It is between these two points that the operations and industry of making boots and shoes are confined ; whatever is there done, and nothing more, is the real product of that industry.

In the making of boots and shoes in that State, for the year ending May, 1875, there were employed 48,090 persons, at an average yearly compensation of $383 44 each, as appears by the report of that Bureau. This gives $18,439,639 as the value of the mechanical work that was performed in that industry. Adding twenty per cent. to that amount for profits and incidentals, will give $21,727,566 as the utmost real contribution which the industry of boot and shoe making has given to the productive occupations of the State, in place of $90,000,000, as claimed.

It makes a very fine showing to carry all the items separately into the account, and then, also, to add the totals as another item. In commercial exhibits such accounting would be deemed fraudulent, and under some circumstances become indictable.

So, also, in textile manufactures. In the second volume of the Massachusetts Census Reports, page xxiii, $136,251,783 are given as the product of that industry. But this sum includes the cotton, wool, flax, dyes, dressings, etc., which are the products of other and distant peoples, as boot and shoe making are made to include great foreign industries. In the manufacture of textiles, as reported by the Labor Bureau, there were employed 78,967 persons, at an average compensation of $320 85 per annum. This gives $25,572,392 as the amount paid for labor. Adding twenty per cent. for profits and incidentals gives $30,686,870 as the amount that the textile industries have contributed to the mechanical productions of that State, against $136,251,783, as reported.

Here is seen a reduction of $105,564,913 in textiles, and $67,648,226 in boots and shoes; an aggregate dropping of $173,213,139, from the imaginary to the real. Leaving for these two employments, as their actual amount contributed to the productive industries of the State, the sum of $52,414,436, in place of $249,308,350, as claimed. See page xxiii, ibid.

It is hardly necessary to carry the examination into other products, all of which are made up by similar methods. These two will serve to show the way in which a foundation is laid for a statement like that found on page xix, ibid., as follows : —

"By this recapitulation it is seen that the total products of the mechanical industries of the State are $592,331,962, from 22,228 establishments, on a capital invested of $282,683,718."

And they will also show the methods by which it is found that "the mechanical industries of the United States amount to five thousand million dollars annually," when they really do not reach one half that sum.

There is a remarkable swiftness to catch up these false statements and to enlarge and exaggerate them, apparent in the columns of a great number of our leading metropolitan daily press ; and, more especially, in a late publication of the great house of the Harpers, in their "Half Hour Series," entitled, "Labor and Capital Allies, not Enemies," by Edward Atkinson, of Boston. In this work the author not only copies and endorses, but adds to them other statements equally fictitious. For example, he says that of the gross product of the mechanical industries of the State, amounting to $592,331,962, as therein claimed, capitalists receive only five per cent., as appears by the following quotations : —

"It therefore again follows that in the very first division those who do the work of production, either of the raw material or of the finished article, must get ninety-five to ninety-seven parts, and the owner of capital only three to five." — Page 64.

"In addition to the general proof already given, that, in respect to the manufactures of Massachusetts, those who do the work now receive ninety-five to ninety-seven per cent., while indirectly working people receive nearly all the remaining three or five per cent., special proof may be found in the consideration of the cotton manufacture of the United States, taken as a whole." — Page 66.

If these statements mean anything it is that of the gross product of $592,331,962, as claimed from the mechanical industries of Massachusetts, capitalists in that State receive not more than five per cent., or $29,616,598, whilst not less than ninety-five per cent., or $562,715,364 are there paid to the laborers in the various mechanical industries; and that "indirectly working people receive nearly all the remaining three to five per cent.," the $29,616,598 that the "owner of capital" had received. For evidence of the correctness of these statements our author forgot to refer to the wonderful fact that the unfortunate capitalist, who really gets nothing, lives in luxury in a Beacon street or Commonwealth avenue palace, and the correspondingly great matter for astonishment, that the most fortunate workmen, who get all, may be found starving in the tenement houses of the North End.

With regard to the first item of $29,616,598 I have no disposition to dispute that it approximately shows the yearly profits derived by capitalists from the productive industries of that State; especially when it is stated by so high an authority as the distinguished author of "Labor and Capital Allies, not Enemies," and representative of that class of capitalists. But the second item of $562,715,364, being the "ninety-five to ninety-seven parts" that is claimed to be "now received by those who do the work," is a gross delusion. The very report from which the author has drawn his pretended facts contains the most abundant evidence of its untruthfulness; and it is most astonishing that one with the large general and special business experience of our author should have the boldness to publish a fallacy that is so transparent.

It has already been shown that the amount paid to workmen in the manufacture of boots and shoes was $18,439,639, and in the manufacture of textiles was $25,572,392, being a total of $44,012,031 for those two employments. Textiles and boots and shoes represent the product of very nearly two fifths of the manufacturing industries of that State. At that rate the whole amount actually "received by those who do the work," in "the manufactures of Massachusetts," was very nearly $110,000,000 in place of the $562,715,364 claimed by the author of "Labor and Capital Allies, not Enemies," and capital received at least one fourth as much as did labor in the whole transaction, or twenty-five per cent. instead of five, as claimed.

Had $562,000,000 gone into circulation through the workers in the manufacturing industries in that State, as claimed, instead of the $110,000,000 which approximately represent the true amount, it requires no prophet to see that there would have been at least five times the volume of trade of every nature, and five times the profit to capital. But our author does not see anything of that kind. Upon the misrepresentation of facts above shown, and upon principles equally baseless, he builds a superstructure of fallacies and sophistries, all tending to show the "beneficence" of concentrated capital, cheap labor, and competition. That if there is inequality anywhere, it is in labor getting too much; and if a division must be made, it must be of that portion received by labor. That our true policy is, not to increase the material welfare of our own masses, and thus improve our market at home, but to so reduce the compensations of our industrial classes as to enable the capitalist to sell the products of our cold and hungry millions to the still more naked and hungrier masses of Eastern and Southern Asia, and famishing Europe, and give large profits to capital. At one and the same operation not only to impoverish and beggar our own people, but to destroy the industries of all other nations.

Mr. Atkinson says that "the lesson which is really taught by the condition of Massachusetts is . . . . . *that the more the rich may gain in wealth the more the poor may gain in comfort.*" — Page 58.

It is impossible to read and carefully examine this statement without feeling the utmost astonishment at its bold defiance of all the facts of history and "lessons" of present social "conditions" of Massachusetts and the whole world. The author of the sentence quoted certainly will not claim that what is true in his own State is false everywhere else; nor that the truths of past centuries are the falsehoods of to-day.

If there is one social lesson, in all history, taught with greater emphasis than any or all others, it is that whenever and wherever the rich have made their greatest gains in wealth and power, there have the poor correspondingly lost in comfort and sunk into wretchedness. Every historian, ancient and modern, who has traced the causes and marked the steps in the decline and destruction of the Roman empire, has placed the growth of wealth in the ruling classes, and the increase in poverty among the masses, as the most powerful of all. The history of every other nation adds its testimony to the same effect. And so it is to-day in every nation on earth. In no country can stronger evidence of the fallacy of Mr. Atkinson's statement be found than in our own.

In illustration of how the poor gain in comfort as the rich gain in wealth, I quote the following from the daily press: —

"VIOLENT CONTRASTS IN LIFE.

"Ned Stokes' bar [in New York City], it is said, takes in $200 to $300 per day (or rather night), as it is patronized by a crowd of fast fellows who drink nothing but high priced liquors. A dinner at Delmonico's and Pinard's can be had at from $5 to $40 per guest, according to the bill of fare and the wine list. A number of dinner parties have been given during the past season at the Fifth Avenue in which $200 were expended in flowers alone. How easy to pay such bills when one's income is $1,000 per day, and this is not a large figure among our capitalists; but just look at the other side of social life.

"Four women were arraigned in the police court for selling vegetables and matches in baskets in the streets. One of the number said she was a widow with two children, and that this was their only support. The magistrate replied that as it was a violation of law he was obliged to fine them $10 apiece, and as they were conveyed to the prison one of them fainted. Such contrasts may be found daily.

"Speaking of incomes, Moses Taylor is rated $400,000 a year. He has no sons and his daughters are all married. Ex-Governor Morgan is estimated at $500,000 a year. Russell Sage is rated at a million to a million and a half, while Jay Gould's income can not be less than half a dozen millions. To come down to smaller men, R. L. Stewart has nearly a million a year, while Robert and Ogden Goelet are each rated at $250,000. Bennett is reckoned at $600,000. D. O. Mills figures at $200,000, and the young Vanderbilts (Wm. K. and Cornelius) are not much below him. The estate of A. T. Stewart & Co. has an income of a million, which renders Cornelia Stewart the richest widow in America. The Astors (John Jacob and William) are estimated each at a million and a half, while Wm. H. Vanderbilt probably has five times that sum; and yet within five minutes' walk of the place where these men live one can find multitudes whose life is but a prolonged battle with famine." — *New York Correspondent Troy Times.*

The picture here drawn of the conditions existing in New York are in no respect exaggerated, and portray in the most vivid colors the way "that the more the rich may gain in wealth the more the poor may gain in comfort." But it is not necessary for the author of that statement to travel out of his own city of Boston for abundant evidence of his bold defiance of truth. Let him compare Commonwealth Avenue, the whole Back Bay, with the South Cove, North Square, and the whole of the North End. If that will not suffice, then a careful examination of the report of the superintendent of the institution for the shelter of poor working girls, who declares that the great increase in the number of young women who are driven to prostitution in that city, because of low wages, is most disheartening, may possibly enable him to find another "lesson which is really taught by the condition of Massachusetts." The lesson taught by the cities of New York and Boston is preached by every city, town, and hamlet in the country. The lesson is universal; and it would be in the exercise of the greatest charity if one could come to the conclusion that when the author of "Labor and Capital Allies, not Enemies," wrote that sentence he was trying to formulate a ghastly sarcasm.

But there is no mistaking the lesson that the author of that little volume is trying to teach; and that is, that the earth and all that it contains was created and exists for the exclusive enjoyment of the rich, and that the poor live only to add to their pleasures. Upon the evidence furnished by Mr. Atkinson's essay there can be no doubt that "under the beneficent action of competition" Capital and Cheap Labor have become Active Allies in the work of destroying all the industries of the people and crushing of the foundations of society.

But to return to the consideration of the Labor Bureau reports, and in view of the above exhibits of the way grand results are reached by the most extraordinary methods, it is sickening to read pæans like the following, on page xviii, ibid. : —

"In the light of the hard and unanswerable arguments of facts as evidenced herein, our anxiety for the future, industrially, of Massachusetts must be allayed. Our great industries are built upon too firm a foundation to be toppled over by any ephemeral, speculative schemes."

The answer to this pæan is found in the examination here made, and heard in the cry that comes up from every industry and interest. On page 24 I find the following : —

"In reality the wages paid for prison labor — $1,624,515 per annum — represent a product of $9,747,090, or less than one fifth of one per cent. of the products of the United States."

A clear net product of $8,122,575 from labor which costs only $1,624,515, appears to the ordinary reader a most excellent thing. But the trouble is, the statement is deceptive, not possessing one element of fact.

So, also, on page 26, the following is found : —

"The product of each person employed in the manufacture of boots and shoes in Massachusetts is $1,858 per year; that is, 48,090 operatives — the number of persons so employed in 1875 — produced $89,375,792 worth of goods."

The product of each person employed in the manufacture of boots and shoes in Massachusetts, is not $1,858 per year, as has been already shown. Yet the statement is continually appearing and reappearing, with similar misrepresentations touching other products, throughout the reports of that State, and in many other authoritative places and forms.

It is well to commend to these popular statisticians a more careful study of that maxim of Napoleon's, quoted on page xviii, vol. II, Massachusetts Census Reports, 1875, as follows : —

"Statistics mean the keeping of an exact account of a nation's affairs, and without such an account there is no safety."

There is one other point in the Tenth Annual Report that I wish to examine. On page 27 is found the following suggestive statement: —

"One large manufacturer stated that he had at one time believed that prison labor must, of necessity, injure outside labor. He knew, he said, that Rice & Hutchings had the labor of 100 prisoners in the State Prison for 40 cents a day — a very small sum to pay for labor, and at first glance would seem to give them great advantage; but the great drawback is, that, by the terms of their contract, they were obliged to pay their men all the year round, whether they are employed or not."

If forty cents a day, for the year round, amounting to $123 20 per annum, is the great drawback upon the employment of prison labor, pray what must be the yearly wages of the average boot and shoemaker when out of prison? Certainly it can not be so large as to change the well known fact that free labor is cheaper than slave, because, in the case of the slave, he is guaranteed his subsistence from year to year for the work he does; but the free man, under present conditions, has no such assurance.

Then upon the point of the insignificance of the effect which the competition of 13,186 persons working in prison, at forty cents a day, has upon the work of those outside, as stated on page 24, I quote the effect of competition as shown in the agricultural volume of United States Census Reports, 1860, as follows: —

"As long as we continue to export wheat, no matter to how small an extent, the price in Europe will regulate the price in this country. The price obtained in England for the 295,241 bushels of wheat which we exported in 1859 determined the price of our whole crop of over 173,000,000 of bushels raised that year. The price of the one and three fourths bushels exported fixed the price of the thousand bushels consumed at home."

Perhaps there is no more deplorable feature connected with the present distressed condition of our industries, and demoralization of trade, than is the favor with which any fallacy, sophistry, or misrepresentation of the matter, or any attendant fact, is received by those who are popularly esteemed the most intelligent and "well to do" classes, and the exceeding disfavor shown towards any attempt to truthfully examine the real facts, and show actual conditions.

CHAPTER XVIII.

WHAT SHALL WE DO?

IT has been shown in these pages that for more than fifty years there has been in our country a constant and rapid development of a power that is irresistibly undermining the demand that, for all time before, has existed for such employment of man's muscular force in this country as would guarantee to him at least his bodily subsistence.

It has also been shown that at this time that power has reached a development that practically throws into idleness at least one half of the working force that found full employment previous to 1830, and that industrial demoralization and distress is seen in every quarter.

It has also been shown that this power has attacked the agricultural interests of the country with a force that has already broken up and destroyed many of the small farms and homesteads of the people, and is moving on in that direction with alarming rapidity. That in their place monopolists have seized upon the lands in vast tracts, and have converted them into gigantic food factories, worked by machinery and laborers, without fixed population — without women, or children — or converted their great estates into tenant farms peopled by feudal slaves.

It has also been shown that whilst the people are being driven from the farms, and vast areas of territory are barred to population, our towns and cities are crowded with hungry, naked, houseless multitudes, without employment, without hope, and sinking deeper and deeper into the abyss of despair and crime.

It has also been shown that the constant struggle of the idle for work, causes an irrepressible conflict and competition between the employed and the idle, which tends directly to add to the ranks of the latter, the reduction of wages, and the increase of the general distress.

And it has been shown that as the idleness has increased, and the demand for work has grown more importunate, that monopolies have developed in every direction, and the tyranny of capital has become more despotic. That whilst labor has become more and more disunited, and weaker and weaker, capital has steadily gained in consolidation and power.

How have the industrial classes, the workingmen, those who should be the real rulers of the country, met the development of this great power, and the evils which have grown out of it? What have they done to avert the threatened catastrophe that is already upon us? or, better still, to so direct and guide the growth of this power as to derive from it the greatest possible benefits?

In the matter of guidance nothing has been attempted, and every step that has been taken to escape the effects of this overwhelming development has been in the direction of proscription, monopoly, and strikes, that have only served to aggravate the evils that have been so rapidly growing.

The first notable move made by the workingmen, when this power was first felt, were in the organization of unions that limited the number of apprentices who should learn trades, prescribing the number of boys who should be employed in shops and factories, and proscribing the employers who attempted to teach a greater number.

Here was the beginning of that unreasoning and heartless monopoly that attempts to seize and hold all the work, and to deny to a portion of their fellow men the equal and God given right and obligation, which rests upon all, to labor for their daily bread — that says to a parent that his child shall not be taught a trade, nor acquire a profession by which he may earn a subsistence, but shall go out into the world unprepared for its duties and fitted for vagabondage only. Here was the commencement of that tyranny of the workingmen over their fellows that has resulted in converting one moiety of that class who are dependent upon labor for the means of life and its comforts, into the veriest slaves, who toil from ten to eighteen hours a day for the most scanty subsistence, and the other half into paupers, tramps, and criminals. Of all the monopolies and tyrannies of capital there is not one that equals the suicidal selfishness of the workingmen. These measures and methods of proscription and monopoly have continued to the present time. Out of them have grown the armies of unskilled laborers in the country — men who do not know how to work — and the consequent evils that find no mitigation in the benefits vainly hoped to be derived by the proscribers and their unions.

The next step was the use of labor organizations in dictating who should be employed and the wages that should be paid ; compelling the whole body of workmen, in any given trade, or in several trades, to strike — to abandon their work — at the command of a few unreasoning, hot headed leaders, and against the counsel of the more prudent and thoughtful, often without cause or reason, throwing hundreds and thousands into idleness and distress, and bringing hunger, nakedness, and want in every form upon multitudes of helpless women and children. These methods of proscription and monopoly, coupled with riot, violence, and destruction, are the only measures that have been relied upon to arrest the evils by which the workingmen are surrounded. Every succeeding year has brought with it a repetition of the past, differing only in a less show of strength, and increasing discouragement and loss of hope. Year after year the labor strikes are followed by a greater development of idleness, the generally increasing weakness and povverty of the laborers, a greater distress of the masses, but with a rapid growth and power of combinations of capital and gigantic monopolies that are truly alarming. So evident are these matters that they have begun to attract attention in quarters where the most persistent blindness has heretofore prevailed, as shown by the following item, found in the New York Tribune of April 7, 1883 : —

"A publicist of large experience and recognized ability gives, in a private letter, this significant warning:—'The great mass of the people are not prosperous. There is unrest among not only the lower classes, but the middle classes also. The concentration of capital and the rapidly acquired fortunes and unwise display of them by the few, are creating dissatisfaction among the many, which will manifest itself whenever there is a decided change in the condition of the country, in a manner that will try the strength of republican institutions as it has never yet been tried. The danger then will not be from blatant and lazy revolutionists, but from men of an altogether different type. The experiment of manhood suffrage has not yet been worked out.'"

During the fifty years in which these methods have been employed practically one half of the working force of the people has been thrown into idleness, a large portion as unskilled labor, and become a power that is constantly at war with those who are employed, and by their competition are compelling an inevitable reduction in wages. To this army of the idle constant accessions are being made from among those who were but recently at work, caused by the more active operation of the forces that first created the idleness. At the same time the centralizing power of the monopoly of capital has become a tyranny that is overwhelming. The increase in all these developments has never been so rapid as within the past decade.

It has also been shown that where, fifty years ago, it was truthfully said that every man owned the soil he cultivated, to-day we have between one and two millions of tenant farmers. A half century of the methods pointed out has resulted in placing the land

and farm interests in our country in a worse condition than are those interests in Great Britain, after a feudal land tenure of more than ten centuries.

The development of large land holdings, through the railroad grants, is marvellous and sinks into littleness the holdings of England; running, as those in our country do, from tens into hundreds of thousands and millions of acres, with single grain and cattle farms of hundreds of square miles in extent. These holdings and farms are scattered throughout the country and numbered by thousands. More than this: quite one half of the small farmers in our country, who hold the titles to the lands they cultivate, have a merely nominal interest in the land they occupy; the mortgages and other liens held by capitalists making it only a question of time and the payment of interest when the titles shall be changed.

Within the same period of time monopoly has seized upon and holds all the highways of the nation, imposing arbitrary taxation upon society for every service rendered, whether the carrying of the mails or the transportation of the produce of the soil or any other industry, or of passengers. So in every other manner capital has made a successful application of the principles of tyrannous monopoly, first adopted by the laborer against his own brethren and children., Where the workingmen, because of their overwhelming numerical preponderánce, had and still have the absolute power to control all the material conditions of progress, and so direct them as to be of the utmost benefit to themselves and to society in general, they have, by disunion, proscription, violence, a narrow minded selfishness and unreason, madly thrown away their great opportunities and become weaker and weaker; whilst the capitalists, insignificant in numbers, but powerful in unity and wise in their methods, have as surely increased in strength, and never more rapidly than at the present time.

The workmen have literally forged and placed upon their own limbs the shackles that bind them and society prostrate before the monopolists of capital.

During the past summer we have had forced upon our attention the fact of strikes of gigantic proportions, said, by intelligent observers, to include more than one hundred thousand workmen, a large portion of whom were among the best paid of all the skilled laborers in the United States.

The average wages of these strikers, before the strike, was not less than one dollar and fifty cents a day; but we will call it one dollar only. This will give a loss to the strikers of one hundred thousand dollars for every day the strike continued. There was a continuance of at least fifty working days, which means a loss to these men and their families of at least five million dollars. Who can estimate the distress thus brought upon these people and their dependants? The mere money loss alone to the strikers can never be recovered, and the increased weakness of the workmen is very manifest. But there are at least two other classes who also suffered from the same cause, and to nearly an equal extent. The producers of all the necessaries and comforts of life which went into the sustenance of the strikers when at work, found the demand and market of their products limited to the extent of the diminished ability of the workmen to buy and consume, which must have been to the amount of five millions of dollars, or the sum of the wages lost; and the transporter, trader, and merchant, suffered to an equal amount in their respective businesses. If the suffering which grows out of strikes could be confined to the immediate strikers, all the undeserved misery thus brought upon society would be averted. But it can not. The loss and demoralization thus inflicted reacts upon the interests of all. These evils are of the most serious character, and the hatred and bitterness engendered and perpetuated among the members of society by strikes and proscriptions seriously complicate the solution of the industrial problem.

Had the industrial development of the last fifty years been directed by some infernal power, with the design of working upon the laborers, and society in general, the greatest possible amount of injury, no more effective methods could have been adopted than those that are now, and have long been, in use by the workingmen.

That the workingmen have suffered; that their sufferings are constantly increasing, and are now greater than ever before, no one can successfully deny. That when they find themselves being hurt, and their families in distress, they should struggle and attempt to strike down and destroy the object that gives them pain, is to be expected, and proper to be done. But in the insane struggles which they make, and the blows which they so liberally shower about them, they never touch the causes of their distress; their wrath is not felt by those who have made them suffer. Their blows fall upon themselves and their families; their anger is felt only by their wives, their children, and their nearest friends. They are made to go hungry, to be without fuel or clothing, and suffer all the miseries of destitution and idleness, whilst the capitalist, against whom they wish to wreak their vengeance, is never touched; nor does he suffer anything more than a slight inconvenience, which is amply compensated in the greater weakness of his workmen that is sure to follow, soon or late, and the greater demands that he may soon enforce.

But for the workingman there is no retrieval, no compensation; what he has lost is gone forever. All that he has gained is on the side of greater weakness, greater competition, less of the necessaries of life, and more of its miseries. The industrial history of the last fifty years, with the workmen relying solely upon proscription, monopoly, strikes, and violence for protection and comfort, is a long list of disasters and story of continuous failures. The weapons that they have used are the boomerangs of self destruction. They will not protect, and much less can they be made to build up and improve.

Manifestly, the experience of the last half century has incontestably demonstrated one fact, and that is, that proscription, monopoly, strikes, terrorism, and violence are not the weapons with which to right the wrongs of labor. But none others have yet been used.

Is it not time that new weapons should be adopted, and new methods introduced? But the present indications are that the new season we are entering upon will be a repetition of the past. Will not the workingmen of the country learn anything from the bitter experiences they have passed through, and abandon the methods that have been so uniformly followed by the ultimate failure of all their efforts? But the great evils by which we are surrounded, and that are destroying the foundations of society, can be removed by the workingmen only. They form the large majority of its members, and in our country they are all powerful. Still it is only by absolutely united action that the workingmen can accomplish any good. By disunion they may achieve any amount of evil. The enemy they have to contend against, though few in numbers are strong in position and possession of great capital. Nevertheless, before the united workingmen of the country, seeking really national objects and noble ends, by methods that are just and in harmony with the institutions under which we live, the tyranny of capital will end. The workingmen will also draw to their support a very large part of the best thought and intelligence of the country, that will be sure to keep even step with the labor of society in its attack upon the enemies of humanity and progress.

Therefore, the first indispensable requisite is union in its fullest and best sense. There must be in the work complete harmony between workingmen of all classes and conditions — society men and nonsociety men — for the common objects of reformation and improvement. Without such union no good can be effected. It is not necessary that any organization should be abandoned. Through them the best work can be done, and the organizations should be strengthened so far as is possible. But proscription must cease, and strikes must end. It is absolute union that must be obtained to rescue society from impending disaster.

There are those now acting with, and to a great extent directing the operations of the principal labor organizations who can easily bring about the union so indispensable, if they so desire, and upon their heads will rest the responsibility of failure if united action is not obtained. It would not be difficult to find twenty-five men in those organizations, who can, if they will, by their position and great influence, start a movement that will unite all the workingmen in a great reform crusade, and bring to its support much the larger part of the best thought and patriotism of the country, and thus within a very short time make effective the necessary measures for protection and improvement in every interest. There are even ten men now working in the labor agitations who can with the greatest ease set the desired movement into such action as will be sure to rapidly increase in strength and command the most perfect success.

Without a commencement that shall come directly from the workingmen themselves, or that shall receive their cordial support, if started by others — the first object being to secure the most perfect union, and the next the adoption of the measures that will be the most effective for the cure of the evils under which we suffer — no good can be effected; and society must drift on to sure destruction.

Having set in motion the machinery for united action, it becomes of the highest importance to determine what are the measures required to cure the great evils by which we are now surrounded, and prevent their revival ; and, also, so far as practicable, to render impossible the growth of other evils in place of those that may be destroyed. The measures must be national, equally affecting the people in all parts of the country. They must be general in their character and operation, and such as will command the approval of all who desire the welfare and advancement of the people of our country. Among those that appear to be necessary, are : —

First. — The redistribution of labor among all, that all may live.

Second. — The restoration of the lands to the people, and their *bona fide* occupancy, by the people, under the provisions of the homestead laws.

Third. — The breaking up and wiping out of every vestige of all systems of tenant farming.

Fourth. — The at least double taxation of all unimproved lands, rated at the real market values, to the end that all speculators in the lands shall pay for the privilege of holding them without improvement, and thus preying upon the wants of society ; and also to compel those speculators and gamblers to bear their share of the burdens and protection of government, which they have heretofore escaped, and to thus offer a premium for the *bona fide* occupation and improvements of the property of the nation.

Fifth. — To bring the highways of the nation under the supervision and protection of the government.

Sixth. — To compel the equal division of estates among all the natural heirs; thus preventing the accumulation and transmission of great estates in single hands, and guaranteeing equity to all the members in every family.

These measures have been sufficiently discussed in this volume to show their importance, and how near the foundations of a truly republican government they lie, in contrast with the feudal institutions under which we have been struggling to develop, and which they should replace.

But to make the consideration and adoption of these, or any other measures, effective before the people, a Central Council of representative men from the leading labor organizations, should be founded, who should invite into the council an eminent representation of the influential, intelligent, and best educated mind of the country — not politicians — to take part in and decide upon all measures for the guidance of action and adoption of means to effect the reforms that must be had. Such a council may be so organized as to wield an influence of the highest power, and become of the utmost benefit.

The work to be done must be sustained by the people. The propaganda undertaken will create very considerable expense, and the workingmen are abundantly able to meet all such charges. When once under way it would doubtless receive material support from other sources; but the people should provide for and lay the foundation. It was the power of Peter's pence that started the crusades of the middle ages, and tested the Moslem power in Palestine. Even so the dimes of the workingmen of this nineteenth century in the United States can shatter the power of the dollars of her plutocrats. The expenditure of millions, through strikes, have brought no good; but a few thousands, for the objects proposed in this volume, contributed by the workingmen of the country, to the amount of one dime each week, with their ballots to sustain the contributions, would be the beginning of a new era for the relief and comfort of labor.

It would open a new page in the world's history, upon which would be written, not the old, old story, that the masses of the people had destroyed another nation; that the workingmen of the United States had pulled down the institutions of that country, even under the most bitter provocations. But a new tale would be placed on record, for the guidance of coming ages — that the workingmen of our country had destroyed the instruments of social and industrial oppression bequeathed by our fathers, whilst preserving all that was good, and lifted society to the highest plane of human development.

Whatever final and effective measures are obtained must be through the operation of legislation, which will necessitate political action. Any attempt to create a new party would in all probability prove a failure; it would certainly bring the movement into antagonism with both the great political parties of to-day, and surely be the cause of dangerous delays. A new political organization is of very doubtful policy. But the adoption, by the Council suggested, of the measures herein proposed, or their formulation of others that would better achieve the objects desired, and put forth as the basis of reforms demanded by the people of the country, will surely compel both parties to adopt them, and become their supporters, to the extent, at least, of making them planks in their platforms. In this way the desired reformatory measures would meet with no organized political opposition, and leave the plutocrats and monopolists without party support, but still not without the great power of concentrated capital and unity of purpose and action that will be found most formidable; not the less so because of the influences which they can and will use in secret, and it may be, also, in open corruption.

The times are now ripe for the action proposed. The questions here discussed are challenging attention in many forms. Already are they being approached by able inquirers among the classes where the best results may be achieved. It only remains for the workingmen of the country to take hold of them unitedly, seeking nothing that is not for the common good, but insisting upon whatever is necessary "for the general welfare" of the country. Setting aside all trivial matters, but firmly advocating all those great measures so necessary to the cause of human advancement.

Here, in the United States, we have all the conditions for eminent prosperity. We have a vast territory, extending from ocean to ocean, and from the tropics to the frigid zone, with soils and climates that are adapted to the bounteous production of all the necessaries of life, and much the larger part of the luxuries. Our seasons follow in such uniform succession that seed time and harvest rarely or never fail. We are never afflicted with wide famines, nor destroyed by general floods. Our mountains and plains are covered with the greatest abundance of useful and ornamental woods, and filled with an affluence of all the useful and precious metals, and, also, inexhaustible stores of building and ornamental stone, coal, and oil. Rivers, streams, lakes, and harbors everywhere abound, giving highways and power upon every hand. The God of nature has dealt bountifully with us, giving, in the greatest abundance, all the elements of health and strength.

We have a population of more than fifty millions of free men and women, governing and controlling ourselves by our united, or general, wisdom or folly. Our people are more generally educated, more intellectually advanced, with a more universal and higher civilization than blesses any other people. Out of our civilization, our general intellectual advancement, has grown a knowledge and use of the forces of nature — the invention of machinery, the adoption of labor saving processes — by which we are enabled, with the expenditure of far less of physical force than in former ages, and great economy in time, to produce, in the greatest abundance, everything necessary to the health and comfort of all. More than this, these new forces have developed, and are continually developing and widening the use of new and valuable productions that could not otherwise have been used. This power marks the highest order of development; but, like every other great power, when perverted, or turned from its proper use, it becomes an instrument for producing the greatest evils, as is now illustrated. By the blessings of our Creator we are surrounded with everything necessary to prosperity and happiness; by our own folly we pervert all our opportunities and powers, and change our blessings to curses. The law of compensation avenges itself. A Divine Providence immutably speaks through all His laws.

Ours is the opportunity to not only bless ourselves, but to become an example to all other peoples; to teach all nations that there is a way in which the highest good of all may be reached, and that in the highest good of all is found the greatest good of the individual. Not that every man and woman can reach the same degree of intellectual excellence, or position of material comfort, but that all shall have at least a liberal subsistence guaranteed from his own industry.

This can not be brought about by degrading our industrial classes to a groveling competition with the pauper labor and slavish customs of other peoples. We have already had too much of that, bringing, as it does, their wretchedness to our very doors. But it is well to look a little more closely than we have yet done, and see the real condition of the labor in that country with which our competition has been most active, and which, undoubtedly, will continue to have the greatest influence upon the labor and industries of our people.

During the time that this volume has been in press, Robert P. Porter, Esq., late a member of the United States Tariff Commission, has been examining the great industrial interests of England, on behalf of the New York Daily Tribune, and making reports of what he observed, and the facts gathered, in a series of letters to that great journal. From those letters

I make a few extracts, showing the earnings and condition of the laborers there employed. The extracts will be necessarily brief, but instructive. The first relates to the great iron industries near Birmingham; the region examined having a population of about 135,000, of which 24,000 are engaged in making nails, rivets, etc. Mr. Porter says, writing from : —

"LYE WASTE, Worcestershire, March 5th.

"The inhabitants of this desolate district are among the most industrious, and yet the most wretched, in England. They are engaged in making all kinds of nails, rivets, and chains. The work is done in little 'smithys' attached to the hovels in which the workers reside, and for which the usual rent seems to be about 2s. 4d. to 2s. 6d. a week, a trifle over fifty cents. These houses, as a rule, contain little or no furniture. They are filthy and wretched beyond description. What spare time the unhappy nailer's wife gets from nursing the baby and preparing the meagre meals, is spent at the smithy fire pounding away at the anvil until late at night. But the extra work that the woman does, combined with that of one child — say a girl of fourteen — will barely keep the family from starvation. For example: An expert nailer, working steadily from Monday morning to Friday night, can only make two and a half bundles of iron rods into nails, for which he gets 6s. 7½d. per bundle, or for his week's work, 16s. 8d., exactly $4. Now, his wife, by working every moment of her spare time and late into the night — neglecting the wretched little children — can make a bundle of commoner nails, for which she is paid 3s. 1d., and the little half starved, stunted girl of twelve, with her brown arms and steady, unerring aim, will hammer out half a bundle, 1s. 6½d. Total earnings of an industrious and hard working family, three at the forge, for the entire work, $5 13.

"But out of this pittance must come 3d. for carriage of iron from the 'fogger's' and returning the nails, 1s. for the smithy fire and 3d. for the wear of tools. Net earning, $4 77 per week — the united earnings of three industrious sober persons. I stood in the 'foggers'' shops of these nailing districts and saw the pale, emaciated women drag their weary limbs up the narrow black hills to the 'gaffers,' and eagerly watch the weighing of the heavy sacks of nails. The 'foggers' do not 'claim' that a woman, who has no family to attend to, and who goes to the forge every morning and works all day as a man, can make more than 8s. a week — less than two dollars. But the truth is they do not make anything like that amount.

"'How many nails have you there,' I said to a pale faced, half starved looking woman, with a fresh looking lass of sixteen at her side. The nails had just been turned into the 'fogger's' scales.

"'There should be forty-six pounds back,' she replied. 'They are a small nail and it is a bundle of rods of sixty pounds made into nails.'

"'How much do you get for them?'

"'Ten shillings, sir.'

"'How many days steady work,' said I, taking up one of the well shaped hob nails?

"'Six days, late and early, sir.'

"'Alone?'

"'Oh, no,' with a sickly smile, 'the lass here has worked steady with me.'

"'How far do you have to bring those nails?'

"'About six miles.'

"'And walk it?'

"'Yes.'

"'What does your fire and the carriage and the wear of tools cost you a week?'

"'At least a shilling.'

"'Then you and your daughter, working all day, six days in the week, at the anvil and the "oliver," make about nine shillings?' ($2 16 a week).

"'That is all we can make, sir.'

"'How do you manage to live?'

"'We don't live; we hardly exist. We rarely taste meat. I don't know what the poor folks in England are coming to. If they as work at other trades be like us God help them, sir, I don't know what will become of us. A many of us have to go to the workhouse. So far I have not taken anything from them, but I may have to do it. Work is very slow here sometimes, and it's hard even to get what we do.'

"The most cruel part of this business is that young women should be allowed to work at what is called the 'olivers,' a heavy iron machine worked by means of two wooden treadles. At Halesowen I saw numbers of girls making large eight inch bolts on these machines, and indeed they seem to work with masculine firmness and with far more vigor than the men. Mr. Ball, one of the largest nail makers of the district, told me that hundreds of women were employed in the little 'smithys' at the back of the houses in making these great bolts, and I visited seven or eight establishments, that might properly be classed as factories, thus employing women. Their earnings do not exceed $1 25 a week.

"In this way mothers, daughters, and mere children toil and slave on from year to year — indeed, one man told me nails had been made here for over a century in this way. How they exist is a mystery to me. They live in hovels, they are poorly fed, and poorly clad. They marry early, and several girls not over seventeen were pointed out to me as mothers of children two and three years of age. The men have an unmuscular look, most of them are 'very pale and lean and leaden eyed.' The small nailers are not protected by the English Factory act, and they work in their fathers' shops sometimes until late at night. The time to see the nailers at work is Friday night. The sharp din of the hammer on the anvil, and the dull rapid thud of the 'oliver,' as it flattened the heads of the nails and spikes, still rings in my ears from last night. I can see the bright sparks from the forge, the red hot nails clattering down to join their cooler brethren, the bending forms of the men, the women, and the girls, little children creeping into the clattering, scintillating nail shops, for the sake of warmth, and every now and then the red flames from the forges illuminating the scene and making more distinct the weird forms of these shadowy creatures, doomed to a never ending industrial treadmill.

"In some cases I found mothers and three, and even four, daughters at the forge. Many of the nailers actually starve, and cases of the deepest sorrow are not uncommon. 'Misery,' as The London Standard correspondent wrote, 'so deep and dreadful that the most graphic pen can but faintly convey its depth of sorrow, are witnessed.' Now that I have visited this region and walked through it, and conversed with at least a hundred of these industrial slaves, I am ready to add my testimony to the facts contained in the letter written from Edinburgh Christmas Day (No. 5). I can simply say that I have not half told the misery of this district, and of a dozen other industrial districts in England, and that if any one doubts the facts, I will gladly take them with me to any of the places I have visited for The Tribune and let them see with their own eyes. It is all very well to gloss these things over and keep them out of the newspapers, as they do in England, but the poor in England are day by day and year by year getting poorer. Not long ago, a journalist of ability undertook to show the desperate condition of the working classes here. I do not mean idle, worthless, good for nothing people, but just such industrious people as those described in this letter. He sent the result of his inquiries to a Liberal journal and the manager refused to publish the facts. He wrote:—'It is better not to call attention to such matters. It could do no good.'

"In this way they hope to tempt the United States to throw down its protective barriers, and, at the awful risk of bringing our own labor to this condition, give back to England the sixty millions of customers she has lost in so many important branches of industry.

"It is time the truth about industrial England is told. The London Standard has dared to speak out on the condition of labor in the Black Country, and when that paper makes the following statement I can say that it actually accords with some of the horrible facts which have come within my observation during my stay in this dismal region.

"'Women within a few days of their confinement have been known to work in the agony of exhaustion, in order to earn a few pence at the 'hearth'— not the 'hearth' of home, but the hearth of the 'forge;' they have been known to return to work in a day or two after childbirth, emaciated in constitution, weak and weary for the want of simple nourishment. Their children, ragged and ill fed, have had to lead miserable and wretched lives, with no hope before them but a life of wickedness and vice.'

"It matters little to these poor fellows what the cost of clothing is, for they can not get it. Taking the net earnings of the man, his wife, and his little daughter, which I have shown in the above tables was less than 19s., and here is what he can buy for it. The man and his wife sat down with me and gave the facts with great detail and care to 'get it exactly right:'

	s.	d.		s.	d.
Rent	2	4	Candles		3
Coal	2		Flour		6
Bread	4		Tobacco		6
Bacon	3		Club		4
Cheese	1	6	Clothing and boots and		
Butter	1		shoes, etc.		1
Potatoes		6			
Tea	1	6	Total	19s.	
Sugar		7			

"And the above is fair wages, not only for the nailer, but for the laboring man in every section of England, without one exception — less than $5 a week. A necessary housekeeping utensil, a pair of boots or a garment, as both the man and his wife assured me, meant total abstinence from meat for the week, while a doctor for a dying baby or sick wife is nothing short of a domestic calamity."

From Bradford, the center of the silk industry, Mr. Porter writes under date of January 22nd, where, during his stay of a week, he had "visited many of the principal mills." He says : —

"The factory people, who live in comfortable houses near the mill, seem contented and thrifty. The silk weavers are a better class of girls than those engaged in the worsted mills, and earn more money. Each family pays about 4s. 6d. or 4s. 9d. a week rent. Their houses each contain one general room, two bedrooms, and a garret. The floor of the lower room is paved with stone flags, in most cases partly covered by a rug, which can be taken up "wash days." Many of the rooms are cosy, with a well blacked grate, white hearth, cheerful blazing fire, green or straw colored Venetian blinds, mahogany furniture covered with horse hair cloth, plenty of shells and cheap glass ornaments, and a profusion of antimacassars. I called at a score or so of these cottages and talked with the pleasant old Yorkshire dames who kept house while husband and daughters were at work. Some were making, all told, 30s. a week by the united efforts of husband and daughters ; others only 22s. They never owned a home, and never expected to. All had heard of the land beyond the seas, and one or two had relatives who had gone out and done well. They complained very much of the high price of provisions in England. Of course those engaged in Lister's mills are a superior class of operatives. The houses in the other divisions of the city were not so good, and the interiors did not present the same comfortable appearance. The inmates of the latter complained of the dullness of trade, of their meager, almost starvation earnings, and longed for something better.

"'By strict economy,' said one, 'we are able to get enough to live upon; but saving is almost an impossibility, unless there are at least three wage earners in the family.'

"In such cases the girls were able to dress respectably, and the family to live more comfortably."

From Middlesborough, in the coal and iron region, Mr. Porter writes, under date of February 20:—

"In this trip I made the most careful inquiries in regard to the actual earnings of the iron workers, and found that the average earnings of 'slaggers' was 4s. and 4d., or $1 04 a day; of 'mine fillers,' 4s. 8d., or $1 12; of 'chargers,' 5s. 3d. to 5s. 6d., or about $1 30 per day, and 'keepers,' 6s. 6d. to 7s., or $1 50 per day. These figures are absolutely trustworthy, and were corroborated in every case, and taken down in the presence of Dr. Hedley. Laborers are paid in Middlesborough 3s. to 3s. and 2d., or about 80 cents a day; but I found several laboring men who said they only received 2s. 8d., or 64 cents per day. House rents vary from as low as 2s. 6d. a week to 5s., and some of the better houses 7s. 6d. a week. The latter houses are occupied by foremen and men earning say $7 50 a week, and who, perhaps, have one or more children employed in the neighboring works or factories. Men working in the Bessemer pits are paid from 5s. 6d. to 6s., or about $1 50 per day."

From Hanley, the center of the crockery interest, Mr. Porter writes under date of March 12th : —

"Here then are about three fourths of the operators at $8 14 and $6 86 a week, if we take the employers' estimate (which is disputed by the men). Then the printers, of whom Mr. Lane says there would be forty in a factory employing two hundred hands in white ware, are the lowest paid of all — only $6 55 per week. All three of these classes, aggregating undoubtedly over three fourths of the entire skilled labor of the Pottery District, receive far less than the average. I have merely gone into these details to show the absurdity of averaging wages. The unskilled hands in those potteries make from 4s., or $1, to perhaps £1, or $5, a week.

"'How much do you make?' said I to a dark eyed young woman in the print shop.

"'Ah moost do a many to mek oot mah dee's work.'

"'How much money a week, I mean?'

"'Oh, we doan't make more than ten shillins.'

"The only fair method of comparing wages is to take the same department of work in each country. For example, plate makers in England average $7 50 a week; in the United States $20 30. English dish makers make $9 62; Americans $19 43. English cup makers, $9 92; Americans $19 67. And so on through the list. It is not so much in the skilled work that the British workman has cause to complain, but I have found throughout England that great suffering exists among the laboring classes and those whose work does not require much skill. For example, in the English potteries, according to the masters, the hollow ware presser, the oven man, and the printer (representing over three fourths of the skilled labor) receive $8 14, $6 86, and $6 55 respectively; while in the United States they receive $17 90, $13 18, and $13 56 respectively. In short, with the additional high pay in the United States for the unskilled labor, and for the lads and girls, it puts what I may call the bone and sinew of the trade on a living basis, where they can live comfortably and save money, own their homes, and be men and women. It is this class that feel more severely than any other a reduction of wages, and it is this class, for they are after all the many, that give strength, character and prosperity to a country. It is an undoubted fact that three fourths of the people of the entire pottery district live on 25s. ($6) or less a week per man. What can that buy them? Consul Lane has kindly given me an average estimate of the weekly expenses of a man with a wife and two children (a small family in England), whose income for the year round averages 25s. ($6) a week. Here it is, and a perusal shows the grotesqueness of the cry of cheap cloths. Admitting there is any difference in the price of the common grades of clothing (which I begin seriously to doubt) at home and here, the bulk of English potters, according to their own statements, have but 50 cents a week to invest, aside from actual cost of keeping body and soul together."

From Leeds, in the great woolen district, Mr. Porter writes, under date of January 23, 1873 : —

"Some of the most trustworthy of Bradford's manufacturers assured me that young persons from thirteen to eighteen years of age never earned more than 12s. (less than $3) a week, and that they descended as low as 6s. (less than $1 50) a week for fifty-six hours of steady, confining, dusty, tedious work, and that men varied in their earnings from 15s., 18s., to 20s. (from $3 75 to $5), but that the latter was exceptional, he said. And this with a family to maintain.

"And so toiling and sorrowing, with no future and little hope, contented to live and die in the shadow of these giant factories, with little or no chance to better themselves; fixtures, in fact, around the mills, as the peasants were to the land in the feudal times, the English operatives slave on, while the mill owner discusses in the club how he can produce an article a farthing cheaper per yard. The idea of cheapness pervades the whole kingdom. It is all some people seem to live for. There is no limit to it. The struggle for cheapness sometimes brings ruin to the mill owner and starvation to the operatives. But for all that the struggle goes on. For example, when in Scotland, in December, I travelled in some cases for less than a penny a mile, first class. In my opinion no one demands this; in fact the public has no right to demand it, for it means the degradation of labor. What is the result of Scotland's cheap railway travelling? A strike — which has unfolded to the public what their so called 'demands for cheap travelling' mean — the suffering that their fellow beings have undergone.

"It is not a mere question, in Scotland, whether the men shall work fifty-six or fifty-seven hours a week; but it is whether they should be required to hang on at important duty till nature is so exhausted that they fall asleep clutching the handles of the critical levers, on the accurate moving of which the lives of hundreds of travellers depend. At one of the meetings of the men, this week, an engine driver stated that in one week he worked ninety-six hours, his Thursday's spell lasting twenty-three and one half hours. A pointsman had two hundred hours duty in a single fortnight. A goods guard for twenty consecutive days had three hundred and sixty working hours, or an average of eighteen hours a day. These astonishing revelations might well make one pause, when advocating that cheapness is the only thing to be considered. Cheapness in railroading and cheapness in manufacturing means the exhaustion or the starvation of the laborers. It can be obtained in no other way. Free Trade may bring cheapness. It will not prevent the degradation of labor.

"ROBERT P. PORTER."

The above may be taken as fairly representing the condition of the industries and working people of England. England is to-day preëminently the country, above all others, that manufactures for the world — that depends upon the markets of the world for the disposition and consumption of her products. That country is the great apostle of "Free Trade," which, if it has any blessings, should have gilded the whole land and made it a very paradise, in the full century it has occupied that position. There, also, the desire for "cheapness" pervades the whole kingdom, and is all that many live for; and competition is their life-blood. But here we have, in the case of England, the indisputable evidence that, for the people, the only fruits of manufacturing for the world, foreign markets, free trade, cheapness, and competition, are slavery for men, women, and children, with want, misery, starvation, and death in all its most horrible forms. These things have made that country an industrial hell.

We, also, have been struggling for the world's markets and for the remainder of those imaginary blessings that England possesses in so eminent a degree, and find our industries and people rapidly following those of the mother country. Indeed, in some things we have already passed them. Mr. Porter reports "fifty-six hours of steady, confining, dusty, tedious work," in a week, as the lot of the mill workers. In our blessed land, in Massachusetts, it is sixty hours, and in Connecticut and all of the other States, it is sixty-six or more. He also reports the excessive labor of railroad employés in Scotland, even to one hundred hours a week. In our country a common and regular time for conductors and drivers on our street railroads is from fifteen to eighteen hours a day. A long list of such comparisons may be easily made up. Nor in the matter of cheapness is England always in the lead.

Nevertheless it is true that the general condition of those who find work in England is far worse than the same class with us. But it is equally true that we are fast closing the gap that lies between the two. How vast have been our strides within the past eighteen years! Unfortunately, we have in our midst a large number of persons, composed mostly of popular political economists, in and out of college professorships, and politicians of all grades, from the halls of Congress, up and down, who join with the foreign trader, and insist that our only path to prosperity is to be found by treading in the trail that England has made — by competing with the slaves of the world, and sinking our people to a depth of degradation from which there can be no resurrection.

Workingmen of America! You have an absolute power of control in this whole matter. It is the first time in the history of the world that the people have so completely held their destinies in their own hands. Shall the good that we have be preserved and transmitted to our children, purified from the evils which now so heavily press, with labor made respectable, and all our industries preserved from all possible foreign competition, not one lost or injured, but passed on to our children as a sure guarantee of long life and prosperity to our country? or shall we continue to drift on as we have been, until anarchy and misery are swallowed up in destruction? You only can answer. What shall we do?

LAND AND LABOR

IN THE UNITED STATES.

By Wm. Godwin Moody.

In this work the great problems connected with the LAND and LABOR of our country are practically and thoroughly examined, showing the remedies that may be effectually applied for the cure of the social evils now so pressing.

One Volume, 12mo., 360 pages.

Special attention is called to the following from some of our most thoughtful and eminent citizens:—

TESTIMONIALS

From the Hon. HENRY W. BLAIR, United States Senator from New Hampshire, and Chairman of Committee on Labor and Education.

UNITED STATES SENATE,
WASHINGTON, D. C., JAN'Y 20, 1883.

I HAVE examined the proof sheets of a new work written by Mr. W. GODWIN MOODY, upon the subject of LAND AND LABOR, and the economic and industrial problems which concern the welfare of the people of the United States and of modern civilization. His book is full of facts of the greatest importance, many of them very difficult to procure, and not hitherto brought to public attention to my knowledge.

MR. Moody is a profound thinker, and is master of a condensed and trenchant style. His theoretical views are many of them very striking, not to say startling, but are sustained with a clearness and power which will arrest the attention of every thoughtful man.

I think his book the most original, and one of the most important contributions to the discussions of political economy made in recent years. I do not mean to be understood that I am prepared to endorse all his conclusions, for some of them challenge close attention, and their adoption requires the overthrow of many of the views which hitherto have generally prevailed.

H. W. BLAIR.

From the Hon. GEORGE WILLIAM CURTIS, of New York.

WEST NEW BRIGHTON, STATEN ISLAND, N. Y.,
DEC. 6TH, 1882.

My Dear Sir:—

I HAVE read the sheets of your work with very great interest and pleasure. It is a treasury of most significant facts which, so far as I know, are not elsewhere so conveniently collected. The work is a valuable contribution to an unavoidable and most important discussion, and will certainly command the attention of all who share the generous hope of harmonizing conflicting social interests.

Very truly yours,
GEORGE WILLIAM CURTIS.

W. GODWIN MOODY, ESQ.

From the Hon. DAVID DAVIS, late United States Senator from Illinois, and Acting Vice President.

UNITED STATES SENATE CHAMBER,
WASHINGTON, JUNE 5TH, 1879.

Dear Sir:—

I HAVE read with much interest and instruction the proof sheets of "The Labor Problem" which you were kind enough to send me.

The facts presented in that paper are worthy of the most serious attention of the Statesman and Legislator. They apply to one third of our whole population, now prostrated by want of employment and of reasonable reward for their toil. No country can expect to flourish with its labor degraded and depreciated. In the United States labor is honorable, and may be said to constitute the bone and sinew of the Republic. In war it is the most sure resource of defense, and in peace it has always been, and always must be, the chief element of National prosperity.

Whoever can solve what is called "the Labor Problem," by which fourteen millions of willing hands will be set at work, with just compensation to elevate their condition and to educate their children, should be regarded the greatest public benefactor. It is my highest ambition to contribute to that object, in any proper way by which it may be attained, in or out of Congress.

With great respect,
Yours truly,
DAVID DAVIS.

W. GODWIN MOODY, ESQ.,
Boston, Mass.

From the Hon. GEORGE F. HOAR, United States Senator from Massachusetts.

WASHINGTON, DEC. 6, '79.

My Dear Sir:—

I HAVE read your papers with pleasure. They are written with great clearness of style, and precision in the use of words, in excellent temper, without heat or bitterness.

I have long ago formed and expressed the opinion that the workingmen ought to get, in greater wages and reduced hours of work, their share of the increased production caused by the invention and perfection of machinery. So far I agree with your conclusions. Some of the propositions which you lay down as steps in your process of reasoning are new to me, and seem to demand further reflection.

I am,

Yours very truly,

GEO. F. HOAR.

MR. W. GODWIN MOODY.

From the Rev. EDWARD ANDERSON, Pastor of the First Presbyterian Church, Toledo, Ohio, and late Pastor of the First Congregational Church, Quincy, Illinois.

STUDY, FIRST UNION CONGREGATIONAL CHURCH,
QUINCY, ILL., DEC. 23, 1878.

Dear Moody:—

I HAVE been thinking a good deal about the matter of our correspondence, and the more I think the more grows on me the importance of the discussion, and of your being in the field at work on it. I am sure you have the only solution of our problem; and that there is no other way out of our hard times. This must be solved soon.

Last night (Forefathers' sermon) I discussed the general question, without statistics, in my service. Our people seemed deeply interested. That interest must grow. Some earthquake must rouse the people. You remember that it took the guns of Sumter to blow the cotton out of people's ears, and to shatter the film over their eyes, at the beginning of our Rebellion. Our people are hard to rouse for a swing; but, roused, they are honest, ingenious, and very prompt.

I want to write more of this, but am now,

Affect'y yr. Friend,

EDW'D ANDERSON.

From the Rev. Dr. R. HEBER NEWTON, Rector of All Saints' Church, New York City.

MR. W. GODWIN MOODY,
          My Dear Sir:—

                    I HAVE looked over the manuscript sent me with exceeding interest. The subject to which you have given such careful study for several years, as I have personally known, is one of supreme importance to the future of our country — that is to say, of the world. I know of no one who has followed the trail of our present tendency in agriculture so patiently. The facts you have gathered will prove to most men, even to most students of social science, a revelation full of warning. They are of such a nature as to engage attention at once on presentation — and will, I have no doubt, provoke a wide discussion. They ought to be laid before the people, by whom they will be read, I am sure, with quick appetite.

          Yours cordially,
                    R. HEBER NEWTON.

All Souls' Church, New York, Dec. 14, 1882.

From ROBERT D. LAYTON, Grand Secretary of the Noble Order of the Knights of Labor of North America.

                    PITTSBURGH, APRIL 16th, 1883.

WILLIAM GODWIN MOODY,
          Dear Sir:—

                    Amid the hurly burly of my office duties I have found time to read the advanced sheets of your remarkable book.

I knew, in a general way, of the monstrous Devil Fish — Land Monopolies — but never really comprehended its magnitude until I began the reading of your exposition.

I congratulate you upon the happy, felicitous style in which you have presented this cancer in our nation. It reads as pleasant as a romance, whilst it unerringly points out our terrible condition. I trust your valuable work will find a place in the home of every son of Adam who toils for his bread, that he may *know* the answer to that universal prayer now welling up in their hearts, What must we do to be saved ?

          Yours for humanity,
                    ROB'T D. LAYTON, G. S.

From the Rev. MINOT J. SAVAGE, Pastor of the Church of the Unity, Boston, Massachusetts.

Jan'y 9, '83.

W. Godwin Moody, Esq.,

   Dear Sir:—

I have read carefully such chapters of your proposed book as you have put into my hands.

Much of it I do not agree with, and perhaps should feel called upon to attack in the proper time and place. But you have put your case vigorously. The subject is most important and timely. And I am of the opinion that such a publication might call out a much needed discussion, and help toward a solution of some very important problems. I know you desire only that the truth should be brought to the front; and so I wish you success in your endeavors.

   Most sincerely,

   M. J. SAVAGE.

From FRANCIS B. THURBER, Esq., Merchant, New York.

W. G. Moody, Esq.,

   Dear Sir:—

Referring to the work on politico-economic subjects of which you have been kind enough to show me one or two chapters, I would say that they are certainly very striking in character, and I believe the present time is a propitious one for the publication of such a book. Many persons have had this line of thought forced upon them by events during the last few years, and it seems to me probable that a work of this kind would be more generally sought for than at any time within my recollection.

   Yours truly,

   F. B. THURBER.

www.ingramcontent.com/pod-product-compliance
Lightning Source LLC
Chambersburg PA
CBHW020309240426
43673CB00039B/754